The

Olympics

of

1972

The Olympics

of 1972 A Munich Diary

Richard D. Mandell

The University of North Carolina Press

Chapel Hill and London

© 1991

The University of
North Carolina Press

All rights reserved

Manufactured in the
United States of America

The paper in this book
meets the guidelines for
permanence and durability
of the Committee on
Production Guidelines for
Book Longevity of the
Council on Library Resources.

95 94 93 92 91

5 4 3 2 1

Mandell, Richard D.

   The Olympics of 1972 :
a Munich diary /
by Richard D. Mandell.

   p.   cm.

Includes bibliographical
references (p.   ) and index.

ISBN 0-8078-1954-9
(alk. paper)

1. Olympic Games (20th :
1972 : Munich, Germany)—
History.   2. Mandell, Richard D.
I. Title.

GV722 1972.M35   1991   90-23544
796.48—dc20   CIP

To
Willi Daume
Hans "Johnny" Klein
Otl Aicher

Contents

Preface

The XXth Olympic Games of the modern era appeared to be, even at the time, a summit in the staging of sports festivals. No Olympic Games, indeed, no public festival of the late twentieth century, seems to have been so convincing and complex a demonstration of new iconographic props for public ceremony. No festival contained within it a more frank admission that in our time the partakers of large-scale public ceremony will be moved by media specialists and will, almost all of them, stay far from the physical site of the theater. I was in a special position at the Munich Olympics. In this book I have observed and reflected on this grand celebration and have employed several literary modes to do so.

My preparation for the Olympics of 1972 began long before I knew it. In Germany in October of 1955 the so-called "economic miracle" of the postwar years was under way. The West Germans were well into a long epoch of fabulous prosperity, but the grandeur of this coming accomplishment could be guessed at by few. The factory managers knew only that there were more jobs than people to fill them.

After seven months of sightseeing, I was tired of moving about yet unwilling to return home to Detroit. Along with several recent refugees from East Germany, I was hired in Cologne to work as a laborer at the Ford factory there. For a few weeks I was on the final trim line applying thin lines of caulking and sealers, which gave off chemical smells that made workers nearby dizzy, on the painted bodies of Taunus 12m's and 15m's. Somehow rumors got around that I was a spy from the accounting office in Dearborn. Why deny them? The already not unpleasant working conditions (I fantasized most agreeably while doing routine work) became more adventurous. I carried messages for managers, took foreign visitors on tours of the plant, and made trips to chemical manufacturers in Amsterdam or Stuttgart to fetch technical information—often about sealers and petrochemical solvents. The pay of 420 marks ($100) a month was low even then, but if I were a spy, a pay raise would have been interpretable as a bribe and was therefore out of the question. I ate big lunches in the factory's subsidized cafeteria where the emphasis was on mounds of boiled, granular potatoes.

Part of my ancestry is Jewish. I had begun my stay in Germany with the partial intention vividly to read Hitler and Auschwitz books. However, in making a life, one is obliged to live agreeably. As my first days of living and working in Cologne went on, I could not bear to look at the faces of the enemy seated across from me on the trams. I abandoned this planned part of my self-education and began an extended marvelous time.

My stout landlady's husband had not returned from the Russian front. During the war she had twice, with her son's help, rebuilt their little row house after it had been wrecked by American bombs. She suppressed the rollicking local dialect when we talked and diligently corrected my grammar in good German. My room was unheated. We sometimes drank schnapps in her parlor as I polished shoes and she mended my clothes. Our jokes were grossly sensual. However, she never gave me a significant, count-of-four stare or the irrevocable, wet-eyed embrace, since she was saving me for marriage with her pretty but stupid daughter, then twelve.

At a performance of the Cologne Opera in a high school auditorium, a student and part-time journalist picked me up. He adored American jazz, for which I disguised my disinterest. Having a strong personality, he forced his many friends on me. He settled me in with the older sister of his lover.

The new friends quickly became good friends. We all hiked, and we drank fruity white wines. I listened in company to a lot of jazz. The friends diligently corrected my German. During Carnival in February 1956 I shouted and danced, got repeatedly lost, and was felt up a lot. Then, like a good Rhinelander, I returned to my work and my friends.

Almost suddenly there were too many parties. My affection mattered too much to too many worthy people. I was moving toward promises to marry. So, sometimes in tears, I gave away the clothes and paperbacks that would not fit into a large rucksack, hugged all around, and hitchhiked to Venice.

There was another trip to Germany in the winter of 1969. Though nostalgic, I was there professionally to warm the historical imagination and to collect materials for a book on the 1936 Olympics. These Games had taken place in the winter in Garmisch-Partenkirchen and in the summer in Berlin.

There were lots of materials on the 1936 Games. I found three pamphlets on the Olympic Village alone. In Berlin in late winter it was useful to pretend that I was successively various stars of the festival of 1936. As the final torchbearer of the relay from ancient Olympia, I loped down the flag-bedecked boulevards (not cold and sooty as they were in actuality) of the capital city. I had to climb and drop from a high chainlink fence, but I entered the Olympic Stadium, continued running a half lap around the cinder track, and climbed up to the enormous brazier that would hold the Olympic flame that I lit. As chancellor of the Third Reich at the opening ceremonies, I was satisfied, smug even, as the world's athletes saluted me. As Jesse Owens, I went full speed over the brittle, icy track and, despite the emptiness of the vast bowl, reveled in my fantasy of the adoring cheers of 100,000 spectators.

Munich is on the way to Garmisch. I stopped to look at the preparations for the second German Olympics scheduled for the late summer of 1972. The site was far from the center of the city and looked dreary.

Snarling bulldozers were everywhere. The only completed building was a television broadcasting tower, Germany's first huge one. On its top was a revolving restaurant serving pallid food at sensible prices. From it I could see the Zugspitze in the Alps, far to the south.

At the nearby offices of the Games' organizers, I introduced myself as a reporter for a major newspaper. All officials were amiable. No one questioned this lie. An ingratiating functionary gave me samples of the only poster then available, an *Erscheinungsbild* or "appearance picture," and assured me that henceforth I would be on all their mailing lists.

Sure enough, astonishing amounts of Olympic mail came to me at my office at the University of South Carolina. Much of this information was strikingly well designed and printed on especially heavy, slick paper. Pictures and statistically supported surveys of parts of the undertaking all demonstrated that the preparations were fulfilling the organizers' desires to project generosity and perfection.

In March of 1971 my book on the 1936 Games, *The Nazi Olympics*, was published. Though by then a working professor with a titular specialty in European cultural history, I now had a base for posing as a sportswriter. But my stuff was sportswriting of a particular kind. I had employed a skeptical, ironic style. I claimed that the modern Olympic movement was ideological in its origins and often unfortunate in its consequences. So, a side effect of my sportswriting was that I became a minor, quoted figure in a subsection of one of the many countercultural movements of the age.

There was, for a while, a "jock lib" movement. The leader of the radical, sports-critical movement was a former college runner, Jack Scott. Jack had published his significantly titled *Athletics for Athletes* in 1969. In California in the summer of 1971, Jack and I took long runs together, talking all the time. Along with a changing group of dissident college and professional athletes, I sat, smoking grass, on the floor in the living room of his shabby Oakland house, which he called in a serious voice and in his interviews with reporters, "The Center for the Study of Sport and Society." I wrote a few historical articles for *Sports Illustrated* and, since then, have been regularly trotted out at meetings of academic physical educationalists to talk on politics and sport.

The Nazi Olympics was well noticed in Germany. *Spiegel* and the *Frank-*

furter *Allgemeine Zeitung* praised it. These periodicals presided, proud but critical, over the ever more solidly established respectability and wealth of the Federal Republic of Germany. On the other hand, two of the few areas of German public life that were never quite cleansed of their Nazi past were public physical education and high-performance sport training. For some elderly personages and some sentimentalists who were neither Nazi nor German, I was a dangerous iconoclast who denied the official myth that any Olympic festival was destined to be an "oasis" in any time of troubles.

The most representative upholder of this view in 1936 was Avery Brundage, who kept his power in the Olympic movement into his extreme old age. In 1971 Brundage was eighty-two and president of the International Olympic Committee. Though Brundage no longer held any sport-bureaucratic positions in the United States, where he was regarded as a fossil, he was pampered by the consensus of German politicians who were eager to maneuver to anticipate hitches in the preparations for the greatest Olympic festival ever.

I visited Munich again in early May of 1972. I was assembling materials for a long article. I planned to talk a lot, listen a lot, and learn more about the ideological and political controversies of media-reported, high-performance sport.

Once again I handed my card to a guarding functionary at the offices of the organizers of the Munich Games. Then things moved fast. The card went through a layer of underlings, and I was led to the cigar-stinking office of Hans Klein, who described himself, coincidentally just as I did as a "journalist." Klein had earlier gathered clout in high political circles as the image maker of Ludwig Ehrhard, the economist and politician who launched the "economic miracle" of the still-booming Federal Republic.

Klein was now the press chief for the XXth Olympiad of the modern era. He pronounced *The Nazi Olympics* "fair," and so we were off to a good start. He brought out his kit bag of jokes, which were good; I brought out mine. This went on for some time. He interrupted our laughter and thigh slapping with some phone calls.

Klein took me to Willi Daume, a former magnate in the steel industry, a well-known collector and patron of modern art, and now, as president of the Organizing Committee for the Games of the XXth Olympics, the boss of the whole Olympic enterprise. Only then did Klein tell me that Daume had imposed as required reading for those below him my recent book on sport and politics. I already knew that a never denied object of the 1972 Olympics was to counter the bad-German, totalitarian reputation of the successful German Olympics of 1936.

I had provided a lively survey of what had gone on before. So, as a figure already known on the site, a self-proclaimed and acknowledged sports pessimist, one of the few Americans Daume encountered who spoke German and was a professor too, I was to be welcomed and, if possible, seduced. Daume's own German was slow and lucid and ornamented with rugged irony. As we talked amiably, Klein almost danced about with happiness.

It turned out that Daume and I had recently been interviewed by Joe Garagiola on the "Today" show in New York. He asked me if I knew his friends George Romney and Richard Nixon. I got back to the preparations in Munich.

Klein quickly agreed with my observation that a technically experienced observer might write an especially lively survey on the 1972 Olympics, the beginning of which was just a few months off. I wistfully mentioned that I would like to attend their splendid festival, which the whole world already acknowledged would be the most splendid ever, but, as a recognized sports critic, I had been the victim of administrative sabotage on the part of American Olympic officials who did not want anyone like me anywhere near them or their charges. In spite of all my earnest endeavors, I had neither tickets nor quarters in Munich.

"Would you like journalistic accreditation?" Daume asked.

"Why of course I would—more than just about anything else in the world. But I'm only the author of a book and an established university professor of European cultural history. My writing on Olympic sport, though widely sold, read, and commented on, is presented in a rather ironic style and is really not journalistic. If I were to be on the site, I very likely would be an especially close observer of the arts, design, ideological issues, and skilled staging of the festivities that almost all the reporters outside of Germany have irresponsibly treated far too casually. It's a shame that many well-placed people who should know better seem to be incapable of appreciating the complexity and profundity of the grand festival you have so laboriously thought out and so efficiently prepared for. Perhaps you would really prefer to have more standard sports journalists on the site rather than one skeptical. . . ."

"If you want to see the German Olympics of 1972, write me a letter marked 'strictly personal' asking for accreditation and all will be arranged, Herr Professor."

As we left, I asked Klein, "Does he mean it? If he tells you to give me accreditation, will you do it?"

Klein's answer was swift: "What the boss says, goes." He was grinning.

The next day Willi Daume got my letter handwritten on hotel stationery. Back home there was an official invitation. I sent my check to cover the $17 a day for quarters and two meals a day in something called the Press City. The flow of printed material, now arriving by airmail, increased substantially.

While I had been in Munich early in the summer of 1972 I had collected a lot of materials on the preparations for the Games. I did, in fact, write the journalistic piece that took me to Munich and led me to Klein and Daume. However, by the time it was literarily good enough for me, it was too late to be of current use for an American magazine. The Introduction that follows is that article, with suitable adjustments to take into account the fact that the matters discussed now lie some twenty years in the past. The article is important as an introduction to the diary that comes afterward because it provides an explanation of what many planners, participants, and observers anticipated for the games and of the expectations that accompanied me on my trip to Munich.

Even before I arrived in Munich as a "journalist" late in the summer of 1972, I had convinced myself that the form that would provide the widest flexibility for saying new things about new things at the Olympic Games would be a literary diary. The diary was shown about in the course of 1973, but I learned that it too was finished too late and was a victim of the "Olympic hangover" of forgetfulness following all of these quadrennial undertakings. When recalled, my festival was most particularly—perhaps almost exclusively—remembered for the atrocity that I refused to discuss at length or in investigative depth, because there was little new that I could say about it. I felt I had to tell a larger story of success, not only one of calamity.

Upon looking at my material years later, I determined that I had—

almost—a work that could still say new and worthwhile things about this festival, about high-performance sport, and about the arts of the time that should not be left lying. I added this Preface and the Epilogue. To finish the book off I added a short bibliographical note.

Introduction

Preparations for the Second German Olympics

I

A potlatch was a complex of activities, including feasts, dramatic displays, public announcements, and the lending, giving and destroying of property. . . . Potlatching was the indispensable means of gaining and maintaining political influence and social position among the rank-conscious Indians of the North Pacific Coast. Its distinctive feature was the distribution of various types of material goods, including food, to formally invited guests to witness their host's announcement of his assumption of a new status.
– *Dictionary of the Social Sciences*

A man might give a potlatch . . . for the purpose of maintaining the standing of his own potlatch position by distributing a greater amount of property than had his rival the year before. In any case, the property distribution was an occasion of public moment; the property to be given away was displayed

ostentatiously; the potlatch was preceded by announcements summoning the people together; the potlatcher and his speakers made rhetorical capital of detailed histories of potlatching, bragging of past achievements as the property was counted out and the names of the recipients called out.
– Helen Codere, *Fighting with Property*

Indeed, in the descriptions of the famous Kwakiutl contests, attention is so completely centered on the antagonistic attitudes of the two rivals that an important fact is lost sight of: namely that they are only the principals in a drama, which like all dramas, is for the benefit of the spectators.
– H. G. Barnett, "The Nature of the Potlatch," *The American Anthropologist*

The Munich Olympics of 1972 had much in common with other modern sports festivals, which, on a simple level, appear to be innocent carnivals of sweat. But, from the beginning, the Olympic Games have been integrated into larger political ambitions.

The first modern Olympics, which took place in Athens in 1896, was a project favored by the Greek king because it was expected to boost the collective reputation of the Greeks after a series of diplomatic humiliations and the bankruptcy of the national treasury. Of recent Olympic Games, we know that the summer Games of 1964 in Tokyo and the winter Games of 1972 in Sapporo were needed to demonstrate the wealth of stable, technocratic Japan. Analogous statements might be made about the Rome Olympics of 1960 and the effort made by the until-then internationally neglected Mexicans in 1968. However, no international meeting of athletes was as charged with political intentions or produced such benefits for its organizers as the Berlin Olympics of 1936. The costly, complex, well-run festival of the Nazis demonstrated to many that the new Germans of that epoch were friendly, generous, and respectable and (since their athletes won more medals than those of any other nation) that Nazism was a wave of the future.

New Germans; new festival. The Munich Games evolved from the grand Olympic festivals of recent years. A particular focus of the 1972 Olympic festival was to allow the politically clean Germans of that time an opportunity to negate ceremonially the bitter memories left behind by the Germans of the preceding generation and a half. These new cosmopolitan Germans were eager to counter the nasty impression left by the last generation's internationalism—athletic and political. In Munich, lettering, architecture, music, and even colors were devised to have no previous ideological attributions. One might, if one wished, have called the Olympics of 1972 (at least from the point of view of its principal organizers) the anti-German, German Olympics.

The president of the Organizing Committee for the XXth Olympiad was Willi Daume, a sixty-year-old former steel manufacturer, a genial technocrat, and a collector and patron of modern art. I talked at length with Daume in Munich before the Games. He wore the dark gray, chalk-stripe suit favored by most important Germans. Daume's jacket had high side vents and was a little tight. The black shoes were pointed. His large office was cluttered with Herman Miller furniture of the sparest lines. Near him was a rowing machine that he said he regularly employed, but I doubt it. He moved ponderously and was pudgy. Sport was for Daume probably an abstraction that allowed him to do lots of tangential, marvelous things. Willi Daume successfully communicated optimism about the biggest sporting festival of all time, scheduled to open formally on 26 August, a Sunday.

Well aware of my allusion, I commented to Daume that, during a tour of the Olympic site, I never saw the color red.

"Red is the color of dictatorship and of totalitarianism, which we all abhor. We are using the colors of a May morning in Bavaria. Friendly colors: grass green, sky blue, cloudlike silver and touches of flowery orange," Daume exclaimed proudly, as though he had recited this often before.

These statements about color could have been confirmed by any observer at or near the many new sports sites in South Germany and in Kiel for the yachting competitions on the North Sea. Black, brown, and red, symbolically indicative of the wicked Germans, those who were bosses at Germany's last Games thirty-six years ago, were scarcely to be seen.

One learns quickly that all of the visual aspects of the summer Olympics of 1972 were ideologically integrated into a scheme of six new colors enforced upon the entire organization by one Otl Aicher. Aicher, a left-leaning Catholic, had had many commissions as a graphic designer in prosperous, democratic Germany. He had been quoted as stating, "One can make politics with color." He probably considered himself a sentimental successor of the pre-1933 Bauhaus, suppressed by the Nazis.

In Munich, Aicher had a staff of thirty-five that helped him apply his colors—two blues, two greens, and two yellow-oranges. These colors—and only these colors—appeared on almost all painted surfaces and the uniforms of some 40,000 functionaries. Some colors had specific indicating functions. For example: security guards wore coveralls of the darker of the two oranges. The colors were on the publicity, including the bulletins sent to foreign journalists which were in a livid green meaning "communication." His colors were on exhibition catalogs, programs, and even the kitsch, such as the official souvenir, a stylized, color-banded Bavarian dachshund called "Waldi." "Waldi" was generally around, buyable as a stuffed child's toy, a paperweight, and on many decals.

"Waldi" posited levity and merriment and was a cute joke with a paradoxical, deeper intention. He recollected in a dim fashion Daume's original stated wishes, dating back to 1962. When the idea of a new German Olympics first circulated in high banking and political circles, Daume assured all that these Games would be cheap and lighthearted.

Die heiteren Spiele (the merry games) is a phrase now used sardonically in an "I-told-you-so" fashion in critical circles in Germany. Until roughly the beginning of 1966, the organizers held firm in attempting to keep it all jolly and modest. However, deeper wishes came forth within the country, which kept getting ever richer. A lot of very important people— ever more of them—wanted the German Games to be big and perfect. Eventually Daume had a circle about him that labored for supremacy and perfection in facilities and display. It seemed that there could never again be a sports festival as grandiose because it was difficult to imagine anywhere else the establishment of a festival accounting system that was so lavishly fueled and so loose. One expects comparable, intelligently channeled throwing about of treasure only in the quasi-sacred military programs of nations even richer than Federal Germany.

Indications were all about showing the importance that the Germans, especially those in or near Munich, placed on what was heralded as their "Olympic Summer." A potentially rancorous election was postponed. All the legal political parties were determined that there would be no opportunistic, domestic obstructions, comparable to that staged by thousands of youthful protesters (hundreds of them now dead) before the Olympics in Mexico City. The Parliament slickly passed a law declaring it a federal offense to have political demonstrations within two kilometers of any Olympic facility. Almost all of Munich was near some Olympic facility.

A posited *clou* or overarching symbol of the whole undertaking was the much-discussed tent (*Dach*), that swooping, translucent, acrylic roof that was an expanded version of the tensed-cable fantasy that covered the West German display at Montreal's world's fair, Expo '67. It spread over several acres. The *Dach* sheltered from the climate only the swimming and diving center and the gymnastics hall—a small fraction of its meandering extent. As a leitmotiv or center of visual attraction (as well as a center for disputation), the roof could be viewed variously. The architect (whose contracted fee was a fixed proportion of the roof's total cost) had long ago won Daume over to the view that his project would be exhilarating, airy, and rather cheap.

Once it was incontrovertibly up, though striking in its novelty, it was esthetically unsettling to move around and under due to the complex mechanisms for rain diversion and the massive foundations, masts, cables, and buttresses. All this support was demanded in case a strong wind came up from the Alps which were visible, when the smog cleared, to the south. Another disappointment was that the swooping roof, once anticipated as a jeu d'esprit, cost more than eight times the original estimate. Its cost was about 140 million marks ($40 million), a significant fraction of the bill for the whole show.

The whole show was expected to cost close to the clean round figure of 2 billion marks—about $650 million. This was about three times the cost of the Olympics in Mexico City and four times the figure that Daume first employed when convincing the federal government, the state of Bavaria, and the city of Munich that they must split the essential subsidies three ways.

One could ponder the metaphoric importance of the open area about four kilometers from Munich's old town that held most of the new architecture. Before the lamented last war, the Oberwiesenfeld (the word suggests a distant meadow) was a drilling concourse for Bavarian and, later, various imperial armies. After the Allied air raids between 1942 and 1945, parts of the area became dumps for unsalvageable rubble from the city. The grandly contoured green, sodded hills that overlooked the Olympic Stadium were therefore, except in their attractive surfaces, wreckage. Among the facilities on the main site, a quiet favorite of some esthetes was the new bicycle racing stadium that seated some 9,000 spectators and 300 journalists. It had an orange, plastic roof covering the performers and an open center. The long curves seen in the main stadium that were so intimidating there due to their extent were here pleasing. The inclines and declines of the Radstadion were, in fact, conducive to ultimate performances by nice bikes and those who propel them.

Some facilities were located away from the main site and indeed far from Munich. The regatta course for contests in rowing and canoeing, new, yet noble as a pyramid or a Sphinx, sat isolated amid some farms near Oberschleissheim, about ten kilometers from Munich. In 1966 there had been no rowing facility anywhere near Munich, so Daume, in an early buckling to yearnings all around him for perfection, authorized the digging of a spring-fed, seventy-five-acre lake more than two kilometers long. Then, planners went ahead and equipped the lake with substantial storage sheds, changing rooms, several restaurants, landscaping, and permanent grandstands for 8,000 spectators. This solid, up-to-date complex could serve no other purpose except for the raising of more trout after those stocking the lake matured. Rowing is neither a participator nor a spectator sport in Bavaria. This whole complex, probably the best in the world of its type, was used for five days of rowing and four days of canoeing at a cost of somewhere between $40,000 and $80,000 per competitor.

The rowing course cost about $23 million or seven times the first estimate. The stadium and attendant facilities, all of them new, for some of the equestrian jumping competitions at Riem, near the airport, cost ten times the original estimates and were used for just six days. The dressage performances were not at Riem but took place on the grounds of the palace at Nymphenburg. The *prix des nations* jumping event took place in the main stadium on the last day of the Games, Sunday, 11 September.

There were no early estimates for the site for the marksmen (total cost $8 million), which was also in a suburb, because the need for a

shooting stadium was just not foreseen until the plans for other structures were well under way.

Two major installations were not necessary to purchase but were
rented. The new Press City for 6,500 media people reverted after the
Olympics to its owners, Neue Heimat, an investment house specializing
in rental apartment house construction. This complex of high-rise and
low-rise structures became a sensible demonstration of urban planning
for 15,000 residents after the Olympic hubbub. An obligatory Olympic
Village adjoined the main site. The term "village" may be more ironic
than apt when such a large number of villagers are encompassed. This
construction for 12,000 athletes and their hangers-on was transformed
into a different new town of privately owned luxury housing for 15,000
civilians after the Games were over.

The planning, the construction, and, perhaps most astonishingly,
the financing for the Olympic Games of 1972 were carried out almost
without a hitch. The high costs and overruns were fully reported in one
of the freest presses in the world. The guardians of the various public fiscs
just opened up. When appeals were made to the German people for
financial help to maintain the desired standard of excellence, they
pitched in to buy special coins and stamps and to participate in lotteries
for what was called, and not always kindly, a *Superschau* or "Super Show."

II

How can one speak of Munich but say that it is a kind of German heaven?
Some people sleep and dream they are in Paradise, but all over Germany
people sometimes dream that they have gone to Munich in Bavaria. . . . The
city is a great German dream translated into life.
— Thomas Wolfe, *The Web and the Rock*

München leuchtet.
— Thomas Mann, "Gladius Dei"

Munich owes its prominence as a religious, art, and administrative
center to the Wittelsbach kings who made it the capital of Bavaria. The
Wittelsbachs long opposed the unification of Germany under Prussian

leadership and only reluctantly joined the German Empire as a quasi-sovereign nation in 1871. Until 1918 Bavaria had her own kings, one of whom, Ludwig II (1864–86), was spectacularly eccentric.

Bavaria has long been a fertile breeding place for the crazier and more menacing sorts of German politics. Hitler staged his Beer Hall Putsch in Munich in 1923, and the Nazis' first useful martyrs were created on this occasion in some street fighting. The city remained a sentimental capital of "the movement," and Hitler's Brown House, a sort of Nazi palace, still stands, near the museums for classical Greek art, but is now a music school. One of Hitler's diplomatic triumphs, the breakup of Czechoslovakia, was sealed with the signing of the Munich Pact on 30 September 1938. The city got some saturation bombing late in the war and fell into the American zone of occupation in 1945. Bavaria is still a gathering place for what remains of disreputable right-wing politics.

My pleasant hotel was on the as-yet unrenamed Dachauerstrasse which runs eleven miles from the old city, past the sprawling Olympic site, and on to Dachau, a quiet town of 20,000. Near Dachau, the Nazis had set up one of their first hard-line concentration camps. Some 238,000 persons were burned in the camp's furnaces.

Some of the many tourists dashed to visit mad King Ludwig's extravagant palaces and others to Dachau to see evidence of the worst kind of German madness. Some did both. One may understand, then, why almost all Germans agreed that the outlay of treasure and talent on the Olympic Games could be justified. The generous undertaking might help to obliterate the impression left by the previous German generation's internationalism.

Old political memories aside, there has always been an ambience of indulgence in Munich. We still felt it, though the city was much busier than usual, torn up with major constructions, and tensed for the great potlatch for which high-performance international sports were offering the excuse.

Some claim that the city's motto is, "Live and let live." An ancient and still current fantasy of some constrained Germans is to dash off to Munich to rut with a big-footed artist's model who, before being encountered and quickly subdued, smilingly strolled in Schwabing, the old university village and artists' quarter.

Many people of Munich are still loose, and some, far from having to be conquered, can be aggressive in the offering of gifts of themselves. But the old Schwabing is no more. It is just that part of the big city which is especially over-boutiqued and discothequed. There are supposed to be thirty gay bars, some of them with specific psychosexual orientations. As in Amsterdam, there are bars where one can readily purchase and smoke hashish for about $2 a gram.

German Protestants flock to Catholic Munich for release. And they do this not only at those sweaty orgies, the Oktoberfest and Fasching (carnival), which, providentially, have placed themselves at the beginning and late in winter when the tourist industry would otherwise find itself in slack times. If one's standards for pop entertainment are not high, the city is, in fact, a safe and cheap place to blast. The Müncheners themselves work and play hard. They tend to have an elevated notion of their home-town's reputation elsewhere. In his ambling the only partially informed visitor will encounter tram conductors, taxi drivers, and museum guards who are enthusiastically eager to help but are also boozy and ignorant of the conventionally elegant aspects of the city.

If one likes museums, Munich has more per inhabitant than any other city. There are museums for motorcycles (at the BMW factory), for china (one building at a complex of structures called the National Muse-um), and for state carriages (at Nymphenburg). These and others might be bypassed, but even the hurried tourist must not ignore the Alte Pina-kothek, the huge place for old, that is, before 1789, paintings. We know they would have done it anyway, but the local authorities claimed that for the Olympic Games they reconstructed and redecorated the war-wrecked Glyptothek and the Antikensammlung, which contain the Wit-telsbachs' stunning (particularly on the basis of quality) collections of, respectively, classical sculpture and the smaller classical arts. The more worthwhile museums have adopted first-class display techniques includ-ing hidden spotlights and glare-proof glass to show off their treasures more vividly. Maybe the Attic vases at the Antikensammlung would en-chant because of their quality alone. Perhaps I would shiver no matter how they were presented, but I never have seen this kind of thing look better. Munich is rich in gigantic canvases by Rubens and many of the best paintings by Albrecht Dürer, the Brueghels older and younger, Rem-brandt, Frans Hals, and the German romanticists. The city possesses Fran-çois Boucher's portrait of Madame Pompadour and at the Glyptothek, the naughty "Barbarina Faun," and the newly mounted friezes from the temple at Aegina.

The Games provided occasions for the good new Germans to remind us of the roles of the good old Germans as art creators, patrons, and collectors. For the "Olympic Summer" of 1972 there was a large special exhibit of "World Culture and Modern Art" demonstrating the influence of non-European cultures on European art since 1800. Naturally the hosts planned a great display of Bavarian art. For admirers of Olympic trivia, there were large shows of Olympic philately and numismatics. The sprawling Deutsches Museum, on an island in the Isar River, housed the exhibit, "Technology in the Olympic Games," that mostly displayed the apparatus, some of it oddly pretty, that specify the meticulous time and space measurements that are essential in critical athletic contests.

Another exhibit at the Deutsches Museum was called "One Hundred Years of German Excavations at Olympia." Since almost all the digging at the site of the ancient Olympic Games was financed by national governments in Berlin, many Germans, particularly those claiming to be especially well educated, have felt that the Olympic Games and whatever they might mean are a special sentimental province of the good Germans.

Munich has a resident (that is, well-subsidized) opera, a ballet company, a symphony orchestra, and several theater companies. All of the city's many facilities for performance were pressed to capacity during the summer of 1972. Munich was loved by Goethe, Heinrich Heine, and Thomas Wolfe. It was long the home of Thomas Mann and Richard Strauss. Munich is a fine place to revel secretly or publicly in low or high culture.

The Olympic Games occupied sixteen days—26 August through 10 September. One day at either end was taken up with the opening and the closing ceremonies. The Bavarians always expect outsiders and love them, and the city is rich in diversions. But Willi Daume and those who took his orders issued relatively few specific invitations. The "Olympic Summer" of 1972 was not offered for the whole world's sports fans and culture hounds but for two particular classes of visitors: the creators of publicity and celebrities.

III

Approximately 4,000 journalists will come to Munich from all corners of the world to report on Olympic activity. Their news will reach one billion people. Do you know how many that is? The large Olympic stadium on the Oberwiesenfeld, which has a capacity of 80,000, could be filled every day for 34 years.
– *Official Guide to the Games of the XXth Olympiad*

As Fresh as a Daisy for the Medal Ceremony
        At the 1972 Olympic Games the lady athletes will be able to turn out spic and span for the medal presentation. For this purpose they are to have the use of little cosmetic cabins that are to be installed in the stadia near the victors' rostrum. . . .
        The cosmetic cabins, however, will not be the monopoly of the sporting ladies. Shot-putters and hammer-throwers, sprinters and marathon runners, weight-lifters and boxers—all these will have access to the facilities for telegenic make-up as will also the ladies and gentlemen who present the medals.
– *Olympia Press, No. 16*

Prior to the 1972 Games, the deputies of the publicity office seemed oversupplied with statistics to make concrete the grandeur of the impending festival. Some statistics were indeed impressive. One splendid statistic was the acknowledged cost—2 billion marks or roughly $650 million. Those on the list to receive publicity bulletins from Munich had long known that the great swooping roof covered some 800,000 square feet. The two scoreboards at the main stadium each weighed thirty tons and contained some nine miles of wire. Within seconds the computer could set and print the results of each event for use by the reporters and could simultaneously send the results to television screens throughout all the Olympic complexes. Hans Klein, the press chief, estimated that the amount of paper required to furnish quick results to the journalists would amount to some 40 or 50 million pieces or a pile three miles high.
        The new lake at the regatta site held some 5,000 trout. Viewed in another way, the lake contained liquid greater in volume than all the beer

drunk in all the Oktoberfests of the past 225 years. I did not make these calculations. Indeed, how could I question them? They were furnished to me. The publicity apparatus seemed particularly stuck on providing, with exclamation points, statistics on the forthcoming consumption of eats. At the Olympic Village during the Games, the athletes and their hangers-on would eat 1,100,000 eggs and some 147 tons of meat. One bulletin of the Organizing Committee had the title "2,638 Facts."

Some other statistics were available—but not easily available and not with exclamation marks after them. With an urban area of less than 1,500,000 souls, Munich was the smallest city since Melbourne in 1956 to host the ambulatory summer Olympics. Though its capacity for visitors was much expanded, the city still had less than 23,000 hotel beds. The main stadium with 43,000 seats and places for 37,000 standees was one of the smallest ever to harbor the Olympics.

The Organizing Committee had publicly proclaimed in a celebratory fashion that there would be almost twice as many tickets issued as there were for the Games in Mexico City in 1968. But they did not add that most of these many tickets were for Bavarians to go to colossal facilities such as the regatta site (which in addition to the seats for 8,000 had standing room for 16,000) or to the many preliminary hockey (field hockey) and soccer games in large stadiums in other Bavarian cities. For a lot of South Germans, it might be easy to experience some sort of Olympic environment, but not many would see much of the best in Munich itself.

On the other hand, everyone knew that television coverage would be thorough and excellent. The best place to watch the 1972 Olympics might possibly have been from an armchair in front of a good color television. The quality of the picture in German color was high, and sets were everywhere.

Still the actual spectators on hand in Munich were overwhelmingly inhabitants of Munich. There was simply not much room for others. There was a rigorous and successful campaign to issue many of the better tickets to locals who could offer beds to out-of-towners. Most visitors therefore stayed in private houses within a twenty-mile radius of Munich. The maximum number of non-Bavarians that the planners allowed for was 150,000, of which less than half could be non-Germans.

Another statistic: the tickets were expected to bring in only about 30 million marks (about $10 million) or roughly 1.5 percent of the cost of the whole jamboree. Still, this statistic was not cause for fear for the established reputation of the chief organizer, Willi Daume, as a business-man. Almost all of the 2 billion mark total cost, much of it consisting of permanent civic improvements to Munich's transportation system, had already been covered by government grants or promises of further ones. The issuance of special Olympic coins and postage stamps, lotteries, the licensing of souvenirs, and the charges to guests using the Olympic Village or the Press Center all brought in money but not very much. Modern Olympic Games cannot be defended as business propositions just as they cannot be presented as merely a series of sporting events. The XXth Olympics of the modern era were ambitious and were a major undertaking in domestic and international politics. The costs of politics are always met.

Another big statistic was the nice round figure of one billion: a good estimate of the number of people who would be reached by sports reporters and by the people behind the radio and television equipment. Almost all the West Germans agreed that the inhabitants of the great globe deserved an outlay on their part of some 62 cents per head. The world would see some supreme sports performances and, along the way, get an honest and convincing picture of the good taste and altruism of the rich Germans of our epoch.

A special category of persons worthy of particular consideration were those through which this stupendous number of people were to be reached. They were the 4,000 journalists and the 2,500 radio and television broadcasters and technicians who would be on the spot. These individuals, if their duties were not too pressing, had an enviable existence while in Munich. Hans Klein provided the journalists with frequent buses and a fleet of 200 cars (no Mercedes or big BMWs) and chauffeurs (actually soldiers in the Bundeswehr) to take them almost anywhere they wished in and around Munich. As they moved about, the journalists were insured: $17,000 for death; $34,000 for permanent disability.

Members of the accredited press lived in private rooms in the Press City, a new apartment complex about a mile from the main stadium. Media makers had at their command more soldiers (a total of 25,000 were used on the sites) to serve as stewards and as fetchers and deliverers. Included in the $10 to $17 per day that the communications people paid for their quarters were two daily meals which were at a somewhat higher standard of bourgeois cookery than that spread out at the cafeteria for the athletes. For example, available to the journalists were red and white wine and beer—all barred from the athletes' quarters.

A hive for the media people was a large cube-shaped building near the Press City. Later the Pressezentrum (Press Center) became a school, but during the Games this place had corridors filled with hundreds of typewriters in all the world's scripts, more hundreds of compliant, many-languaged hostesses, a restaurant seating 1,000, a place to buy the world's newspapers, telex machines, banks of long-distance phones, conversation pits with deep upholstered furniture, acres of carpeting, and bars with deliberately enforced low prices. Much of what has been described or listed above constituted the integrated details in an official (but almost secret) attempt to keep journalists *away* from the competition sites. This last was a sort of tiny paradigm of the official, yet never quite stated, intention to keep tourists away from Munich and the Games.

The Press Center had many, many television sets. In some places lethargic reporters were able to watch twelve color sets at once, including all the material that ABC and NBC sent out. There was free photocopying, free yogurt and milk shakes, and free developing of photographers' film by the Agfa and Kodak companies. For those journalists who forgot their cameras, the Leica and Nikon firms competed to urge the renting of any of their models for fees so low as to be derisory.

Each accredited journalist had a letter and color-coded pass (designed by one of Otl Aicher's team according to the prescripts of the *Erscheinungsbild* or "appearance picture"), which indicated which areas at the site he had access to. Everything was not open to everybody, but the freedom given to the 6,500 journalists and technicians was far more than that of anyone else, and they were able to move about with an ease, if not rapidity, that assured each one of his long-suspected importance.

One place which the journalists were to see little of was the Olympic Village, where the athletes and those, such as coaches, who lived off them stayed. Almost no journalists knew prior to the Games that they would have but limited access of their choosing to the essential human substance of their callings.

The Olympic Village was more than a kilometer from the main sites and an equal distance from the communications hive specified for media specialists. The athletes had a separate bus system. The so-called Village was surrounded by a high, chain-link fence, and all the entrances were guarded to prevent the entry of the unauthorized. Almost all athletes and officials were housed two, three, or many more to a simply furnished room. Tickets were given to the national teams for the events in which their athletes were competing. One assumes that each athlete received tickets only to the events in which they competed—presumably for their mothers. No efforts were made to furnish the athletes with passes or with tickets to events other than their own specialties. The athletes were entertained at their residential sites. They were given no tickets nor were they furnished even minimal knowledge of the extraordinarily rich cultural program that was intended to keep a lot of other people in the old city of Munich during their stay and away from the athletes.

The Village itself was to be fun. As stated in all the publicity sent to athletes, their town was to have its rich program of movies, a chapel, a discotheque, a rich array of shops and boutiques, saunas, swimming pools, Ping-Pong tables, chess boards eight meters square, and lots of possibilities for freeloading on Cokes, energy drinks, and athletic equipment such as shoes and training suits.

One could well have assumed that the clean-living, beautiful athletes would prefer solely the company of their own rather than the autograph hunters, souvenir stealers, and tobacco-stinking reporters. But there is a lesson in modern life to be learned here. More than ever before, world-class athletes were to be quarantined creatures. They were thought to be resources too rare, fragile, and undependable to be allowed to move about in the distressed real world. As symbols or conceivably even weapons in submilitary wars, they were considered valuable ideological troops. They had to be protected from confounding notions and haphazard experience.

Besides the communications men and women—those whom the organizers posited as the routes to the minds and hearts of a fourth of the world—there was a second, smaller group on the spot for which there had been more calibrated, quieter preparations. The welcome that was set up for these people, when compared with that for the tourists and athletes, makes one suspect that these latter classes at the XXth Olympics were something like indispensable nuisances. With singular determination and consistency, Willi Daume and his immediate assistants sought the endorsements of the world's great names for their party.

German for "very important person" might be Ehrengast or "honored guest," but all Germans who watch television know "VIP," which they pronounce "fipp." Otl Aicher's staff of designers even made a "pictogram" for VIP containing those letters and indicating that these three letters had entered visual Esperanto as well as verbal Esperanto. Anyway, nothing was left to chance. Planners at all levels of this greatest of all sports festivals worked to bring in especially well-placed individuals from anywhere who represented the top levels of taste and power. Their presence at the Games would authenticate them.

Especially high-ranking VIPs were the members of the International Olympic Committee's (IOC) executive board. These worthies were titled, rich, and old. They were to stay at the Vier Jahreszeiten and the Münchener Hof, the city's best and indeed magnificent hotels. Their chauffeurs were to be real chauffeurs (not the soldiers put into service for the journalists), and they were to ride in big Mercedes and BMWs—some of them with little sliding draperies across the side and back windows. High (as high as can be obtained) bureaucrats of all the world's governments and the diplomatic services were to be company for the IOC board members. Keenly sought decorations as VIPs were the world's cabinet ministers, prime ministers, and presidents. Even choicer were the princes, princesses, and above all kings and queens the organizers tried to rustle up. Members of the royal families of Belgium, Denmark, Great Britain, and Holland would be on hand. They were still hoping Richard Nixon would come. Daume and indeed, new free, generous Germany sought to entice and make evident the world's walking and talking symbols of continuity, stability, respect, and safety.

During the Games there were to be platoons of guards to protect the VIPs from photographers and autograph seekers. Their limousines would travel on roadways free of hindrances. They would have exclusive entrances to the athletic facilities and once on a site, would have wide seats with fleecy throw rugs to protect them from drafts and drizzles—in short, a whole (though temporary) elevated sort of existence apart from that of all others.

The color dictatorship that the leftish, ideologically inspired Otl

Aicher decreed for the rest of the Olympic facilities did not hold for the VIP quarters. Red, of course, was not permitted. But at the enclaves for the singled-out, the VIPs on the spot were soothed by earthy tones of brown and tan, waxed woods, and sumptuous hides. At the main stadium the great ones sat on portable chairs covered in ecru mohair, and the concrete beneath them masked with thick beige carpeting. I saw plans for several VIP restaurants and examined the one at the rowing and canoeing site. It was odd to see wood surfaces used on low tables and bars—but only because I had seen wood only once before at the Olympics.

The Ehrengäste had at their restaurants table service with trained waiters and small vases of fresh flowers. Though large, these restaurants and lounges were unviewable, almost secrets kept from the hubble-bubble of the athletes and the spectators by windows of smoked glass. Each of these special restaurants was fixed up quite without regard for cost, taking furniture or materials from the best designers from all over Europe. The results were a series of interiors different from the mood enforced in all the other facilities. These attempts to be modern and conservative at the same time recalled the lobbies of four- and five-star hotels anywhere.

There was a lot of employment for interior decorators here. Yet each of the VIP establishments was intended to be employed for a maximum of two weeks. The one at the regatta site would fulfill its object for just eight days; the one at the archery center for a shorter period.

The much-touted cultural program was staged essentially for the use of the VIPs (if they desired it). The best seats were never sold or even known about and were being put aside for presentation to the internationally substantial after they arrived. Some few seats (in view of the size of the whole Olympic undertaking) for all the opera, theater, and dance were being released at very high prices for people of Munich who claimed education or wealth. From the beginning some of Munich's best rejected the Olympics as vulgar, though necessary. The Munich Lumpen bought up the remaining places. The 6,500 non-VIP image makers had for years been learning about the cultural ecumenism and tasteful vitality of modern Germany by means of all the publicity handouts describing the cultural programs that were indeed rich. On the other hand, no effort was made to provide journalists with tickets which were dear and had long been sold or were otherwise unobtainable.

Still, one could promote what *others* might do. To endorse Germany's festival, Willi Daume sought out the world's greatest orchestras, dance companies, and opera companies. La Scala of Milan will do *Aida*. The Moscow, Vienna, and Berlin Philharmonics were to be on hand. Munich would be the scene of puppet theaters, folklore performances, film festivals, and jazz concerts. Besides almost countless performances of chamber music, there were to be several series of special concerts in Bavaria's castles and in the rococo churches in the nearby countryside.

When the chief organizer sent out invitations for a special edition of art posters (apart from Aicher's official posters printed in the official six colors and used officially all over the sites) to celebrate this sports festival, he favored submissions from known artists. Indeed there was for this sporting occasion a so-called *Edition Olympia* of prints, posters, and miniature speed-press pictures that were supposed to deal with sport. Sales of these graphics by some thirty-five artists were expected to bring in a little money and did. The pictures were not seen as much on the site as Aicher's were.

Most of the artists in this special series were abstractionists who had had their heroic periods decades ago: for examples, Max Brill (born 1908), Josef Albers (born 1888), Oskar Kokoschka (born 1886), and Marino Marini (born 1901). Here, especially, one sees that the cosmopolitan technocrats in charge of this affair wished to give the impression that they were avant-garde—but safely so. And the skeptical critic also suspects that the artists who supplied these pretty images merely reached into their storage files and fished something out. Almost none of the pictures had any discernible connection with sport, the Olympics, or the particular time and place.

There was no single official Olympic film of the 1972 Olympics as there was in 1936. Then, Leni Riefenstahl, secretly financed by Joseph Goebbels's propaganda ministry, produced the most original sports film ever made. Her *Olympia* was not only an artistic triumph but an organizational *Gesamtkunstwerk*, a grand and original summation of artistic power and arguably the greatest film ever made. But this stunning monument was an embarrassing one for the German anti-Nazis in 1972. Daume invited a mixed bag of ten acknowledgedly good directors whose artistic reputations were unassailable and asked each of them to do a ten-minute segment on some aspect of sport of their choosing or impulse.

Some of these directors were: David Wolper, Milos Forman, Mai Zetter-ling, and Arthur Penn—none of whom had shot a sports film before. Therefore, Willi Daume arranged that the representatives of political power and of established taste joined the molders of public opinion to skew the views of half the world in favor of the Federal Republic of Germany.

While on the scene, knowing well that I provoked, I asked Daume and "Johnny" (though his name was Hans, he insisted on being called this) Klein, the press chief, if there was any organized or expected oppo-sition to the Games. As the late preparations went on in Munich, Chan-cellor Willy Brandt tried to normalize or at least to de-menace further the clumsy relations between the German Democratic Republic (GDR) and the Federal Republic. The papers and news magazines were full of relevant discussions. I was anticipating ideologically leftist agitation. Daume assumed that I was referring to the East German question.

Daume answered, "We will be hosts for the festival and the GDR will win the most medals. Everyone will be satisfied." This was a pat response. This done, Daume moved on nervously to ask me what kind of protest he should expect from the American athletes. He was fidgety, and I knew that he feared lapses in protocol by American blacks that, in turn, could detonate upheavals on the part of Avery Brundage and, subse-quently, the international press. The Mexico City Olympics were vividly recalled for such brouhahas. I told him what I believed and that, if there was to be an American protest (I knew then only of a plan to smuggle some peace buttons into the Olympic Village), it would be against the United States and not against Germany or the Olympic Games. Relieved, Daume sighed and fell back into his $500 Eames chair. Another difficulty buttoned up!

At another meeting with Klein, each of my queries regarding poten-tial critics within Germany provoked enthusiastic assurances. But he did not understand what I meant. For example, he responded that the undig-nified sex tests for equivocal ladies that had caused such a ruckus in 1968 had been replaced by a new and infallible examination requiring the ladies or putative ladies to surrender one hair so that the follicle might be subjected to conclusive microscopic examination.

But I had already collected some clippings from the left German press showing opposition that was more various than was officially ad-mitted. Due to the expectations almost everywhere that the Olympics would be a prestigious triumph, all the politicians of the four major parties had been shouldering each other aside to claim particular sponsorship. They wished to hog the lights of flattering publicity and, later, happy memory. Even the Communist party issued press releases that did not attack the Olympics but accused the bourgeois regime of being rotten and of misusing the "Olympic idea" for imperialistic purposes.

Outside of journalism, but still taking advantage of unhindered expression and low-cost publishers, a vigorous and clever (or so they seemed to me) group of young Marxist sports critics had for five years been claiming that the "Super Show" was the festive climax of the usual bourgeois strategy to use sport as a "system-stabilizing" diversion, thus masking the need for social justice and political transformation. These last two objects were assumed to be justifiable objects of politically sponsored public activity. Moralistic social critics whined that money might have been better spent on care for the aged or the insane.

Other protesters were Germans who could not forget that this festival required the honoring on sacred German soil of the Soviet mutilators (even if they were young athletes) of traditional German territory. Some youth groups might have protested against the presence of the American murderers of the Vietnamese. Another debate concerned something fundamental about the modern Olympic movement. A few elderly officials of the Catholic church in Bavaria objected to several ceremonial aspects of the festival, most particularly the torch ceremonies, because they are pagan, which, of course, they are.

But no hitches were foreseen. Perhaps one did not *want* to foresee hitches. The money and the talent and the materials were there, and the organizers behind the computers planned everything. Whether in Munich or before our televisions at home, we would be delighted spectators at the finest sports festival of all time.

Munich Diary

1

Getting Ready

Morning, Tuesday, 22 August 1972

The cycling stadium has been praised by the early critics. It is on the periphery of the main site, north of the many huge constructions of various sorts united, sort of, by the oppressive and not airy (as claimed) acrylic roof. Since it is independent of the rest of the site, it is also exempt from the rules for colors and surfaces imposed almost everywhere else. The architect-engineers conceived of the project as a piece of sporting equipment. It is a big piece of sporting equipment intended to provide optimal conditions for the achieving of optimal performances by smaller pieces of optimal sporting equipment, track bicycles.

The landscaping of sodded lawns and low shrubbery around the cycling stadium is characterless. There are brown, structural beams on the outside. High up on the outside rim there extend panels of orange plastic sheltering the track and leaving the center area open. Inside, the feeling of aloofness, of inhumane separation, is made stronger by that translucent roof which alters the daylight. The inside of the cycling stadium is one of the few places anywhere around here where one sees a surface of a natural material. The oval that the cyclists rush across has a surface made up of bonded narrow strips of a desirable African wood that is hard and dries quickly. There is a roofed, submerged area at the end of the infield with racks for the hanging of cycles and benches for the teams and their supporting staff. Most of the infield is a grand sweep of untrodden, sodded grass. All colors are muted.

All the curves, which are everywhere, are long, slow ones. There are banked grandstands for 9,000 spectators and an elliptical roof of tensed, arched panels. Dominating everything are the longest curves of the canted track—an awesome, endless, correct-according-to-formula ribbon that swoops, rising high at the ends of the oval, tilting low near the spectators along the short straightaways. All these are pure, mathematical curves, apart from life and apart from art. That we are enchanted is a fine dividend. But all this was assembled for performance—of a useless kind. The tilted, altered, otherworldly planes diminish the sightseer.

Though the fact was not announced in the press, most of the competition and practice sites are open before the Games for the casual visitors who are speckled about the grounds. I am alone in the press "tribune" at the stadium for track cycling. Some idlers are on the other side of the track. A couple dozen people chat in the infield. They are here for serious matters.

Two hunkered-down athletes, Trinidadians, alternately sprint and coast. As they make motions to leave, a waiting group of six Netherlandish men push their machines to the track. They will practice for the team pursuit.

The track bikes add to the impression of grandiose austerity. The instruments are immaculate, polished machines of minimized essentials. No brakes or gears. Though they can be propelled swiftly, they are hushed even when passing before the observer's nose. These bikes make little noise. The air they part makes more. One just perceives the continuous engagement of the heavy chain against the drive sprocket and the continuous, steady kiss of the pared skinny tires on the buffed wood surface.

The Dutch circle at full speed. They perform so intricate a training maneuver that one must stare to grasp that humans of tendon and brain, like ourselves, are capable of such preconceived, calculated logic. It is visible calculus. At each end of the oval, number one rises and slows and, as he does so, a place opens up so that, as he descends, he becomes number four. Simultaneously, number six has eased forward, rising yet higher, and sprints ahead to become briefly the wind-slicing leader. The others tailgate. This mechanical switch amid a steady whir, this bit of tactical virtuosity, occurs every half revolution and every few seconds.

The déjà vu experience is piercing and I will not let it go. Then I recall a hypnotic observation as a child at some General Motors "Futurama" or other. The display was in a case, at my eye level, in which two streams of marble-sized ball bearings fell periodically from opposite directions. They bounced and then crossed paths through a rotating, synchronized small hoop. Useless ingenuity. Inhuman rhythms. I got seasick then.

It must be otherwise in competition, but I hear no grunts. The cyclists wear light, leather harnesses to protect their skulls in the event of a spill, which one must assume is unlikely. Their faces are low, and one sees only their upraised chilly eyes, no grimaces. It is impossible to make any ranking esthetic appraisals of their bodies or even their spinning legs as they flash past my grasping eyes and ears. The composition of stable and dynamic elements produces an abstract composition of frightening power. There is no time, only pure motion in this setting of powerful spaceless curves.

An old professor of poetry once spoke of the esthetic shiver test. When one is immersed in a self-proclaimed work of art and one occasionally shivers, the attempt is either very good or very bad. Here in the cycling stadium at a practice session, I am traversed by waves of shivers. Risking more self-abnegation, I start leaving myself to look yet harder at those figures moving in nonhuman curves in nonhuman architecture accompanied by nonhuman, reverential, noiseless noise.

I am altered. I went too far. Frightened, I push myself from the rail my chin is on and rise quickly to save the likelihood of subsequent rational thought. As I stumble from the stadium, I feel like I have been made negligible by the disorienting beauty within pure sport. The close watching lasted about five minutes.

Later, Tuesday, 22 August 1972

What follows is a consequence of the artful vertigo of the bicycle stadium. For years now I have felt almost alone in my taking of pleasures I feel are keenly esthetic from some—usually the best—sports equipment. The following little joke has long been assembling itself in my projecting imagination. The heuristic device is a multicopy letter.

Olympic Games 1972

Directors and Curators
Museum of Modern Art, New York
Victoria and Albert Museum, London
Musée des arts décoratifs, Paris
Deutsches Museum, Munich

Dear Sirs:

I propose an exhibition to be called, "Sport as a Determiner of Form." I offer myself as the chooser of what would be shown, but would expect generous assistance from experienced, self-effacing display designers in setting up the show and especially the lighting. I would write the explanatory prose for all parts of the exhibition, including the brief captions accompanying the objects and the historical, justifying essays in the richly printed, small catalog.

A major role, less in the number of examples displayed than in their central significance, would be taken by bicycles, particularly the spare, track machines. The track bike is one of the purest examples of elegant form currently being made and readily available for purchase. The present form of the competition bicycle is the product of a history worth here reviewing. The "safety" bicycle, having two wheels of equal size with pneumatic tires, the rear wheel being driven by a continuous chain connected to a drive sprocket amidships, was invented about 1880. So keen was the interest in this wonder, that the "safety's" evolution (by this I mean the angles, curves, general size, and proportions of wheels, frame, handlebars, and seat) was accomplished in about ten years. During this short period a sizable fraction of the world's engineering talent, particularly in France and in the United States, was devoted to perfecting the racing bicycle. Minor, continuous improvements came along in the form of thinner tires, lighter alloys, and the recent addition (for road-racing machines) of derailleur gears.

It is worth pondering that on first or even second glance the ten-speed cycles adopted by flaunters and flaneurs in Central Park on April Sundays appear much the same as the refined machines employed by champion Belgian and Dutch road racers. One singles out the best road cycles by their delicate, costly refinements: slimmer frame members, quick-release hubs, titanium pedals, drilled-out chain wheels, ultrathin tires, and suede (rather than plastic or hide) saddles. The track bikes are similar in configuration, except that they are lighter and more austere, having no gears, brakes, or freewheeling.

The competition-bike makers are individuals who proudly apply decals or hand lettering to their products. Many fine bikes take the names of their makers. In our exhibition we will salute Harry Quinn, Geoffrey Butler, Poliaghi, Lejeune, Gramagli, Neri. The admirer of fine bicycles can enjoy some poetic names: Favorit, Allegro, Goldia, Saxis, Tigra, Plume vainceur, Paramount.

Unfortunately for the glory that we want to accrue to the painted or decaled devices, only the frames can carry a grand variety of names. Almost all the bikes use similar, nearly identical running components of the lightest metals consistent with infallible strength. The most carefully finished and expensive derailleurs, handlebars, head sets, seat posts, sprockets, and chains are acknowledged to be those of an Italian firm, Campagnolo. The Japanese are coming up fast. The best road bikes cost up to $500; the best track bikes $350. Whoever pays more is giving some retailer an undeserved profit. It is difficult to get the weight of a reliable road bike below twenty-one pounds or that of a track bike below eighteen pounds.

Returning to a main point: Individualism among makers is made manifest in decorative colors or fanciful striping around the lugs, the critically important junctures—really the slim basis of the maker's "art,"—that hold the tubes of the frame together. Some frames are entirely chromed.

The fine competition machine is an enchantment for the eyes because as a whole and in its parts it is a refined product meeting a refined purpose (which, we remember is not *really* useful). The two-wheeler used for going to school by a Tucson fifthgrader or the black lummox used by a Dutch housewife to fetch cabbage is not beautiful. Indeed, we would agree that to offer these pedaled tools to a craftsman's care or a striper's frivolity would be in bad taste.

So then, the best competition cycles (excepting tandems and some special machines for hill climbing) are very much like others of their sort. In the races, the different bicycle finishes last. If one were to finish first with a different machine (something that has not happened in decades and that we do not expect ever), we can be sure that the radically new bicycle would be most exciting to contemplate as an object and that in a few months, all other competitive bicycles would look just like it, except for the surfaces, machined, painted, or upholstered.

Nicely maintained bikes of the best quality are not often seen at the shopping centers of Cincinnati or Wolverhampton, but at the Olympics (where this is written), the collector of fine visual pictures sees them in clusters leaning against walls about the Olympic Village. The clean, polished bikes attract passersby who give the objects the unselfish admiration that the art teachers plead for us to feel before canvases of Mondrian, Rauschenberg, or Albers. This justification of the bicycle is a paradigm for what would be included in the rest of the show.

There are objects less commonly known than the bicycles to a potentially art-consuming audience, yet perhaps of keener interest to a beauty-seeking public than the gallery art of jokes, philosophized disorder, and contempt. We might mount for consideration some of the various (here again I must insert the word "useless") rowing machines. The single and double sculls; the larger (yet astonishingly tiny) boats for four-man and eight-man crews.

It is worth adding here that the first international sport competitions were in rowing, usually British collegians against teams from America, Belgium, and France. The continuous refinements in these narrowly particularized craft date from about a century ago. A great technical leap forward occurred before the Olympics of 1936 when German engineers applied their wits and energies to the task of getting a projectile through the water by means of harnessed human power. Without the German medals won in rowing in 1936, the Berlin Olympics would have been less of a Nazi triumph.

At an international competition such as the Olympics, one sees the very best. The forms of the prettiest boats, low, precarious in the water, and useless for anything but their purpose, have been settled. The craftsmen fashion them of light woods, fiberglass, and duralumin. But here again the surfaces are dazzling. Glossy acrylics in optimistic, chemical-ersatz colors, design motifs of expressionistic vigor drained of expressionism's anguish, pearly lumber. All sculpted to hold tendoned behinds and to maintain desperate grips or cupped, as the oars are, to seize and exploit the water. All surfaces are protected by polished translucent or opaque epoxies that glisten variously in the sunlight like Brazilian butterflies or Australian opals.

We can bring up here the competition canoes of fiberglass, sometimes veneered in pearly woods. The delicate kayaks might be yet more attractive for our examination if we could look at the spare frames stripped of the fabric coverings. An ambitious, spacious exhibition might include some of the smaller craft used in Olympic sailing competitions.

Instructive for the sports art critic might be the shows of the various sports shoes manufacturers: Adidas, Puma, and Tiger. The shoes for wrestlers, boxers, football players, and the several classes of track and field athletes must be lightweight, super durable, and super comfortable. Each manufacturer has succeeded in satisfying the athletes' needs and cannot long maintain an engineer's jump on the others. Competition is largely in terms of eye appeal. Puma's shoes employ the most garish combinations of colors, but for all the shoes the forms at any time are apparently settled, while the particulars of surfaces or applied stripes are not. The best of the sports shoes as new, clean, unused objects are worthy of conscious display to elicit celebration.

I will go on in this fashion. The rifles and pistols used by

Olympic marksmen are already evolved wonders of precious woods carved to hold the world's steadiest grips. Their matte-finished metal parts are massive, curiously and even fetchingly shaped. On first viewing we might suspect that some delicate combination of control and fantasy went into their design, but this notion must be rejected, since the firearms are coldly purposeful and narrowly so. Those few of us who have been permitted to examine, to fondle, the fabulous wood and plastic assemblages that are the bows of world-class archers must admit that these strange objects merit exposure to an esthetically tuned crowd that can get close to them and even feel them.

As examples of sports objects suitable for display in the round or for wall hanging, we can offer the foils, épées, and sabers of world-class fencers. Or further: hockey sticks, footballs, and basketballs. Wall hangings might be the fabrics used on some racing swimming suits or sports parachutes.

Some of the sports architecture used in the Olympics of 1960, 1964, 1968, and 1972, and indeed, at non-Olympic sites has been responsibly photographed. While most athletic architecture (excepting for a few medium-sized stadiums and some ski jumps) has been hampered by overseeing cost accountants, blowups of certain photographs might be suitable two-dimensional subjects for our exhibition.

Since the much-cited, never-specified "Olympic idea" becomes over the years a little more tarnished, we can easily expand the exhibition and include objects, really whole classes of objects, that are non-Olympic and might merit mounting in a consciously sensitizing milieu, that is, in an art gallery.

The surfboards made for use by teenagers on the Pacific Coast of America have received but little establishment praise. In their magazines, the surfing poets and photographers have made minor contributions to the ecumene of the human spirit. But surfboards deserve much greater exposure for much greater praise. I feel that the older, longer models dating from about 1963 are more appealing as sculpture than the newer, stubbier boards. Perhaps we could show ten boards illustrating characteristic stages of what surfers thought was perfection over the last few decades.

What about ski equipment? Not only the skis themselves, but the boots and poles and most especially the costumes. Lightness and warmth are the without-which-nothings for ski outfits, but the interpretations (colors, surfaces, cuts, appliqués, etc.) have long provided scope for original wit and insufficiently applauded invention.

More items might be tennis and badminton rackets, cricket bats, and snowshoes. Boomerangs are far more various and more amenable to individual creators' invention than almost anyone suspects.

A certain cachet of the whole show is worth noting here. It is not necessary that it be a "hands-off" operation. It might be instructive and conceivably exciting for some jaded gallery-goers or some habitual gallery-avoiders to spin the silvery wheel of a precious bicycle, to lift a javelin or a discus, to bounce a patchwork soccer ball, or to test the bend-ability of a vaulting pole. One might try his footing in the starting blocks, mounted, appropriately, in yielding artificial turf. Being not unique, all the displayed tools for uselessness of course would be well made and therefore difficult to vandalize, and all would be replaceable in any case.

I am well aware that by proposing in locales traditionally reserved for celebrating the desperate innovations in modern art the declarative display of such objects as I have praised, I am launching a calculated defense of form as a means of channeling the expression of individualism of an artistically original sort. And I wish to undermine the opportunists who pick and choose for the galleries of New York, Paris, and Düsseldorf and who order the obfuscating prose of some of the so-called art magazines. I wish to demean the desperate work and the unplayful purposefulness of the dominant, high-toned, art-progress milieu that has imperialistically charted and claimed murky, possibly diabolical, areas of human endeavor that cannot be of interest to any pleasure-seeking public and that (it goes without saying) cannot be beautiful.

A difficulty in staging the exhibition is that for our modest rhetoric, needed in the explanatory prose in the catalog, we must begin almost from point zero. It is superfluous to note that bicycles and single sculls are beneath the notice of the hard-pressed word smiths who criticize and usually defend conceptual art and its preceding and succeeding fads. The best sporting goods have not received the rationalizing devotion of the wordy admirers of Danish rockers, French perfume bottles, Italian 200-kilometer-per-hour cars, or jewelry for millionaires—all of which adapt to various modes.

I think that the lack of accessible rhetoric devoted to sports equipment is due to several reasons—all sad. One is that the final users of the very best sporting goods are nonverbal, specialized humans, and the nature of their professional preparation demands that they be isolated from esthetically sensitizing and justifying literature and ideas. Encapsulated in the above sentence is a judgment of the world of high-class sport that is meant to be more severe than my judgments against the world of high-class art.

There is no existing connoisseurship regarding sports equipment. This lapse is a small aspect of another large problem: intellectuals and searchers for the lovely refuse to examine sport. Even our best critics and the bourgeois society in which they flourish cherish sport and encourage its evolution as a pseudo religion. But they remain unwilling to recognize or analyze a final area for the indulgence of their childishness.

Perhaps a third reason is that economically the makers of the best sporting goods are almost all small concerns serving small clienteles. They might want to but cannot pay an advertising man. Our exhibition and all the attention it gets are unlikely to increase the demand for $500 bicycles or for $5,000 eight-man racing shells.

In closing my prospectus, I must add that the show would be cheap. A year of my salary and modest traveling expenses would be significant items, but the whole caper, including purchase (which might not be necessary for a lot of expensive objects that could be readily borrowed), should cost far less than a shabby Pollock or a half-dozen Picasso ceramics. Total cost, including the production of that curious catalog, would be very much less than a Philadelphia highboy or a Duesenberg.

One last matter. I will anticipate the first satirist by excluding underwear. Jockstraps, though useful as a pejorative leitmotiv, are not meant to be seen.

Respectfully offered,
R. D. M.

Wednesday, 23 August 1972

My running here is useful for more than the maintenance of general tone. Training, it turns out, can be a passkey through gates locked to others.

From the point of view of those required to meet deadlines for the sports pages at home, the means used by the organizers to protect the athletes was a silly error. The number of journalists in the Olympic Village at any time was to be severely restricted. The Press Department here (which covers the radio and television reporters as well) set up a system of priorities and passes that is just, indescribable, unworkable, and maddening. Despite the fact that the competitions have not yet begun, thousands of journalists are here with "ink" or pictures to produce. The "meat" of their profession is in the Olympic Village, behind chain-link fences, under guard and officially inaccessible.

A Canadian photographer whose anger has not hindered his ingenuity approaches the drivers of garbage trucks or maltose delivery vans, proposing to do photo essays on these callously overlooked contributors to the Olympic dream. He gets his subjects to chat earnestly and, seated beside them, snaps away with an empty Canon as they roll past the security guards, vigilant with their orange-colored suits, beaked white caps, and walkie-talkies. Once inside, the cameraman waves farewell and, a-dangle with long lenses, seeks out for the Canadian public their athletic darlings.

There is another method. I lace tight my smelly Tiger "Bostons," pull up my baggy nylon shorts, and smooth down a navy-blue T-shirt with a sewed-on pocket. After a two-mile lope about the practice fields, I pick up the pace for a quarter-mile or so before approaching the little-used back gate. Then, as the third-ranked marathoner on the Peruvian team, flailing sweat and coughing lightly, I skim past a guard who looks suspicious while glancing up from a comic book. He cannot break into this earnest workout.

Once around a corner, I jog, then stroll until the sweat becomes merely moist, push against a stuccoed wall to stretch the leg tendons, and seek a corner to sit, there to pull from my pocket a Bic "accountant's fine point" and a folded sheet of yellow foolscap. The runner's high has set in. All around is the sprawling, irreplaceably enchanting Olympic Village with its generous girls handing out dairy products, ladies from Ceylon in saris giving away tea, mechanical cows squirting Coke and Sprite, the swimming pools, and the saunas. The unexcellable eyeballing is mine as long as I want it.

Sometimes little kids with slightly swollen, yellowish faces, autograph seekers, stay beside me for a few paces as I am jogging about the whole Olympic site. Outside of the fences identifiable athletes are, in fact, seldom seen. During the first autograph encounters, out of an honest desire not to exalt myself, I kept my pace, shouting, "I'm not an athlete." Which has to be puzzling, for, if I am not, I could surely pause in my nonessential training to add my name to the dozens already scrawled in their smudged booklets. But then, if I were to stop, would it be good manners to sign, since I am, indeed, not an athlete, though uplifted here to be mistaken for one? Tourists with rolls of film to finish snap me, and I giggle at the knowledge that I will reside forever, pointed out as God-knows-who, in photograph albums in Dijon, Hull, or Gummersbach.

This morning, in the course of a long, purposeless run around the whole site, I had as company Mike Ryan who visits for a couple days in the course of hitchhiking from Germany to Venice. Mike was a student of mine and had been a chatty companion for frequent four-to-eight-mile runs all last year in South Carolina. We are shirtless and attract lots of attention since, to the undiscriminating eye, we appear authentic. Mike, with a wicked smile, cannot resist the temptation to sign "Ryan" (Jim Ryun is a charismatic, though almost never-seen figure on the site) in a couple of autograph books as I wait, jogging in circles.

Near the end of this workout, we see ahead a dense crowd of arriving spectators coming out of the subway station. We do not even have to discuss our joke but simultaneously lengthen our strides and our chuffing. We are almost amid them, and then, quite suddenly, no joke, I stumble and, shouting with anger, hit the dirt. I roll over a couple of times on a rise of tramped-down, sodded grass. Horrified, empathetic, grown men gasp, and some ladies scream. The cynosure of public attention, I rise, shake a bit, and then jog off with a limp, slowly picking up the pace. With sorrowful intonations, Mike stage-whispers, "Dammit Freddie, there went your chances for that gold medal!"

Early afternoon to late evening, Thursday, 24 August 1972

Since we are in the outside lane of the Autobahn, the driver is able to hit 170 kilometers per hour in the dark blue Mercedes that is taking me from the Cologne airport to the television studio in Bonn. I must go back a bit to recall the circumstances that brought me to here.

There were phone calls to me in South Carolina after I returned from Germany in the spring. One in early July was puzzling. I had to conclude that the cultured (German spoken by an elegant woman is as elegant as French ever is) woman questioning me was actually trying to determine how slick my spoken German was. She hung up and, sure enough, the next call, an hour later, was to get me to agree to appear in late August on a national television program, "Journalists Ask; Politicians Answer" (Journalisten fragen; Politiker antworten). I did agree, but with some misgivings. Could I, a former *Gastarbeiter* (literally "guest worker," a term now of common usage), carry off the role of "journalist" accustomed to ask bold questions of Germany's grandest political figures?

"Journalisten fragen; Politiker antworten" takes the form of a sort of round-table discussion. The moderator, Reinhard Appel, is deft and strict regarding the sharing of floor time and the limits of rhetoric. Established government figures have long been using this program to launch new notions and, along the way, perform grand roles before what is known to be an alert, well-placed audience. The program is respected because here, where few journalists are buyable and politicians at the highest levels are not normally expected to have much to hide, Appel deftly manages to keep the contents of the questions and answers substantial and entertaining. I am to be on the program as a "journalist" to ask questions about the political significance of the German Olympic Games—to begin the day after tomorrow.

Appel has assembled the major politicians of the major parties.

Chancellor Willy Brandt's representative is his foreign minister and fellow Social Democrat, Walter Scheel. Another high-ranking Social Democrat is Helmut Schmidt, generally conceded to be the smartest and least foolable person in Bonn. German friends have warned me to beware of "oil-smooth" (oelglatt) Rainer Barzel, the leader of the opposition Christian Democratic party. These same envious friends hoped I would be alert to opportunities to diminish what they feel is the insufficiently diminished stature of Franz Josef Strauss, leader of the South German–based, conservative Christian Social Union party. Strauss is carefully watched by the younger people (who always exaggerate) on the left as a bad German, an effective, though out-of-date, authoritarian militarist, a loud patriot, "the most feared German since Hitler."

The independent yet government-subsidized broadcasting company wants all this to be slick, and so there is a sort of preliminary meeting in which all present will do a little eating and some drinking—in this case, open-faced sandwiches, salted nuts, and a fruity white wine and pulpy orange juice.

I was not forewarned, but I was about to witness—indeed, to join—an "Olympic truce" in high politics. This would be an integrated (gleichge-schaltete) manifestation of the larger, transcendent, national truce. Our edition of a prestigious program with critical significance in national political life was to have a festive, "Olympic" theme. The usual, critical questioners were not on hand. Instead, there would be five foreign journalists, each from one of the continents symbolized by colored rings on the Olympic flag. The first member of my team introduced to me was yellow, in this case, a Japanese. He lived in Bonn, was senile, and could scarcely speak any language whatever. Blue (Oceania) was young, an Australian with bouncy cheeks and reddened eyes. His fluent, rapid German sounded remarkably like Australian. He was full of information, but when he talked he interrupted himself. He heard my questions but never waited for my answers. Green (Europe) was a Finnish lady knocking back lots of pale wine from fluted glasses. She told everybody her odd dress was a traditional, regional costume, the very same dress her mother wore when she attended the Games in Berlin thirty-six years ago. Black was a tweedy man from Ghana. Red (symbolizing in this case the American continent and Indians who banged on tom-toms and lived in wigwams) was yours truly.

We were told that Strauss would not appear due to urgent business in Bavaria. Perhaps he early knew something we did not know.

After some boisterous, ritualized greetings to the five continents, the three remaining politicians ignored us and compared memos with their aides. Putting away the eats and drinks, we, the whole world, talked of ourselves. The Finnish lady usually stays home turning out human interest stories for a liberal Helsinki daily. The Australian is a "stringer" for a couple of syndicates at home. These two are the only "journalists" among us. Just one of us speaks German with the rich, grammatically correct incorporations of foreign phrases, the verve and sardonic wit that the big boys deserve. This is the African who confessed to me that he is a civil servant of the federal government. He lives in and loves Bonn. He was rounded up for this occasion the day before. The gentleman from Japan used to do something else but is now retired in Germany.

We move to another room. The ceiling is lower, the chandeliers bigger. We sit about an oval, mahogany-veneered table. Appel suggests, imposes really, the order in which we will speak. There are waitresses now. Will I have a cigarette, Scotch, or more wine? We go down a corridor to yet another room where we are all made up. There is a scramble for a dark enough pancake for the elegant African whose skin is rough like a thick-skinned orange. The pancake cannot be found. Will he go on prime time shiny or buffed and lighter than usual? There are arguments among the three make-up girls, each of which presides over an immense barber's chair.

More confusion. What will they call me? Up to now, I am "Professor." But this will be a giveaway that I am not a "journalist." I cheerily accept "Herr Mandell," foregoing also "Doktor," by which I am also honorably singled out in Germany. But, is it correct, if I am so demeaned, to use "Doktor" before the last name of the Bundesminister (minister of economics and finance), Helmut Schmidt? I defer to everything and everybody as the paparazzi arrive with their long lenses and lots of film.

Appel gave me the opening question: Did the German politicians see parallels between the Olympic Games of 1936 and those scheduled to open in two days? Off they went. The three pros dominated the proceedings completely. They nodded at and then ignored all of the questions form the outside world. Soon there were two big talkers, since Schmidt abandoned the field to Walter Scheel and Rainer Barzel, neither of whom would answer even gentle questions put by the putative journalists. Appel, just as he did when there was no Olympic truce, abruptly cut in, but then they started over and re-orated clichés—in this case, the clichés of Pierre de Coubertin's Olympism of international understanding.

The Australian, who grasped only late that we were all paid and pampered participants of a freshly devised, pre-Olympic ritual, pressed the politicians and got impolitely angry when his questions were interpreted and not respected. We others knew we were there to be polite.

A few things did come out. Appel and Scheel revealed that Willi Daume and other Germans had tried to lessen the perilous visibility of national banners and anthems in Munich. Pressure for continued emphatic national identification came not from the big, dangerous powers but from the smaller socialist countries and especially the new countries in Africa. At one point Helmut Schmidt recalled his fearful forebodings in 1954, as the Germans won the world cup in football. It was not the victory (which pleased him) but the frightening significance drawn from it by the until-then humbled Germans and the joyous violence of their celebrations. German enthusiasm and pride had already caused the world too much trouble.

During the (inevitable) buffet (called a "cocktail") afterward, Scheel, despite his claims on the air that he remembered nothing of Nazi sport, revealed an amazing statistical knowledge of star performances at the 1936 Olympics. A couple of assistants of the big boys were especially pleased that I had defended the expense of the 1972 Olympics by stating that, though indeed costly and of equivocal utility, the Games, with all their cost overruns, still cost less than two American aircraft carriers, "the ugliness and uselessness of which there can be no doubt."

For the next morning, the day before the opening, the organizers and the politicians in Munich had scheduled a curious and noble ceremony at the site of the Dachau death camp, just a few miles outside Munich. Small notices in many languages had been on the bulletin boards in the Press Center. There would be an interdenominational religious service to give solemn recognition that none of us could pretend away, even now, the worst episodes in recent German history. There were burdens to be acknowledged and carried. Semitically tinged, a lover of German high culture, a self-appointed scholar of contrived ceremony as politics and art, and a self-posited and accepted critic of the deeper issues in the second German Olympics, I knew in advance that my observations would be especially worthwhile. This manifestation of German responsibility had been on my calendar for weeks. I had a reservation on the late plane back to Munich.

As I leave the television studios, some visiting Finns in the diplomatic corps and a couple television functionaries ask me to come along to seek action in Bonn. There is no action in Bonn. All we can find open in the capital of this great nation is a roof-top restaurant with almost no one in it but our noisy selves. A sullen Tunisian serves us onion soup, tinned sausages, and yet more wine. I missed the plane and slept under a down comforter at the Hotel Tulpenfeld.

Friday, 25 August 1972

A sorry spectacle in the sauna this morning is a small, mottled African boy who has lots of bristly hair on his high behind. His eyes are far apart, and he has a horizontal crease across the bridge of his nose. A running river of sweat, he is miserable and scared and, I feel, is staying in the deep heat far too long. When asked where he comes from, he replies, "Malawi," very likely dwelling on the last syllable, so that I will not confuse his homeland with Mali, another small, African nation.

"What is your sport?"

"Box," he answers with explanatory right and left jabs in the hot air and a nice, ritualistic smile. But the smile fades almost at once, and the face returns to its pathetic, original form.

Unwilling to drop the matter, I determine that his bout is the next day but conclude that he would prefer not to talk further about it. I decide then to seek out Paul Martin, the accredited journalist from Malawi, with whom I had exchanged Munich addresses when we were both being driven about, much too far and circuitously, by a confused soldier, the chauffeur of an Opel "Rekord" sedan.

2

Opening

Morning, Saturday, 26 August 1972

Using a janitor's door, my intimidating pass with all the open-sesame, coded bands of color on it, and some bluffing, I am in the press stands at the stadium before almost anyone else. I can brood about the integration of ceremony in these recently invented and now-so-venerable rituals.

One must begin at the beginning, which in this case is Pierre de Coubertin (1863–1937), who is widely attributed, with a good deal of legitimacy, with having initiated the modern Olympic Games. The Olympic movement has subsequently manufactured a splendid Coubertin out of a man who was indeed fascinating to investigate but who does not merit his growing reputation as genius, prophet, and saint.

However, we must allow that the modern Olympic Games have assumed some of their present forms and have fulfilled some of their present purposes due to Coubertin's foresight and stubbornness. A most enduring contribution of Coubertin (and one he shares with the prehistoric inventors of the bullfight and the more recent impresarios of intercollegiate American football) is his maintained and enforced conception that sport actually does not appeal to mobs disinclined to enjoy playful, agonistic efforts either on their part or on the part of others. Sporting contests always have been integrated into socially affirmative festivals and were just aspects of staged, sacred celebrations. This integration of agonistic contests with cult rituals was most emphatically true of the many athletic meets of the ancient Greeks. It was and is most famously true of their most prestigious meets, the quadrennial Olympic Games.

We must remember that the varieties of sport that Coubertin first witnessed and subsequently admired were the special tastes of a narrow stratum of the young and wealthy in England. Coubertin wished to use sport in order to toughen all Frenchmen. He assumed in advance that sport was not a universally transferable taste. Coubertin's objects for convincing (at first Frenchmen, later the world) had to be "seduced" (he used this word in this context) and charmed into being participators or vocal supporters of mass physical training and large athletic meets.

Coubertin began at the top. He knew that to hold the attention or grasp the respect of influential, middle-aged aristocrats, politicians, and financiers, his novel advocacy of physical effort of an imported kind had to have gracefully carried (if at all possible), lulling, and reassuring ceremonies with the declarative ranking of dignitaries, inspiring and not-novel slogans, symbolic banners, allegorical medals for awards, and all the pseudo-classical trappings so enjoyed by even slightly educated nineteenth-century educators and intellectuals. Accordingly, in Paris in the 1890s Coubertin's first rowing meets, gymnastic competitions, and "cross-countries" (the English term had to be used) were preceded by banquets and conventional oratory. Athletic events were interspersed with parades and more speeches and assemblies and the prominent display of personages to suggest the support of established social position and political strength. If Coubertin could not have the actual presence of princes, presidents, and prime ministers, he would settle for their acquiescence as "honorary" members of titular committees. These names he placed on various letterheads and charters.

Since only the participating athlete (always a member of a tiny tribe) can, in the truest sense, enjoy the sweetness of victory (or, by extension, the bittersweetness of well-contested defeat), Coubertin's meets had to have victory ceremonies showing to everyone the transfer of awards. Meets, for him, were required to begin with parades and rhetoric and to be finished off with solemn assemblies, which, if possible, should take place at night out-of-doors and be accompanied by firework displays or torchlit processions. It was this stoutly (and ultimately cynically) maintained view that sport also must be theater that Coubertin most triumphantly succeeded in implanting among the putatively athletic bureaucrats of international Olympism. His flags, rings, and orders of precedence became venerable when still very young. And his campaign to seduce the French led steadily to the seduction of the world.

The Frenchman had little to do with it, but the royal family of Greece projected themselves into many ceremonies of the very first modern Olympics, which took place in Athens in 1896. At one point, the chubby queen inaugurated a specially built shooting gallery by firing a pistol engarlanded with chains of little flowers. The first modern Games that took place more or less as Coubertin wished were in Stockholm in 1912. Here the Swedish royal family and Europe's princes and other nobility played elaborate ceremonial roles in affirmative, synthetic rites having no conceivable connection whatever with athletics. The whole affair was assumed ever afterward to have been a festive and political triumph. Succeeding Games gathered more trappings. The absence of titled names did not hinder the Americans in 1932 when the Olympic Games took place near Hollywood in Los Angeles. The organizers revived an exodus of pigeons first used in 1896 and added an "Olympic flame" (for which there were no historic precedents) to burn in a big brazier over the main stadium until the closing ceremonies.

In splendor and in heaped allegories, all previous athletic festivals were surpassed by the 1936 Olympics in Berlin. Actually, invented festivities began months before and included special traveling exhibitions to the German countryside intertwining traditionally classical, German, Nazi, and fresh symbols intended to elevate mindless physical training.

Carl Diem, organizer of it all, was the enthusiastic supporter of a completely invented and now hallowed torch run from ancient Olympia. Diem also concocted processions, anthems, titles, badges of office, bells, and towers—almost all of which have since fallen from use. The Nazis were good at this sort of thing. They had already learned a lot from the experimental staging of the Nuremberg party rallies.

It is worth noting that purposeful, pagan, or even fake as they were, no one in any prominent position objected to the bogus theatricality of the Nazi's international sports festival at that time or at any time afterward. Just as the Olympic Games grew in political utility, they took on mythic legitimacy and dramatic power. In Berlin in 1936 the opening ceremonies took up a whole day.

While the supreme international festival of the twentieth century gathered symbolic paraphernalia and a theatrically sensitized audience, other sporting festivals did as well. The middle decades of our century witnessed the establishment of regional, national, and international championships for all the old sports and for many new ones. One might study, for example, the continuous alteration of the dramaturgy of college football in order to accommodate different audiences between 1870 and 1970. The pure (in an athletic sense) football game cannot alone absorb spectators who may be indifferent to sport but who subconsciously, or atavistically perhaps, yearn to be a part of socially affirmative rites.

The uncritical acceptance of festive innovations in public performances of team sports, and most particularly in the Olympic Games, should be seen as evidence that most of us crave and, in fact, may need festivity. We may prefer complex festivity. Massed, periodic celebrations are elements in almost all social life and serve the socially stabilizing function of demonstrating to a participant in vivid form the power of the political conglomerate of which he is a contributing member.

The individual alone or in a primary group such as the family cannot in an epistemological sense perceive the existence of the larger society of which he is a part. A person will need to participate in periodic, symbolic reaffirmations of the controls (I speak as an ethnographer) that protect him from demons or raiders and, on the other hand, prevent him from indulging in his beastliness. We might say that a political festival, fantastic though it may be, legitimizes the enforcers of reality. But the participator in a grand festival is not entirely an individual at all but is part of an organism, a temporary, living body affirming and celebrating the enforcement of rules and assuring that periodic time will go on. Though exciting and outside of the regularity of boring daily life, a public ritual is paradoxically a protection against chaos. Gustave Le Bon (*La Psychologie des foules*, 1895) was not the first or the last to perceive that a crowd is both less and more than the sum of the persons in it.

In Western society, the sponsoring bodies or at least the legitimizing authorities for festivity have for millennia been either the established sacerdotal hierarchy or, in more recent times, local or larger secular political bodies. An illiterate individual living in an isolated place has depended upon the saint's day, the joyous entry, the harvest feast, or the fair to demonstrate the glory and the power to punish or reward of the larger universe and its distant overseers. Festivities may also be the ornaments of grim lives in that they regularly force the expression of joy.

There has never been a less publicly festive age than our own. There are explanations for this. One is that when we participate in a festival, we are in a heightened, suggestible, unprivate, and more or less irrational state. To celebrate, we must at least partly disbelieve. This is the emotional basis of all theater and civic religion. Nineteenth-century, bureaucratic politicians (who were very much like twentieth-century bureaucrats), fearing the might of the laboring classes whom they knew they were cheating, opposed gatherings of almost any sort and were battlers against any irrationality. Antifestive political technique became almost official in the industrial, urban world. This all evolved at the same time that mass schooling and mass publishing provided the literate and quasi-literate with entirely novel connections with larger collectivities. Thereby the growing proletariat was assured in quite different and private ways of the power and stability of existing political structures. Television is a further reinforcer in private of the actuality and strength of the regnant systems of authority. However, these particular manifestations, while they may have obviated much of the necessity for parades, feasts, fairs, rallies, balls, and the theater, have denied us the visceral pleasure, the social euphoria and intoxication, of the participator in the flesh. Few of us have, for example, experienced the still-accessible revels of such occasional things as hours of Balkan line dancing, drugged immersion in a colossal rock festival, sweaty hymn singing, or even the all-out, mindless giving-up of good sense at some sports victory celebration.

For a long time now, the dominant, technocratic, professional, and, most especially, the educating classes have rejected all religious superstitions and all other systems of ideological nonsense, including patriotism.

Sport as we know it postdates the theoretical positions of the nineteenth-century social critics and reformers. Sport as a political reinforcer and as the occasion for affirmative social rites is too new, and conceivably over-whelmingly (literally) successful, to have been subject to critical analysis. Its fresh rites are untarnished and accepted, though in essence still in-authentic because they are not based on accepted notions of the sacred. In no profound sense do football games and the modern Olympics mean much. But for a lot of us, they are all we have.

The above was inspired and allowed to be written down by the slow filling of the stadium. Some people, like myself, had come very early. And this sort of reflection is in keeping with my self-imposed role in Munich, which is to be an above-it-all skeptic. As a philosophical conservative (as most historians are or come to be) I have been saddened by the decay of usable, affirmative tradition.

An object of my book, *The Nazi Olympics*, was to expose as bogus the most ambitious assemblage of contrived ceremony the world had yet seen. I had become a quotable campaigner for the truncating of festive trappings for sports—particularly the dissonant and possibly dangerous, provocative clanging of mutually antagonistic national anthems and ban-ners. I was one who said that athletics should be for athletes. As a sports critic and specifically a critic of the Olympic Games, I was invited to Munich to be "seduced."

Noon, Saturday, 26 August 1972

Still three hours to go. I am at my spot, section Y, row 20, seat 19, in the press and radio swath of the stand near the right or south end of the roofed side of the stadium. Before me is one curved end of the 400-meter track upon which sit many large cages of rustling doves, which my program says are Bavarian and number in all 5,000. The end-field parts of the stadium are already filled with standees, and the rest of the place is filling slowly. It has become apparent that the light blue, four-foot-high band along the top rim of the opposite side of the stadium is a row of hostesses in their dirndls of the leading official color. In being allowed to be at the stadium today, they are being given part of their nonmonetary pay. Above them are the hundred or so national flags, which are neither hanging limp nor flapping in agitation but, responding to a possibly auspicious breeze, are extending themselves in languid waves.

The weather in this part of Europe has been until now too cool and gray. Today, from the beginning, the air has been warm and lucid. Is it a meteorological conspiracy, perhaps an augury of happiness? I have to reflect that the weather here is much finer than it was for the opening ceremonies in Berlin thirty-six years ago. If I squint, before me I can see or at least interpret colors close to those prescribed officially: a light blue sky streaked with a few silver clouds; the perfect green sward below. The bright sun has made all colors declarative and shimmering.

The press section, where each of us has a desk and a television set, has filled up more slowly. On my right is a plump Venezuelan lady who pants with pleasure and recites her observations into a hand-held tape recorder that she must pound episodically to keep going. On the left is a slim, very dark man in a fine-fitting blue cashmere blazer. He is the Paris correspondent for a Senegalese paper. Just above are six overweight Canadian journalists. Below are six almost disturbingly similar-looking East Germans with massive abdominal folds. A little off to my right are some choice parts of the spectator stands. They are separated from us by a glass partition I can talk over. And so I chat a little with a group of middle-aged or older Japanese. The men wear hats of a limp white cloth and wave white flags with the familiar red disc in the center. One crone, the only quiet one in the bunch, is wearing a faded, though still magnificent, kimono. It is of gray silk with large embroidered storks. She first wore it when she was a spectator in Berlin thirty-six years ago. All protect and aim single-lens reflex cameras, most of them with 135 mm lenses. The focal lengths of the lenses fondled and poised by the dozens of professional photographers on the field below us are much longer.

2:00 P.M., Saturday, 26 August 1972

My mood and that of all of those around me is one of alert, amused excitement. Though almost nothing has occurred, we watch keenly. The stadium is not yet full. On the opposite side, orange-suited ushers and guides are taking assigned places along the aisles, adding stripes of regulation color to the rustling blocks of grass, sky, banners, and humanity around me. The scene as panorama alters slowly; yet everyone flicks their gaze about—watching the flags, occasional officials on the green field shift their positions, and the thickening membership in the VIP stands where the unidentified and presumably powerful greet one another with gentle handshakes and quick hugs. We also watch the growing crowds of free-loading, pathetically distant viewers on an overlooking, landscaped, green hill, just outside the stadium.

Suddenly there is action. Some files of children enter. The program tells me they are from Munich, are between the ages of ten and fourteen, and number 3,200 in all. They carry bowed arcs and bunches of crepe paper flowers. The boys are in a declared "Olympic" blue, the girls in an official light orange. They seat themselves on the grass all around the rust-colored, eight-laned, plastic-surfaced track.

Our announcer, an actor, Joachim "Blacky" Fuchsberger, has begun nearly continuous announcements in German, French, and English—in that order. The announcements of real things in orderly, nicely modulat-ed "high" accents of the respective languages seem ever more like recidi-vist elements in an environment that becomes more sensuous and thought altering. We are leaving the time and space of ordinary experience. We do not like the vulgarity and obtrusive statistics. Fuchsberger has obeyed the peculiar commands of the publicity directors and recites some eating statistics of those lovely animals in the Olympic Village. The cafeteria or Mensa seats 2,600, and in the course of the Games those beasts will eat 23,000 pounds of steak, 12,000 chickens, 43,000 sausages, and more than one million eggs.

Fuchsberger jams us into the push-and-shove real world when he tells us that the police of Munich are supervising prices to protect us from gougers. And the fine voice thrice makes me wince and slap my right rear buttock as he tells us all that Munich is notorious for its pickpockets: "Make sure the hand in your pocket is always your own."

Blacky's voice is loud but not jangling or irritating. He begins his German remarks with, "Meine Damen und Herren" ("ladies and gentle-men"), and not repetitions of the severe "Achtung!" (attention) that so grated some visitors in Berlin in 1936. A remark that makes us grateful for our location is that seventy television stations are sending to the world the scene of which we are becoming participating units. We feel ourselves to be like chosen celebrants. We must show our worthiness. Fuchs-berger asks us to applaud the guests in the VIP section, and everyone with a gesture new yet ritualistic does so without having any idea who gains in stature by this. Skepticism ekes away.

2:55 P.M., Saturday, 26 August 1972

We are now in a mood of extended, happy expectation. Every-where is the hubble-bubble of cheerful good order. If one concentrates on a section of the whole scene (an act wrenchingly difficult to accom-plish for me now), it is clear that there is incessant movement. Flag waving and organized patriotism are ripples in certain sections. Mexicans and Brazilians waving their national flags and appropriate pennants make themselves distinctively seen and heard, but these are sweet little jokes in this great bowl of people.

The president of the Federal Republic, Gustav Heinemann, as "pa-tron" of the XXth Olympiad, comes with an entourage from a dark pas-sage, standard in an Olympic stadium, called the "marathon tunnel." As we watch, he climbs into the VIP stands. Happily, there are no speeches. I know what is taking place because of the aforethought program in my hand. But then I am angered into a sharp headache by the playing of the local national anthem, forbidden until only recently by the occupying Allied forces here. It hurts because the music is so beautiful. Joseph Haydn fooled sublimely with that rapturous melody in the slow move-ment of the C-major, "Emperor" quartet. The West Germans sing only the conceivably inoffensive third verse now, but until 1945 they all sang the first verse containing those ghastly lines, "Germany, Germany, over everything, over everyone in the world" ("Deutschland, Deutschland, über alles, über alles in die Welt"). It still recollects Bismarck, the kaiser, and the Nazis to me and, I suspect, to many foreigners around me. The overwhelming majority of the spectators are West Germans. They stand. We stand too, willing to please. We want to keep pleasing. The headache passes.

I am not above the panorama of joy and order. But I cannot lose myself, for there may be trouble ahead. As the program forecasts, imme-diately before us is the portentous marching-in of the nations with the "traditional" playing of more national anthems, many of them, for any number of historical or artistic reasons, squalid or wicked. Then a stupendous, happy, overwhelming joke!

But first I must set the stage a bit. Greece, land of the ancient Olympics and site of the first modern Games, begins each parade. All the other nations follow in the alphabetical order of the host language. We have been watching for some time a lot of rustling in the deep parts of the marathon tunnel. As the flag bearer of Greece comes out, there is a slam of loud music—like in a magnificent disco. Cymbals and hammered big drums throb my spine. Joy! Release! A smashing bouzouki march! We get the point dimly and then vividly that this brassy, sarcastic music is a pinching ethnic joke! Dignified, radiantly happy despite the musical trick played on them, the Greeks (I am sure that some of them are winking at us) march on. Music to the rescue!

Out of the dark and into sunlight so bright it sharpens, chisels almost, all outlines emerges another flag, another column of marchers—Egypt (Aegypten). More assured, maintaining the bombast and snickering cynicism, the opera buffa stance, the orchestra (pre-recorded, of course) slides into tickling, belly-dancing bazaar music. Egypt has not had its feelings hurt and projects delirious happiness as that nation's athletes display themselves to the world. This mischievous accompaniment continues for the entries of Ethiopia, Afghanistan, and Albania. The stalwart athletes and stout officials all accept this depiction of themselves as burlesque Middle Easterners. Then the huge team of Argentina comes out, happy as can be—to a cymbaled, silly tango.

There would, then, be no national anthems. Relieved, we submit ourselves to the designers who offered this unprecedented and delightful ornamentation. The marching goes on. Successive armies of athletes are demilitarized by music. Each legion of ecstatic youths induces accompanying, circular applause around the track until the teams assume predetermined ranks in the stadium's infield. We cannot see (perhaps are unwilling to see) corrosion in the happy mood. We smile to the point of delighted tears. If I and, by extension, if my cocelebrants are sad, it is for the world's billions who cannot be with us right now.

The Afghans advance in a precision goose step that rouses indulgent titters. The Australians are big people. So many of them are out of step. The Brazilians walk in good, steady order despite an accompanying,

off-beat, not-altogether-respectful samba. Inevitably, in their alphabetical order, the enormous team of the German Democratic Republic (here
Deutsche demokratische Republik) files in, the boys in démodé-cut suits
of dark and light blue; the girls in pastel pink pants suits. They march
around to affectionate, appreciative, if not enthusiastic, applause. No
hand grenades; no hisses. We do not expect them. We, all of us together,
have, with our forbearance, disposed of the most bothersome issue for
the politicians of Bonn and East Berlin. The world can be good!

Interspersed among the many small nations are the advancing, sinu-
ous rectangles made up of hundreds of French, British, and Indian athletes. All the marchers give back to us the smiles that, with sweet love, we
beam on them. The athletes on the infield jostle, barely keeping order
and preserving us with their cameras at the same time that we photograph them. Always sassy, fast, smashing, and loud, though still folkish,
the music slickly changes its ethnic tinge. We cannot, however, maintain
the mood of astonishment and exaltation. Peeking at our programs, we
are stifling our fear.

Indonesia, Iran, Ireland, and then . . . Israel. A small team of burly
officials, tall girls, and squat-faced boys marches past. The sleeves on the
jackets are too short. They are quite stern and undistinguished except for
what they mean to us in this place at this time. The welcoming applause
and the responsive waves are dutiful, proper, respectful—but we cannot
love with abandon where the symbolic burdens are so variegated and so
frightening. One yearns for some suitable (Would it be even conceivably
possible?) public manifestation, a cathartic public apology, sympathy for
the persons before us who are tough enough to carry what they carry. But
with the entry of these Jews, Olympians like the rest of us, it becomes
clearer that the desire of this enormous concourse of celebrants is to
offer a welcome. Nothing held back. I, perhaps more than most, am
pleased that we together are trying to destroy history. Amid riches, order,
and gratitude, we must all start again. The Jews must shrug the burdens
they force us to acknowledge. We, by our love, our joy in the present, will
help them do it.

As the parade progresses, there are summits of stimulation. The
welcoming of the Israelis is fundamentally powerful, though calm on the
surface. The relatively small numbers of Japanese spectators have a dis-
proportionate number of large, white and red flags, and men bark strange

exhortatory commands at their darlings, a large team with some astonishingly tall men. Are they breeding these like they do sumo wrestlers and pop-eyed carp?

The kolo march for the Yugoslavians (Jugoslavien) has retardandos and accelerandos so sarcastic as to force some of us to guffaw aloud. The team from Liechtenstein gets ironic applause because it is so small. Then pass more little groups of quicksteppers: Madagascar, Malawi, Mali, Malta, Monaco. What do these teams and those back home who have sent them expect to get out of all this? A mood of skepticism is returning.

The assembly from Mexico—very few of them look like athletes—is really too large. Is this a declaration that the legacy of the sports festival there four years ago was one of durable happiness? A giant trailing a blue silk cape and carrying the flag for Mongolia is nearly naked, despite the fact that he wears a peaked wool cap with flaps to tie down for the subzero winds of the steppes. There was a comparable giant in Berlin in 1936.

The Austrians (Österreich) are boisterously greeted. They are, after all, the third Germany but are not well known for past atrocious international behavior. Norway, with a population less than that of North Carolina, has a very large team. The teams from Poland and Switzerland are yet larger. The flag bearer from Portugal wears a riding outfit and is the sole member of the team.

The gap between Puerto Rico and Romania is no wider than that between other proximate teams. Therefore, the space that would have been occupied by Rhodesia, a basis for the keenest pre-Olympic anxiety, goes ceremonially unnoticed. In a freshly devised festivity, one is not alerted to the *absence* of symbols. Perhaps if we had all attended opening ceremonies yearly and Rhodesia had been there each time before, we might now have felt incompletion, dismay, and even anger. But here all is new, ostensibly nonchauvinistic and affirmative.

With the entry of the Romanians, the music again intrudes and helps us. It is something underhandedly Eastern and yet music-hall Latinate. The long column of Swedes march along with a clopping hambo containing snide syncopation. The Spanish team struts to mock-hysterical bullfight music. The proud Turks cannot be as majestic as they surely wish to be. Still, they determinedly try, stepping to the off-the-beat rhythms of Terry Tunes seraglio music. All during the marching-in,

Fuchsberger coordinates his cordial announcements of every team with the emergence of the national flags from the tunnel into the now truly dazzling sunlight. The German names of the nations simultaneously appear on the high scoreboards of intense little lights at the ends of the stadium. The tiny teams, such as those of Tanzania and Upper Volta, both of which have their athletes march in folk costumes that look like chain-gang uniforms, get his same enthusiastic intonation—just like France and Great Britain. The music, the scoreboards, and the announcer simultaneously declare a leveling justice for small and great.

But all of us know there is trouble ahead. Imminent are the introductions of the teams of the Soviet Union, the United States, and Vietnam. How might one even briefly suggest the complexity, particularly the historical memories, evoked by the Soviet Union here, now, in central Europe? Russ, Tatars, the Slavic East, czars, the knout, freezing steppes, purges, Stalin, Stalingrad. While the Germans around me have long reconciled to their American victors in the regretted last war, they have never done so to the figurative new Turks of Europe who have divided Germany and isolated Berlin and have never forsworn total conquest. And they will reap the biggest harvest of medals in the sports battles to come. Rumors, not countered by other rumors, are everywhere that the Soviets are just now conspiring to be the hosts in Moscow for the Olympics of 1980.

And the Americans! Charismatic culture creators and culture destroyers. Vietnam is on all our minds. These American beasts are the unopposed vandals of an entire subcontinent. Lovely, wicked genocides, the amoral Nazis of our epoch. Some of us are ashamed to wander the earth now and shudder when forced to defend any action single-outable as "American." I notice on the program that, though alphabetical order would require the United States (Vereinigten Staaten) to be directly before Vietnam (and all that might signify), the clever organizers have seen to it that my country is to come in as the USA but still, somehow, after the USSR.

Within the American team is a hot case—ready tinder. Stinging the paternal United States Olympic Committee (USOC) and the coaches, the American youths have elected as their flag bearer Olga Connolly. This matron is perhaps one of the most symbolically potent individuals on the site. As Olga Fikotova and a Czech, the lady was the victor in the woman's discus in Melbourne in 1956. There she defected to marry Harold Connolly, himself a winner of the hammer throw. Olga Connolly then won prizes and admiration as an American athlete. She is a splendidly handsome mother of four and at thirty-nine is one of the oldest women competing. She has been in most European newspapers of the left as a quotable supporter of Jack Scott's mischievous and much-publicized pronouncements for reform in sport. She is a well-photographed demonstrator against American atrocities in Vietnam. Connolly has smuggled contraband peace buttons into the Olympic Village. Her name is at the top of a letterhead for the provocative Olympic Project for Peace. Naturally the reporters, and picture takers pester her for yet more interviews. She has a shtick rhetorical performance that enrages the sports authoritarians who are frightened of any sort of disorder. Some American studs, reporters and officials are insulted that Mrs. Connolly should be the carrier of our holy stars and stripes.

"We must be led by a male warrior, a hero," they grunt to all who care to listen. And part of the fury is at the snotty-nosed kids who would vote for someone who personifies corrosive antipatriotism.

These antifestive reflections, producing the tightened neck and swollen hands of fear, are cut short by the entrance of the Soviet team, a snaking column of marchers six abreast. And their power is at once diminished by balalaika sounds and melodies that somehow soothe though they are in a march tempo. Here the music is not roguish. The stadium is quieter than it has been since the ritualized entries began. Will we, even a few of us, show our bitterness? No, they walk around to our light applause, and as they pass me at about one-third of their trajectory, they collectively look like Americans to me. Our relief at the music's kindness and our own self-control are broken by the slippery phasing of troika music into loud, bombastic jazz—"When the Saints Come Marching In." The champion wreckers, the slovenly rulers of the world, are upon us.

The greeting starts warm and builds up. And the rejoicing is not only by the Germans and the many compatriots on hand but—most astonishingly—by the resident critic on the site, me! At the sight of that ravishing Nike carrying that awesome flag and the immense rank of Yanks in red and white under the blue sky, I slip into a fit of aggressive pride, a blind trance, a shivering transport in the course of which I revel and project complete love. I grasp in their entirety and profundity whole strings of meaningful clichés. I understand as though by revelation all that the phrase "American dream" was ever supposed to promise. I know without effort what is meant by American dignity: a vast, rich land to use as we Americans wish, our limitless possibilities for defending the world's victims—all those skinny, lethargic fellahin less fortunate than I, an American. I bellow, standing, then jumping up and down, jamming my clenched fist into the air to give witness to the guiding forces of the universe, my limitless approval of those American ranks, loving me, before us.

Happy tears expiate the guilt I may heretofore have suffered due to what others, foreigners and putative Americans, say is evil about my country. I feel rich racial harmony in the Afro hair masses like shakos and the modest Orientals with big shoulders. How sad, tragic even, that another hundred million Americans, their patriotism now also dimmed, cannot be with me! I shudder in my mystical experience and can bring from memory only pale impressions here. I know that the American surrogates appear in the brightest colors I have ever seen. Olga Connolly holds that fabulous, dazzling banner straight out before her. Her warrior's face is stern and responsible. She bears the terrible weight of meaning with perfect American grace.

During the later stages of this noisy episode, it is clear that I have become a side-spectacle for observation by the East Germans below, the Canadians above, the Japanese nearby, and the sleek Senegalese on my left. In a gradual re-installation of cosmopolitan shame, with my face soggy wet, I begin to nod around mumbling a little, but, I feel, giving adequately the message, "I am really not this kind of person."

This is cut short, for, providentially, the Venezuelan lady saves me by going into shrieking ecstasies as her team marches in. Slumped, trying to figure out what happened, I miss Vietnam and barely notice the pervading emotional gift that was the whole stadium's welcome for the West German team, which as the host nation is last. Unrecoverably embarrassed and in a state for which there are no words, but which must be something like *post coitum tristis*, I penitentially leave my eager-to-reconcile festive companions to go to the rim of the stadium for a grander vista and a spot where I again have no past.

The athletes are all in the infield now. The children in Olympic blue and orange who had been seated on the grass strips outside the track now move onto it for a gymnastic dance, reminiscent of a *Turntag*, those enormous synchronized demonstrations of the previous century, of welcome. They wave their crepe paper ornaments, and the recorded orchestra accompanies a recorded chorus singing, "Spring is icumin in," with the reiterated lines, "Sing cucu, sing cucu." So, spread below us is a vast panorama demonstrating, by means of the assembled athletic representatives, the harmony of nations and, by means of the synchronized dancing of thousands of innocent children, hope for the future.

All about, the esthetic supersensitivity and incandescent vitality have vitiated. There comes an unchoreographed and unchoreographable progression of fanfares, speeches, and presentations. Avery Brundage speaks briefly in German and pronounces "der" as "dur." Of course many foreigners are pleased that so many of us speak badly. Gustav Heinemann, president of the Federal Republic, the "patron," gives a prescribed announcement: "I declare the Games celebrating the twentieth Olympiad of the modern era as opened." Somehow, this effigy of West German respectability places extraordinary emphasis on the middle syllable of the last word, "eröffnet." A little personal gesture, a German gesture, that the stadium loves as a deft insertion of national specialness in a neutral party piece. Or am I overly delicate?

Eight rowers on the German regatta team hoist some grand, white "Olympic" flag. The vast band, of some 300 members of the Bundeswehr, plays an "Olympic" anthem composed by some Greek for the Games of 1896 and rearranged by some American for 1972. Dull. Much of this action is overdescribed for us by the announcer working in the three languages.

There is more switching of old flags and symbols between civic officials of Mexico City (scene of the previous Games), officials of Munich, and Avery Brundage. The crowd greets every bit of announced action impartially; they are dutiful regarding the five Olympic rings and all other Olympic reiterations. The athletes in the center field, most of whom had been waiting outside for hours to march in, look great to us, but they are not well placed to see what is going on. They start to break their ranks in order to observe what they suspect is of gripping interest.

Sensuous interest revives with the display on the track of Mexican folklore dancers and mariachis who, alas, wear the cheap serapes of striped aniline dyes that our neighbor has brought back from Tijuana or Juarez for his nieces and nephews. This happy ballet that takes place largely before the press and VIP sections merges into a dance of infiltrating, larger numbers of Bavarian heel-slapping dancers called Schuhplattler in circular groups all about the whole track. This, in turn, merges into a startling display of loudly snapping bullwhips by more folklorish Bavarians. One is amazed and approving, not so much at the details of it all, but due to the ensemble. Clean, alone, unknown, and high above, I am becoming once more merged into the festive unit. Once again the sequential dramaturgy moves on in a sensuous area of celebration raised above words, details, separable items, and logic. Surely more marvels will occur.

Creeping, self-abnegating men in gray move forward to pull pegs from hinges on the cages holding the pent doves. In many thin streams the pigeons dash quickly forward in nearly horizontal trajectories. For a while the birds are an aimless series of flapping specks, and then, as they meet over the teams in the infield, the thousands of individuals begin to coalesce in a swirl going way up. They grow into a mass of curving motion, like incense smoke. We smile wistfully when it becomes apparent that all are avoiding the underside of the glistening roof to make for the blue sky and silver clouds of Bavaria. Some of us laugh uneasily and some gasp with unease when the sole failure in the pack gives up his effort to be part of the escaping group and falls as though dead into the front ranks of an athletic team.

As the doves become shimmering specks merging with the distance, sixty men in Bavarian costumes (my program tells me they are Goasslschlalzer, which is meaningless to me) positioned around the track shoot in near unison, three terrific shots from big antique pistols. They must be announcing some sort of climax. Suddenly, five runners, dressed in white, lope in a "V" formation from the tunnel. There are an African, an Asian, and one man from Oceania. The biggest by far is Jim Ryun, the American. The leader, carrying the sacred flame lit a month before at the site of the ancient Olympics in the Peloponnesus, is a fair German boy. As I watch the conclusion of a piece of theater that I know better than anyone is unhistorical and ersatz, indeed, an opportunist's concoction for a Nazi extravaganza, I am seduced. Just another chump, overcome by choreographed splendor—one of many thousands, perhaps billions, of victims of art.

The quintet glows due to the world's adoration in the fine moments during which they run, the vessels of our abject wonderment. Most of us are gasping or weeping. A smooth run of a lap and a half and then four of the five who are the world stop before a carpet of "Olympic" light orange (not red!) that proceeds up a clear aisle on the far side of the stadium. A holy light leaves the four stopped runners and intensifies the radiance of the German athlete. That polestar bends his head down as he springs, as though inspired, up the steps. He grasps securely his flaming message binding ancient Greece to us, today, now.

He continues up. Then alone on a tiny platform he stands before the world's destination. All the world's spiritual aspirations are harbored in that elevated figure. Still, with his torch aimed at the heavens, he extends the jeweled moment and then slowly lowers his little flame to the silver salver, which explodes in a big flaming beacon. This is the fire that will sanctify our activities for the next sixteen days.

Minutes may have passed before we notice that several persons, the outstanding among them a girl in a short skirt, have assembled on the tribune before the VIPs. Forcing ourselves to read we learn from the program that she is a German track athlete who will symbolically swear for all the present athletes that they will compete "in the true spirit of sportsmanship." The translations and the soberness of this playlet are unamenable to dramaturgical exploitation. Having left the state of selfless ecstasy, I glance up to observe that the beautiful carrier of the last torch has vanished, ascended perhaps.

Now some polyharmonic, electronic music of merging, long chords comes ever more oppressively over the loudspeakers. Our program tells us that this is, "An Oracle of the God Apollo," by Krzysztof Penderecki and that it had been prerecorded in Warsaw. While trembling in an amalgam of art-induced pleasure, of aural eeriness, and of fear and emotional fatigue, I understand that this peculiar, modern element must be an insertion on the part of Willi Daume who was determined to inject contemporary chic into our traditions. Furthermore, I am certain that Penderecki is an established contradiction in terms, that is, he is an avant-gardist of impeccable credentials. The music is not liked. Many are restless. Perhaps this caused the precision of the whole enterprise to begin to slip. The national formations of the athletes had broken up so the earlier marchers could better observe. Hastily, most, but not all, of the athletes and officials who had marched resume their earlier positions for a presumed quick march out to a medley of snatches of the same mocking music that brought them in. Then something we prefer to believe was unplanned occurred.

A timorous, though brave, few of the blue-and-orange-dressed children of Munich who were inert before and after their precision dance with the hoops and pom-poms dart out from their places to present their dance apparatus to members of the German team who happen to be nearby. The idea catches on. Slowly and then more rapidly, others thrust their bright ornaments at the athletes nearest them, not necessarily German since there are no Germans near some of the kids. Then this becomes a very pretty sight as little groups from the entire periphery of the stadium dash forward (against the rules?) to offer symbols that could easily be viewed as gifts of peace and harmony to stalwarts from every part of the world from the hands of children who have no German history.

The emptying of the stadium of the athletes and most of the other participators takes just a short time. The stands become empty. But I hang around to lean against things and to watch a couple thousand other pensive stragglers. What, in fact, just took place? We will never know.

Evening, Saturday, 26 August 1972

A couple of days ago, while on some excursion far from the main Olympic site, I took a leaflet from the offering hand of a pale boy. He had many little red pimples. I walked on reading. The mimeographed sheet announced, "OLYMPIC EXHIBIT 1936–1972: DEVELOPMENT OF THE CLASS STRUGGLE IN THE FEDERAL REPUBLIC," and gave as the location of the display a sidewalk and a wall near a cemetery in Munich. The text was an angry scatter shot at the domestic and foreign policies of the hosting government of my festival. Having a professional interest in the Olympic Games of both 1936 and 1972, I turned about and introduced myself to the kid. He was a member of the Basic Workers' Group for the Rebuilding of the Communist Party (Arbeiter-Basis-Gruppen für den Wiederaufbau der kommunistischen Partei), an illegal, though evidently tolerated, organization that has as its heroes Karl Marx and Nicolai Lenin. His group, he hotly declared, was orthodox. They were to the left of the German Communist party, which, as a tool of the Soviet Union, was despised because these so-called Communists had abandoned their independence and, of course, with it, their revolutionary energy. I could not get to the display just then, felt bad about it, and told him so. Then he invited me to a counter-Olympic "Opening Assembly" scheduled to take place after the official opening of the Olympic Games. I told him about myself and gave him my card. He would tell his colleagues to expect me.

Accordingly, following the official opening ceremonies, I lace myself with several cups of coffee and shake my head a lot. No cars or taxis are on hand so I take a subway and then a near-empty bus that traverses the Thalkirchnerstrasse past some construction supply yards and some stuccoed, four-storied prewar apartment houses. Shabby, respectable, quiet: a part of the metropolis no tourist would ever seek. In this part of the city, there is no trace of the celebration the preparations for which have for five years convulsed the cosmopolitan center four miles to the west. The main road and the side streets are damp, cobbled, and silent except for an occasional small car going too fast. From the bus I approach a gathering of uncolorful-looking people—about fifty of them. They shift and mill about the pub, Zunfthaus. Since I had no time to change into revolutionary clothing, I approach them in orange tweed jacket and striped silk tie and so am regarded with some suspicion by the few older people present. On the other hand, I inspire warm curiosity in the majority who are thin but healthy-looking teenagers.

A large, bearded lad in a well-cut but old suit is unloading from the trunk of a rusty Peugeot some long flags with poles at either end. When asked to do so, the boy I saw several days ago who gave me that tract takes me to the leaders. They are two fellows, of whom one is the largest present. The other is one of the smallest. They are indeed expecting me.

"We were going to have our rally in this tavern, but the owner locked us out when some neighbors heard of our plans for a meeting and threatened him. Such is our reputation! To hell with them all! We'll march anyway!" The short one shouts all of this and more as he unrolls the long parade banners that are of a soiled, unapologetic red with sewed-on block letters of gold-yellow. The one he first inspects carries the slogan,

"AGAINST IMPERIALISM AND FASCISM: FOR THE UNITY OF ALL PEOPLES!" Some other kids unleash a pennant with the motto, "YANKS, GET OUT OF INDO-CHINA!"

One child asks if I am a Communist, is pained when I reply that I am not, and is astonished when I explain that I am a bourgeois, American journalist besides.

"Will you not be seized and punished by the FBI and the CIA, if you demonstrate with us?"

"The FBI and the CIA don't care even a little about me. Though I am not entirely unsympathetic with either you or your projects, I am not here to demonstrate. I am here to talk, watch, and pick up documentation. I am writing a book."

The suspicions, if there were any, are subsumed in delight. Growing darkness softens the features of my companions.

"Where are you going to march to anyway?" I ask as I look down the long, empty street at the other end of the city, far from the mobs of Germans and foreigners who might be impressed by this display of courage and power.

"We'll march to the Sendlingertorplatz where so many trams and buses meet. We'd be marching on the Olympic Stadium, but the authorities long ago passed a law forbidding any sort of demonstration near the place. Still, we will not be beaten!"

Rather happily for the purposes of my listening to talk and noting it, the confusion due to the deprivation of an indoor meeting place gives me access to the leaders as they attempt to agree on details for a suitable manifestation for this important day in the history of the Federal Republic of Germany. Not only do they scorn the politics of Franz Josef Strauss, Rainer Barzel, Helmut Schmidt, and Willy Brandt, they will also heap scorn on the Communists.

"All the party does in face of these so-called Olympic Games is issue press bulletins. Makes one furious to hear them call themselves Communists. All the revolutionary vitality of Germany now resides in us."

Another street-wide banner has the legend, "AGAINST THE OLYMPIC FRAUD: FOR THE FRIENDSHIP OF PEOPLES!"

"What are your particular objections to these Olympic Games?"

Two reply almost at once, "Oh, we're not against the Olympic Games! Of course not! It's just clear to us, as it should be clear to the world, that the Olympic idea is being used to mask the aggressiveness of the imperialistic great powers and especially to cover up the corruption of the present regime in the Federal Republic."

"I believe your own book is against the political misuse of the Olympic Games," a studious-looking boy remarks.

"My point was less subtle than that. It seems that the modern Olympic Games are essentially ideological and therefore political in origin and have long since proved to be usable by just about anyone. In fact, any organized sport is employable by politicians—but that's going outside our discussion here. If it were possible, wouldn't you like to use the Olympics for your kind of politics? Certainly every political party in Germany is attempting to gain some sort of credit for staging what appears already to have been successful. Isn't it likely that what you think is the 'Olympic idea' is really some sort of notion that will promote your view of what society ought to be? Coubertin, incidentally, was himself a French chauvinist and a praiser of imperialism."

"No! Coubertin always dreamed that the Olympic Games should lead to the greater friendship of people, not the repression and murder of them."

"Who is being murdered?"

"Vietnam."

An inappropriate, though effective, stab. The single word wrecks for a period the possibility for a moral discussion with an American when he is under way elsewhere. As I mumble and shuffle my feet, a procession is actually forming. I desperately shift the subject to inspire more declarations. The Communist kids read. After all, one read my book, and several knew of it. It would be useful to know if the intelligent polemics of the younger neo-Marxist sports critics have anything to do with their theoretical stance against the present festival. I am also curious as to whether there has been any sort of protest movement or a critical restlessness among the German athletes themselves. Do they know of Bero Rigauer's *Sport und Arbeit* (1969), Ulrike Prokop's *Soziologie der olympischen Spiele: Sport und Kapitalismus* (1970), Gerhard Vinnai's *Fussballsport als Ideologie* (1971)? These, but especially the first book by Rigauer, were all brilliantly incisive analyses of the role of modern sport, at all levels, in stabilizing and legitimizing modern, industrial, urban life. I had been attempting to get my American colleagues to read these books for some time.

"All the so-called critics you mentioned are salaried academics. As such, they are held to their jobs, which in turn are dependent upon the generosity of the Federal Republic's bureaucrats—repressive, all of them. Though that kind of writing is progressive, it's not political."

It is not necessary to inspect the wan, earnest children with care to know that they are neither athletes nor fans. Not a mesomorph in the bunch. Their posed, dirty clothes would make them repulsive to all the mindless clean-cutters at the German sports academies. They say they know of some eccentric individuals but of no radicalized athletes in Germany.

Several standard-bearers span their banners across the column, which looks like it will be about four persons abreast and about fifteen persons long. Since they may be starting, I hurry about to collect propaganda and to write down stuff in a brown notebook about the size of my hand. Several more times they reverently mention that "Olympic idea" attributable to Baron Pierre de Coubertin which could lead to the "Friendship of Peoples" that is a component of several of the slogans.

Just two hours before I had been seduced by the groundless, optimistic staging of the official opening. Almost fully recovered, I remark, "I'm far more pessimistic than you are about the Olympic Games."

"Oh, we're not pessimistic at all," replies a girl with clean little teeth and dark hair parted down the middle.

I am writing her words down when something sudden, scary, and astonishingly erotic occurs. The girl jams herself close to me so that her fine, firm breasts clasp the right side of my rib cage. Simultaneously, a fair boy presses close like a dancer at my left. His genitals are like gristle against my hip. I gasp with frightened astonishment and pleasurable anticipation, "My God! What's happening?"

"That policeman wants to see what you are writing in your little book."

Looking over their close heads and shielding, nourishing bodies, I see, smiling with embarrassment, the stupid, scrubbed-pink face beneath a narrow-brimmed Bavarian hat. This man had indeed been hovering and trying to look into my book. The generous embraces as well as the notion that anything I might be doing could be of interest to a spy are powerfully boosting to my notion of myself here. And so I am now fully recovered after a shattering piece of theater that had reduced me to a cipher trusting none of his judgments. Bravely, a manful critic again, I stare and the cop walks off. We un-embrace.

For some moments the nascent procession has approximated precision. I am now holding them up. So I make a stack of the magazines, mimeographed polemics, and pamphlets they have on hand and respond with ten marks to a prettily hesitant request on the part of the dark girl for a contribution. Part of the stack is a dozen or so lick-and-paste stickers—almost the sole anti-Olympic graffiti one sees in Munich. The stickers depict a four-sequence progression showing the five-ringed Olympic logo being transformed by the addition of a few lines into a tank with a stubby, menacing gun turret.

With many "auf Wiedersehens" we separate. I jog briskly ahead to a large café and some Saturday evening customers. I rush to the back to be alone and to write all this stuff down. But it turns out I am on their line of march. And soon I hear the advancing hordes that would tear the new Germany down. They are relentlessly marching and chanting in the precision of high German the phrase:

> A - gainst O - lym - pic Fraud: For Peo - ples' Friend - ship! A - gainst O - lym - pic Fraud: For Peo - ples' Friend - ship!
>
> (Gegen Olympia Betrug: für Völkerfreundschaft!)

No one pays any attention to them.

3

Developments

Once past the guards I give up my pose as a has-been distance runner making a comeback. Sweat evaporated, I wander about as free as the visiting mothers and fathers, the onlookers in groups from the youth camps, and the few legitimate journalists who have gotten a rare pass into the Village for the day. I may pose as a Costa Rican coach on a coffee break.

The well-planned architecture of this huge complex, its playful landscaping, and the number of installed entertainments are all worth inspection. But what is most emphatically worth watching are the human beauties. The thousands of summit-accomplishment-athletes (German is better here: Hochleistungsathleten) are the most stimulating visions of all. Their demographic density establishes the general atmosphere of sensual beauty that is still somehow distant, clean, and nutritious. A voyeur's ephemeral paradise.

They are bigger than the rest of us. The grand majority of them recall or approximate the proportions and the skin textures of the ideal beauties whom most of us glimpse once or twice a week on the sidewalk, in some fast-food restaurant, or in a crowd. Those of us lucky enough to have employment on an American campus see the type with greater frequency. Here there are a lot more of them, and they come in a lot more sizes and colors. And only a few on the site carry the blush showing that they are aware that they are being regarded as fine fleshly sculpture.

The usual outfits are training suits of brightly colored stretch fabrics, which, happily, cling to magnificent thighs and sometimes slide up into the crease between the buttocks. The uniforms are variegated, though classless—or at least make the wearers unplaceable in a bureaucratically structured social scheme. In training suits with stripes and national emblems and in training shoes of lollipop colors, the strolling players suggest geographically remote creatures like reef fishes, tree frogs, or jungle beetles. Arrogance is exceptional. Thoroughly accustomed by years of directed training to doing what they are told, they are self-effacing.

The precious commodities are having a marvelous time. Our organizers have provided a fenced utopia of amusement and nutrition. The athletes must be kept out of the way of those who have big political stakes in the larger festival. Here the beauties are under the surveillance that the coaches demand to keep them in good fettle.

There are movie houses with continuous programs, parlors with pinball machines, and new pool tables. Most popular are the banks of televisions turned on for each of the sites and for all the national emissions. No need for them to go elsewhere—unless, of course, they must perform.

A little while back, this aggressive looker joined several dozen others on a balcony to observe a pair of tanned, chamois-skinned light-heavyweight wrestlers, stripped to the waist, play Ping-Pong. They dashed about grandly, sweatily, gesticulating in the pauses of play and bellowing good-naturedly in some Scandinavian tongue. Everyone anywhere near the scene was pleased.

Here and there in landscaped clearings are oversized chess "boards" with pieces of half-gallon-bottle size. Each game draws shifting bundles of kibitzers. For some time I watched a winning African sprinter. He was entirely still except for the twitching tendons along his complexly veined and striated bare legs. One recent evening I dawdled in the Village discotheque, a meandering low hall, routinely illuminated as form demands with dim colored lights and furnished with lots of low, occupied couches. The rock music was not as slamming as a jaded American might have desired. The very few smokers (coxswains and marksmen, one guesses) looked ashamed. Consequently, the ambience was not as dreary and frenetic as these places are in all big cities. On the other hand, the dancing was far below the Manhattan level of joking and sensual abandonment.

The American does not expect that there will be so many female athletes on the site. And those here—this was a particularly delightful astonishment—rarely approximate the pallid, stringy, or bulky type an American professor expects on his campus. More often they look like the babes one sees on the covers of Elle, Jasmin, or Sie. The women, hundreds of them, are thin, highly colored, vivacious, and (as my fantasies directed me) presumably loose. Among the men I watched and envied, the British, Australians, Scandinavians, and Americans move in this territory, filled with potential adventures, with enviable ease.

All are surpassed in panache by the American blacks. They have the most pick-outable walks, the frankest stares, the most mobile hips, and the most presumptuous openers ("Hi baby. What's happ'nin'?"). In the disco one sees only the big American black men dancing. They pop their fingers. When they dance, circles of watchers form.

One might see a cheeky Pole, a noisy Japanese, or a dark, sashaying Brazilian dancing, but most of the athletes from out-of-the-way places are, like this writer, quite satisfied to watch. Or maybe they just do not know what to do. Groups of spectacular-looking African males sit together and point laughing at the suggestive antics of others. They look like they could do it but certainly do not know how to carry themselves with derring-do in a disco.

It is worth noting here that the quarters for the female athletes are apart from those in the Village. They will be student dormitories after the Games. In this area the security works. I just cannot get in to look around. Nor can other males or other journalists. One hears that the quarters are yet more austere and crowded than those for the males. But, in any case, females are not barred from the male quarters.

A stimulating atmosphere. It would be difficult to separate the elegant, the erotic, and the rough fantasies of sexual completion from the hot moods of the many lookers. Perhaps there is not as much actual rutting as the consorting and foreplay—figurative tips of the iceberg—suggest. Perhaps the finely tuned good health, contained physical energy, and best-available loveliness make me want to believe that as soon as a pair turns a corner out of my sight, they are tearing at one another, moaning and drooling.

Whatever the athletes may do, there are others on the site hunting something substantial. I wasted too much time today watching a woman with a high sprayed hairdo (I guessed that she was a waitress in an Ingolstadt *Konditorei*) cruise in front of the band shell near the main entrance of the Village. She wore a red wool miniskirt and no underpants. For some twenty minutes she sat on a green fiberglass bench, spewing cigarette smoke and showing more and more. Then she snagged a middle-aged Romanian coach in a training suit. He introduced himself with many bows. She appeared to be in more of a hurry than he was. They strolled a bit but were moving with some speed as I lost sight of them going around a corner.

Much of what takes place seems enchanting and guileless. There are some souvenir shops and quick-service laundries occupying cubicles that will be boutiques once the area becomes expensive housing. The athletes can spend money here, but so many things are free that we seem outside of an economic system based on allocations and scarcity. Coke and Sprite spigots are all over the place. The Nestlé people give away from kiosks on the pedestrian malls an endless number of plastic containers of Milo, a chocolate-flavored, protein- and vitamin-fortified dairy drink that smells like dog food. The label tells us each serving has 188 calories of which ten grams are protein and three are fat. It can hold off hunger for about two hours. Ledges everywhere have Milo containers, many of them sucked for only a few sips, with the skinny pipettes sticking out.

There are little carts staffed by sari-draped ladies from Ceylon who smilingly give away tea from that country. Enclosed, clinically clean shops hand out oversweetened, fruit-laced yogurt in white cups. Olga Connolly told me, as she was simultaneously being filmed by Polish and German cameramen, that she had downed so much yogurt on the run that she longed for the time she would never see it again. At the swimming pools on the first floors of the larger dormitories, an attendant dispenses one-at-a-time items from crates of spotted bananas, tough-skinned Israeli oranges, and grainy German apples and pears.

My pass will not take me through the guarded entrances of the Mensa. So I enter through an exit. The distribution of the food is brusque and businesslike—like in a students' cafeteria. The athletes eat off shiny, off-white disposable dishes and operate with throw-away cutlery. The cheerless attendants offer the food from stainless steel basins with big spoons and great speed. My lamb shish kebab is lean, nicely cooked, and agreeably hot. The bib lettuce is not wilted. The dish of chocolate ice cream is large. Unlike the cafeteria of the Press Center, there are no sauces. Nor is there wine or beer.

Like my young companions, I loiter at the spigots above glass-pressed valves that release streams of orange and grapefruit juice. I never heard any complaints from the Villagers regarding the food. They might have groused, though, if they knew of the superior pampering the journalists got.

The establishment of a moneyless environment does not eliminate commerce, however. There is a doctoral dissertation or at least a statistically buttressed article to be written on the informal market in national lapel pins that is steadily under way on the Helene-Mayer-Ring near the Village's administrative offices. It is (or should be) well known now that the correctly outfitted Olympic athlete arrives with several dozen stick-through, enameled brooches about an inch high and emblazoned with symbols of his nation. He barters his stake for the pins of other nations—as many as he can assemble. These pins are displayed on lapels or tams. Some showmen, not athletes, have whole costumes containing hundreds—in a couple of cases, thousands—of these pins, collected from past international meets. The economist would know that the pins of the United States, the Soviet Union, and Australia are in oversupply and must be offered in multiples to get the recherché emblems of Chad, Mauritius, or Iceland. All this commerce takes place in the highest good spirits accompanied by ingenious sign language and is much snapped by the Prakticas, Minoltas, and Voightlanders of the trading athletes themselves.

Nervous-making, ostensible extensions of moneylessness are the boutiques of the Adidas and Puma sport shoe manufacturers. The struggle for beneficial public exposure on the part of these large German concerns, run by mutually despising brothers, is a spoiling element at many internationally televised sports contests. The competition is especially severe and odd here, since both are using the same dishonest techniques to get around Olympic prohibitions against the athletes' sponsorship of brands of athletic equipment. Nevertheless the three stripes of Adidas, the distinctive speed molding of Puma, and the motif of Japanese Onitsuka Tigers that cunningly combines both are all variously hustled in their respective pavilions. Onitsuka has an establishment nearby but outside the Village.

All of these places have large staffs, disgusted with their work, whose duty is to determine which of the beggars are famous (that is, might possibly receive televised or photographic attention) and are therefore worthy of free shoes, training suits, tote sacks, or other materials carrying the company names or unmistakable logos. Avaricious minor athletes, coaches, and even journalists crowd the shops fingering merchandise. All seek the confirmation of prestige attending a free pair of Adidas or Puma distance-running shoes.

A Jim Ryun or a Kipchoge Keino does not have to go through this groveling. Their sort are sought out by other staffers of the big equipment houses who carry for distribution not only the merchandise but also packets of used bills in small denominations. Tales of such payoffs were some of the noisier scandals at the Mexico City Games of 1968. On the other hand, some unnoticeable athletes and officials will attempt to buy certain shoes in order to indicate in public that they merited the getting of them free. The smell of nervous sweat is oppressive here and is uncharacteristic of the air anywhere else around the Village.

For civilians who crowd about the guarded gates, lean against the fences, or patrol the nearby practice sites, some athletes are rather easy to see, if not too easy to touch. An explanation for this visibility is that there is little reason for the athletes to spend much time in their rooms. These places are damp and bare and have thoughtlessly arranged furniture of martial simplicity. If there are stewards (such as patrol the journalists' quarters), I saw none. But like the women's dormitories, the sleeping quarters of the Olympic Village in Munich were not intended to be seen by anybody. The athletes themselves will not be writing for the world's newspapers about West German coziness.

Evening, Sunday, 27 August 1972

This is my first Olympic competition, ever.

I am in a long, narrow hall where the weight-lifting contests are being held. The hall itself is part of an existing complex of buildings in Munich called the Messegelände. It is sort of a state fairgrounds regularly used for large trade shows. The buildings here were remodeled and equipped in order to house Olympic weight lifting, wrestling, fencing, judo, and some other sports—the sort of competitive activities that in a large American university would be called the "minor" sports. Here in Munich they are the sports that do not attract the kind of journalistic or massed spectator attention that track and field, gymnastics, and some team games do. These latter are offered for more numerous watching a few kilometers from here at the main site. Everybody gets to these halls by means of frequent army buses.

One cannot suggest that the facilities for performing and watching are anything but well carried out. The specifications of the international federations of every internationally practiced sport told the Munich organizers to do things right, and, costly though it might have been, the Germans did things right.

We are in the press section directly before a raised dais. This platform for performance is carpeted and awash in filtered, fluorescent light that casts no shadows. The whirring Arriflexes all about can be certain of keeping the registration of their color film within the depth-of-field gauges on their long lenses. At our left are tables of judges and many other officials whose functions one can only guess. Hostesses serve them pitchers of water and give them lots of messages. The 3,600 spectators in back of me are entertained in the awkward pauses between various parts in the program with known pieces by Herb Alpert's Tijuana Brass.

The weight lifters (like the boxers and wrestlers) begin the run through their many weight classes from the bottom. So we will witness the struggle for medals among the very smallest power lifters, the fly-weights who weigh less than 52 kilograms or 115 pounds.

Intervals of familiarity with Herb Alpert notwithstanding, the first amazement is the sound of it all. Contributing to this is the emphatic presence of small groups of prepped cheering sections from various nations. One helpful guide, an experienced journalistic observer at European championships, nods toward a group of especially agitated, raucous people and tells me that he knows already they are Hungarians. A half-dozen mutually reinforcing screamers are from the Philippines. Among a larger group of Japanese, some kimonoed ladies ululate in high-pitched songs. The call of the Poles is merely, "Polska! Polska! Polska!" in long cadences.

The buzzers that announce the acts of the successive actors are much too loud—perhaps to startle the cheerers. One hears always the whirring of the Arriflexes or the automatic winders of rapidly shooting hand-held reflex cameras.

The most astonishing, quite unanticipated, noise of all is the battering ram of the dropped weights. For the athletes, once having raised and briefly held steady the attempted number of kilograms in one of the three required fashions, are allowed to settle the burden in any way that they wish. The efficient method is abjectly to surrender to gravity. And down the weight comes—a bar with from 100 to 200 pounds at either end of it. There is a tremendous thud and an anticlimactic, but still loud, bounce. Once under way, the competitions produce lots of these bangs—always louder than the last one you remember. Each bang produces a suspension of the sense of ongoing time.

One companion is an American bodybuilder. The one who instructs best is a thirty-year-old German with a bushy mustache that curls into his mouth. He is a magazine writer who has been to many such meets, which can last a week. He says that one cannot get used to these bangs because they are never rhythmical; each one is different. As the contests go on, the weights are greater; the subsequent jolts are worse.

One sees here far more than a contest of physical power. In fact, the presentation of it all seems to distract one from the hoist that, though the object of it all, is rather quick. The emotion displayed is a keener, more moving, and more naked display of psychic excess than one might expect of a stage actor. The performing weight lifter plans to put himself through lifts that surpass the accomplishments of his practice hoists. Records—personal, regional, or at the levels of world competition, as here—are done by tiny increments of previous bests, and these little increments are unleashed by letting go an exceptional gathering of psychic force.

Before some reforms, it used to be the case, my informants tell me, that a lifter could spend as much time as he wished preparing inwardly for a crucial effort. Now, in important competitions, the athlete is allowed only three minutes on the stage after he leaves the team preparation room.

These are intense, three-minute playlets. Confidently, the men strut on, stalk about, stamp, and compulsively raise their arms parallel toward heaven, the source of all spiritual power. Some stop, hands on hips, to stare in loathing at the enemy, which is a weight greater than any they have lifted before. An athlete might make a snarling approach to a bar and then retreat from it. They stand a foot in back of the weight, clinching and unclinching their fists, perhaps hedging their bets with prayerful looks alternatively to heaven and hell. Their faces are moving contortions of hatred, rage, and terror. Time passes. Suddenly the athlete stoops to raise the weight, having drawn from the atmosphere all the electric power he can gather for the brief summits of his emotional and physical existence.

A spectacular performer was a tiny Japanese who dashed from one side of the stage to the other. Simultaneously he went through several shades of skin color as he did some gasping breathing exercises. All this went with interludes of slack-mouthed peering at a hole in the ceiling that only he could see. Zen Buddhism—with a touch of hysteria, we guessed. This man, Tetushide Sasaki, also sniffed from some slender tube, and, due to his earnest psychic distractions, his concealments were fumbling. Furthermore, he seemed to be the most demanding in urging—I do not know how he did it—some sort of spiritual help from all the spectators. The Japanese projected spirit, and perhaps I reluctantly did so toward him as well. He was fatiguing.

A risky attempt when the weight gets only partly up puts the lifters' compressed, knotty bodies into unsymmetrical twists. And then the weight falls. Upon failure—sometimes the bar never even leaves the floor—there are temper tantrums, the grimaces of furious three-year-olds.

Nervous collapse is common at large meets. A great weight gets no further than the shoulders, stays there, and then falls. Here too the noise is terrific. The sufferer of a calamitous failure may nod politely as the weight rolls about behind or in front of him. Consider, I was asked, the self-loathing ever afterward of a world-class athlete whose breakdown, watched by all, occurs after he has been publicly praying for another issue to the affair. He cannot even grasp the bar.

When a power lifter does succeed in a grand effort, the emotion sucked from the audience is yet more intense. However wearing this all is for me, a successful hoist releases the coaches and cheering claques for further paroxysms. The failures sulk through doors at the sides in the back with the merest shoulder touch from a coach.

I am observing the performances of flyweights—that is the smallest of all weight lifters. A surpassing lift causes the coaches—all of them giants—to pick up the little men and carry them about joyously as delightful toys. These are some of the oddest sights I have ever seen.

The evening of the flyweight Olympic weight-lifting competition is also the occasion of my first Olympic victory ceremony. Three light blue boxes are put on the dais—the middle box higher than the flankers. There is also a portable apparatus with three flag poles—the middle one higher than the flankers. While this goes on there is rhythmical clapping on the part of the organized fans. Some German sailors affix the appropriate banners to the flag masts. A band of the Bundeswehr plays some unidentifiable arias as the Musak goes off. The successful athletes wait, subdued, in their training suits. There are murmurs and movement among officials of the IOC and international weight-lifting federation, all of whom have their names mentioned by the same official who coolly mentions the name of each athlete, his nation, and the grandeur of his accomplished lifts. Three girls in *völkische* dirndls approach, each carrying a tray with a case containing the appropriate medal.

The official awarder at this event is the Polish minister of sport, which is appropriate since the winner with the combined total for his best lifts in each of the three classifications—press, snatch, and clean-and-jerk—is Zygmunt Smalcerz, one of his clients. Wild Polish jubilation as the 114-pound Pole has a medal hung around his neck.

Second and third places are Sandor Holczreiter and Lajos Szucs, respectively, who ignite, yet again, the Hungarians on hand. Despite his appeals to Far Eastern powers and imperious demands for spiritual forces in the immediate area, Tetushide Sasaki is but fourth.

Disappointments are smoothed over by lots of handshakes and smiles for the big lenses of dozens of photographers. The Hungarians keep jumping up against each other and kissing.

Noon, Monday, 28 August 1972

"Six-thousand-five-hundred calories at the very least!" With a combination of a groan and a shout the big man pushes himself, still seated, away from the table. One does not expect such loud talk from the East German journalists as they work away at the large white plates heaped with meat. He is a fast eater, ahead of his three companions, who are smaller but also heavy and dressed in poorly fitting suits of a gray synthetic fabric. Chomping, slurping, and sucking, they enjoy the bounty more sedately. The provider of the calorie statistic soon skootches his chair forward to dig with a soup spoon into some little plastic cups of yogurt and quark mixed with summer berries. To watch with one's peripheral vision the Eastern Europeans at their nourishment is an instructive spectacle—for the Olympic critic, possibly a political one.

I had first noticed two of the East Germans a week ago in the course of a breakfast at the central cafeteria in the Press Center. One of them was stubby and porky, and the other had a crafty face with red blotches. They must have freshly arrived for they looked frightened before moving to the short serving line. They left the line, platters heaped with link sausages, sliced lunch meat, and foil-wrapped packet cheeses and butter. They had lots of bottled juices. Near me, each staked out a far end of the same formica-topped, rectangular table intended to seat six. After they had settled in, a teenaged waitress, new at the job and dressed in a regulation dirndl, approached them. She gave them her rehearsed line: "Café oder Thé?" The first and last words were pronounced in the French she was raised with and would speak the rest of her life.

"Kaffee und Tee!" snorted the thinner man, scarcely interrupting his chewing and swallowing. Then he clenched his knuckles together above his head as he looked up and about while gulping rapidly, as though guarding against predators. The plumper man kept his head down in order to make shorter the distance to traverse with his fist, which moved like a piston. They looked happy and grim, as though asking themselves, "Can this good fortune really be ours? We must get it all down before someone comes to take it or us away."

Can food serve political purposes? It might be instructive to stay with this proposition for a while. For the hosts—and in employing "hosts" here, I mean the government bodies providing money for this undertaking—a deeper motivation for the whole Olympic undertaking is symbolically to demonstrate power. A specific object within the larger theater here is for the West Germans to overpower their Communist brothers from the east. In more than one of my talks-in-passing with Hans Klein, I was told that the East Germans would win in terms of Olympic medals but that the West Germans would win in terms of everything else.

Early on, in the vile green monthly bulletins of the *Olympia Press* sent to all pre-enrolled, registered journalists, there were communiqués that combined a ticlike focus on big statistics and on a preoccupation with food. Two pages dated February 1971 describe conditions to be anticipated by the guests at the Olympic Village. The headline read, "1,100,000 eggs—147 tons of meat," and the article continued:

> At lunch on the first day, for instance, they will be able to choose among these dishes from a menu card printed in German, French, English, Spanish and Russian:
> Cream of Tomato soup, with croutons or consommé garni; as hors d'oeuvres: sardines in oil, stuffed ham roulade, herring with mustard sauce, salami and tomatoes, or "Carmen" salad; as main dish: curried veal, roast leg of turkey with fruit stuffing, fried liver with apple and onion, with a choice of rice, mashed potatoes, french fries, peas and carrots, leaf spinach, asparagus and three dif-

ferent salads; as dessert: hazelnut mould, pineapple jelly, stewed
fruit, cakes, yoghurt, three kinds of cheese, ice cream or cassata.

This announcement goes on to describe specifically how exception-
ally large the "catering centre" is, tells of its five shifts, gives more figures
of foreseen consumption there such as 11 tons of rice, 31 tons of celery,
"90,000 bags of Indian, China, mint, fennel and camomile tea," and provides many, many other such details. Though both the athletes' and the
media members' eating establishments are wait-in-line eateries, the former is called "Mensa" (a usual term for a European students' subsidized
eatery) and the latter, "cafeteria."

No proof has appeared, but I am almost sure that hidden from us,
but not from Daume and Klein, there is a food commissariat, comparable
to Otl Aicher's team in charge of vision, to see that victuals are integrated
into the effort and kept purposeful. In the early hours of the day of the
opening ceremonies, the genial announcer at the stadium, in the same
tones of voice employed to warn us of pickpockets, occasionally and
repetitiously, as intrinsically required by the several languages employed,
would offer us some statistics, such as the fact that in the next two weeks
23,000 pounds of steak or 12,000 chickens would be consumed. For me,
several competitions (though this was more characteristic of practices)
were marred in their esthetic or erotic impact because the judges and
coaches were supplied fruited yogurts or small salads by dirndled hostesses with little pushcarts. The glass containers on them rattled. This was
especially nettlesome at the gymnastics meets.

Only a little of this pushing of food has to do with commercial
sponsorship. The names of particular supplying firms are on the labels of
wines or the cylinders of fruit juices, but only because it would be difficult to take them off. Food is subsumed into a colossal, centrally directed,
theatrical enterprise—a governmentally run *Gesamtkunstwerk*, or encompassing artwork, whose chiefs are obliged to earn a political profit. The
fact that so many people are stuffing themselves so much of the time and
seem to be reveling in the consumption suggests that food, as foreseen,
may be contributing to the feeling among us that details on the whole are
working out nicely.

It may be the case that a drama-within-a-drama is being worked out here in an inner celebration for the West Germans enacted before representatives from the whole world (though I recall no remarkable media-presented praise of the food oblations). The privation (most Germans near my age recall vividly the lack of fats and sugar) of the mid-1940s is only a generation behind us. The famine of 1915–19, a generation before that, was deadly because of the critical lack of fats. The potlatch of nourishment under way about us may be a pervasive piece of theater semisacredly offered to put those horrors of scarcity and famine behind us.

As stated before, if the offerings of food can be in any way viewed as a kind of bellicosity rather than self-congratulation, it is part of a little war without weapons against the torpid dependencies of the Russians and against the Soviet Union itself. The journalists of that part of the world cannot even consider leaving their homes unless every sort of guarantee is in place that they will return. They are loyal, reliable citizens. But they are overwhelmed here by the costly comforts, and most voluptuously, the food, around them.

These socialist journalists also know that the socialist athletes in the Village are not special objects of lavish attention. In the high-performance training centers in Leipzig or elsewhere in the Eastern bloc, the best athletes are regularly pampered, getting oranges and bananas from Central America when no one anywhere near them can. Though the Communist sports journalists have higher relative prestige than those of the West (they can, after all, travel), they are only marginally favored working stiffs. Here in Munich the positions of the socialist athletes and their chroniclers are reversed. Writers for the Sofia, Warsaw, or Budapest sports newspapers can be swollen with satisfaction that here they are the ones with the larger apartments and the more costly fruits and cheeses. Here in Munich, in the West, the athletes are crowded three or more to a room. In the dwellings for the press, we all have quiet apartments and our lackeys, members of the Bundeswehr, no less, are nearby.

There is little anecdotal chat or intrusive introductions at the cafeteria in the Press Center. One looks for and awaits this in the conversation pits before the banks of television sets and in the twenty-four-hour scrimmages at the bars. The clinking of cutlery and the queries, "Café oder Thé?" notwithstanding, this huge eatery is a handy place to think and write things down. One can dawdle over fetched small bottles of Italian white or red wine or delivered coffee—all as good as we expect them to be.

Just now, as several times before, I watch reporters, photographers, or television technicians returning from the steam tables with plates only lightly cargoed with meat, cheeses, or decorated pastries, but these are third or fourth helpings.

In one way, the cafeteria scene is tastefully and morally repugnant to this observer. The American bourgeoisie has long been trying to be rid of an ancient demonstration of class status and class disdain. The many Europeans now, as never before, capable of traveling slowly and paying for really large meals served in public still employ a showy method to demonstrate, actually for their own inner benefit, elevation above the time-constricted laboring classes, presumably (but now, in fact, not) mired in shameful scarcity below them. Here the media specialists leave lots of usable food behind. They are not plate-cleaners as I was raised to be. Chunks of prime rib, backs of chicken, the lee sides of whole grilled fishes, lie openly in pools of dappled fat—even as the Hungarians or Czechs return for third helpings. They do not bus their own plates. The valuable garbage lying about is hideous—but, because this spectacle of gluttonous generosity is a part of the overall strategy of the goal-oriented organizers, we can consider this repulsive demonstration of great wealth yet another indication of anticipated success.

This is a place, perhaps as good as any, to say something about the smells of a very modern Olympic spectacle. These are not the whiffs of good food or the fragrant breezes of distant Bavarian nature that are rhetorically brought forth to legitimize the artificial colors imposed on the whole site. We never even get a sniff of the rancid, erotic sweat raised by extreme sporting effort—this last is effectively banned—readily disposed of by the dozens of saunas, the thousands of showers. No, the smell in our apartments, the cars, the spectator stands, the locker rooms, is that of synthesized, volatile, petrochemical solvents, those stinging, dizzy-making thinners of caulking used to close the narrow gaps where one sort of construction plastic meets another. This is an incessant reminder that the enormous architectural complex that we are using has just been hastily, possibly frantically, completed. But for me there is a further evocation. These odors rouse a not unpleasant nostalgia for the beginnings of my first working stay in Germany seventeen years before when, as a "guest worker," I applied industrial caulkings to the bodies of new small Fords.

4:40 P.M., Thursday, 31 August 1972

An unpleasant tension has set in here in the crowded press section of the main stadium. A few minutes ago we heard the starter's pistol for the first heat in the third round of trials to determine the eight finalists for the 100-meter dash—the Olympic winner of which is, as we all know, a particular sport's prince and hero, "the fastest man in the world." In classical Greece the victor in the dash of one *stade* in Olympia added his name to the ensuing four-year period of time, an "Olympiad." In our times the man who wins the shortest race at the Olympics has usually been a black American. We all could, if the modern Games continue their mythic momentum, someday refer back to the period 1968–72 as the "modern Olympiad of James Hines."

American blacks are, in fact, registered in each of the first three heats of this five-heat series. For them, the "man to beat" is Valeri Borzov of the Soviet Union in heat number three.

A touching element at this already symbolically overloaded session is the presence of Abebe Bikila, the now-crippled (in a nonsports accident) Ethiopian Olympic hero, another sport's prince, winner of the marathons in Rome in 1960 and in Tokyo in 1964. He watches, scarcely moving at all, from a big wheelchair at the start, off to our left.

Ominously, only seven men appeared in the lineup for heat number one. On the official scoreboard of shifting tiny lights, after the name "Robinson, USA" appeared the initials, "n.a.," for "nicht angetreten," meaning essentially, "no show." This produced a foreboding rumble among the press corps, understandably mostly American, and in the sprawling crowd at large. Reynaud Robinson has been clocked at 9.9 seconds, a time equal to the world's record. The Americans became the targets of eager questions, and all questioners accepted the quickly passed explanation that Robinson's recently pulled muscle must have been more serious than was first assumed.

We are now watching the preparations for heat number two. An irrepressible, nauseating fear gets substantiation as we see, far off to our left, at the starting blocks, only seven starters for this heat. The great scoreboard gives us the legend, "Hart, USA, n.a." Another, worse rumble rushes through the press section, the whole stadium, and, we must assume, the live television watchers of the world. The same American mavens who made themselves noisily known shortly before are mobbed with questions in many forms of broken English, but the question is one that has been trembling there for a long time. That query is, "Are they protesting?"

This time there are no explanations. The answer might very well be, "Yes." The dominant mood is one of terrified anticipation. Eddie Hart's heat is won by a man from Madagascar with the splendid name of Jean-louis Ravelomanantsoa and the poor time of 10.47. But no one pays any attention to him or his jubilation, for we notice on our schedule, listed with the Soviet, Borzov, the name of a third American, Robert Taylor.

Severe general agitation. Are these specks of persons, these fools, going to sacrifice years of preparation, whole lives almost, to make silly ideological points and thereby damage themselves and the Olympic movement? An American photographer, pale with rage, remarks that Hart (as we all know already) had been clocked at 9.9.

"By a hand watch, please," a German characteristically interjects. "By a hand watch."

What kind of spiritual commitment would give athletes the courage to pull such a trick? Well, not a trick, really, but a powerful act with powerful results. Why always Americans? How could they be so self-destructive, so inconsiderate of us? We all wanted this to be a fine party.

To our astonishment and partial relief, eight men hunker down for the start of the third heat. A false start and the announcer tells us that the responsible party is "Taylor, USA." The race unrolls, and Borzov wins with the time of 10.07. The best in the competitions so far. Taylor's time is 10.16.

No Yanks in the next heat. An agitated middle-aged American leaves for the telephones and returns a few minutes later. The explanation, though implausible, eases somewhat the fears of a "protest" or a "demonstration." Some coach had given all the American sprinters the wrong time to appear at the stadium. They missed a bus.

Fury. A newspaper reporter barks with anger, "Irresponsible! Crazy!

For the hundred-meter dash of the Olympic Games you don't wait for a bus; you get there in plenty of time!"

With this incident, it becomes oppressively obvious that by the occasional exercise of egocentricity, as in the now-legendary cases of Tommie Smith and John Carlos at the Olympics in Mexico City four years ago, and by carrying themselves in a provocative fashion, the American blacks have established themselves as creatures of frightening symbolic power.

An unforeseen disruption of this world festival could have severe consequences in the hearts of all those taking part in or, by means of the media, consuming it. Americans in these days, myself included, are much watched. But the big blacks overpower us all.

7:00 P.M., Thursday, 31 August 1972

The self-assigned task to observe a little of much takes me to the swimming hall. The upcoming event is the 4 × 200-meter freestyle relay. Mark Spitz is anchor on the American team and up for his fifth gold medal; fifth world record. The hall is warmer than any other site. The serried, moist crowd, as usual here, mostly German, is emotionally primed to observe a great moment.

After the starter's shot and the eight splashes that sound like one, there is a vague, restless quiet, as usual. But this stretched pause is brief. For the West German team is keeping up! Sections of the crowd begin to scream and bellow, revealing an effort to will the Germans to victory against, yes, the companions of Mark Spitz. For eyes desperate to believe what they do indeed see, there is an inspiring sight, for after their turns, the first two swimmers touch at the starting end at the same time and then—miracle! The second German edges ahead of the second Yank, while all the others are far behind. The tumult around me is such that it demands that I watch the masses and, less so, the race.

The human noise is utter, complete. The lead of the second boy lasts through his turn and I can make distinctions. The younger people are merely shouting all-out, but I believe I see some mature women, aged thirty or more, who are out of themselves, hysterical, insane. In their howls they seem to be biting at the air. Their chaotic outpourings of emotion and desire are at the limits of life's possibilities. We have read that some women sometimes are capable of a complete, devastating orgasm that exceeds the possibilities of any male's abandonment to ecstasy. We must believe this.

The extended moment of excitement passes, for the physiology of the women and that of the swimmers demands that it pass. The third American builds up a lead that Spitz, as anchor, lengthens into, yes, a new world record. The Germans are not unhappy that their darlings have won silver medals.

It is curious that the swimmers, the objects of all this willed passion, while in the water, can hear little of the howling.

9:00 P.M., Thursday, 31 August 1972

At an intercollegiate wrestling match one's attention is kept at the single mat and on the narrow spectacle there of strength and tactics. One expects the alert, somber judges to be correct. A contest can be pathetic in a sped-up, dramatic-tragic sense as one watches the better tactician slowly wilt before the endurance of a more powerful man. The spectators, experts themselves, are in dim light. They are partly out of themselves and express their empathy in unconscious agonies of body English and instantly regretted expletives. One hears the grunts of the strugglers and the rasp of their skins and jerseys against one another and against the mat. No one gets hurt.

Here it has been already conceded that one can best feel or perceive some essence of the world's best wrestling by watching the work of the German color television cameramen who are dependably responsible. Nameless, knowledgeable cameramen zoom in, zoom out, to offer us the wrecked faces, the clasped bodies, or, pulling back, the immediately near spectators of a match. We can and do turn off the sound to wipe out the crowd and thereby purify and dehumanize the contests.

I am merely one of a long procession of esthetes who have concluded that the medium-large wrestlers show the furthest development toward a certain physical perfection—that zenith being a masculinity so pure as to suggest the absence of spiritual qualities. The late Hellenistic and the Roman sculptors immortalized some of these wrestlers as individuals. They were inspired by these athletes who merited detailed examination of their physiques, but who were not notable as wholes for artistically exploitable harmonies. One can see Heraclean beauty in the so-called "Barbarina Faun" here in the Glyptothek in Munich. The sprawling, naughty male, representing a drunken reveler, was clearly a wrestler. So was the model for the "Belvedere Torso," so much admired by Michelangelo, which is now in the Vatican Museum.

At a provincial wrestling match one can ponder as connoisseur, esthete, or eroticist the wrestlers and their sport. The ensemble here at the Olympic wrestling hall during the preliminary matches defies critical sorting out. At any time there are four matches in different weight classes going on at once. Each is in a different stage of march. The whole panorama, audience included, is drenched in too much artificial light. There are gongs, buzzers, flashing colored lights, and shifting, speckled, electronic scoreboards in too many places. All the wrestlers wear either red or blue, one-piece, knit tricots with no identifying marks or numbers. Loudspeakers mispronounce the names of Africans, Asians, or South Americans in the three European languages. To learn what is going on at any one mat requires a continuous consultation with the program and a growing supply of rapidly printed handouts, all of which are deciphered only with difficulty. Bad theater.

Since there may be four matches in process, there might be as many as eight different, variously sized, whooping, partisanly critical groups of celebrants. Whole waves of congratulation, flag waving, whistling (meaning approval on the part of North Americans, condemnation from most others), stomping, and outrage pass through the spectators without the likelihood that this cool observer will discover what caused a certain piece of excitement. As a consequence, I watch little. There is a whirlpool of unsortable impressions and an occasional distraction outside of it. Occasionally there is a familiar American shout, "He's gonna pin 'im! He's gonna pin 'im!"

The most arresting scenes are the farcical ones. A standing athlete holds one foot of his opponent who hops on the other. They spin about the axis of the planted foot. Two frightened men swirl, their arms circling alternately for long seconds. They are afraid to risk a grapple.

One pathetic sight is that of a big Cuban, brownish gray, who is in appearance quite unlike the clean college kids most of us have watched wrestle before. He looks about thirty and is scarred from battle. His big ears are almost closed up from the buildup of cartilage. He is frightened, appearing as though he had no comprehension of what he is supposed to do in such a place. He is expeditiously pinned. Just afterward as he looks from his corner for compassion from his judgmental trainer, he resembles the over-life-size seated pugilist, the Hellenistic bronze supposedly by Apollonius now in Rome. Frightened himself, he frightens his surroundings. Another of many déjà vu experiences for me on the Olympic site.

The blue-corduroy-suited, fair, hook-nosed youth at my left is watching with almost hypnotic concentration a portly, balding wrestler. Then it is clear that this figure is a polestar of the Germans present. At first the lights altered my perception. The grappler who at first looked ordinary, as somber as any athlete present, is a giant, and he communicates businesslike assurance. A timid query brings lots of information. The man is Wilfried Dietrich, the "Schifferstadt crane." He won a silver medal in the superheavyweight class in Mexico City. Dietrich is thirty-eight years old; this is his fifth Olympics. He has already won five Olympic medals. He has won twenty-eight German championships and three international championships. He is a national hero of titanic stature.

"He's supposed to get something for us" ("Er soll uns etwas holen"), my informant slyly tells me.

As at the other sites, one is steadily wondrous at the cool expertise of the Soviet trainers. For them as for their charges, this is not a time for emotion. After the winning of a medal perhaps, but not right now. Here they are flapping moist towels and patting thick arms and shoulders as they hiss sibilant advice to athletes during pauses in the bouts. One sees no terror or will-diminishing depression among the Soviets. They have realized and practiced for years on the assumption that all counteracting psychology has to be trained out.

Gradually most of us in the hall are attracted to the spectacle on mat D, the furthest to the left. Here are two superheavyweights—that is, each weighs over 100 kilograms or 220 pounds. The one is square-headed, tanned, and moves with our characteristic American looseness. His thin, unmarked skin exposes his stringy, heavy, gracefully shifting musculature.

My easily adopted German guide tells me that the man in blue has the musculature and the coordination of the smaller wrestlers, favorites of the experts who are tuned to enjoy speed and cleverness.

Pitted against this picturesque example of physical harmony from the American gene pool and outweighing him by 150 pounds is a yellow-pink beast whose knitted suit is the red of Russian totalitarianism. He has overhanging, Cro-Magnon brows, brittle fair hair, and a face torn with adolescent pox, though adolescence is long past. The bigger man drools, snorts, and is so bulky and difficult to grasp or move that the other, an adept, superbly trained and conditioned man, cannot throw him for the mat work that will be an unequivocal demonstration of sporting skill. They dance, they grip, they bump, some in the audience titter. But not much happens, though a judge gives points (on the basis of decisions that I cannot appraise but that I inwardly applaud) to the better, smaller wrestler.

This is not a fair match. I brood about the crafty opportunism of the Soviet sports commissars who, in order to produce international victories, groom these poor unfortunates for international display. It is an ugly match that should have been prevented. Power against inertia. Grace against mass. Beauty against the beast. Hellenism against barbarism. I am not alone in my refined distaste. Smirking with patriotism, I turn with eyebrows raised to my knowledgeable German companion who responds, "That Russian, Medved, is behaving with extraordinary skill and composure under such difficult circumstances."

My fury is visceral, immediate. I gasp, "But the match is unfair! The American man is a much better wrestler."

"No! Medved is far more skilled. The big man can't wrestle. He's strong, but it is his bulk that keeps him upright."

Desperately leafing through the programs, I check names against the color-coded red and blue suits and verify my nasty findings with the electric scoreboard above the ring. The graceful, classical athlete is the Soviet, Alexandr Medved; the lummox is an American with an American name. What was all that speculation on the moral authenticity of American sport? Shamed at my patriotic presumptions, I mumble farewells to my generous informant.

I wander about outside in the dark. While pausing at a curb, I see coming at me an army bus with the legend, "Olympic Village," on it. It stops and a door opens. What adventure will be ahead? What the hell. My companions are Japanese and Turkish weight lifters. They are jolly. We cruise by a bored guard, and I appreciate that I have found yet another way to get around some rules. By climbing into Olympic Village buses at athletic sites, I (and presumably others) can enter paradise. As tonight, I can look like a bourgeois and am not required to pose as a South American distance runner.

At the base of the high towers that are the Soviet men's dorms there are idlers peeking through cracks in a wooden fence around a nasturtium-lined terrace. A girl is singing, accompanied by a piano player. Both performers are loud in force and languid in style. Seated in a semicircle are thirty or so athletes in blue training suits decorated with white, felt letters, "C.C.C.P." I want to bluff my way past yet another security guard but can invent no other explanation than, "Amerikanski journalist." The Soviet guard waves me through at once, and some young official in a shiny black dress—she is kindly, chubby, and ravishing—leads me to an empty chair.

The singer is heavily made-up. She sings so clearly, unself-consciously, and sweetly that she and the pianist have to be professionals. Then a thin athlete who has a nose like a scoop and a blonde brush cut relieves the lead singer. He also sings songs with some slow warbling at the ends of the phrases that produce a mood I noted then as weird, nostalgic, and Russian. My pleasure in these sad songs is certainly not diminished by my incomprehension of the no-doubt sentimental lyrics. He stops, bows, and, impulsively and inappropriately, I clap. Obviously Russians do not do this. My nearby fellow concertgoers are so pleased by the gaffe that they seem about to clap for me.

Other athletes rise to sing between the numbers of the chanteuse. Athletes leave and return with Cokes or Sprites. The membership of the audience changes. The tempo of the songs varies, but always the moods on the attentive faces are serious, appreciative. During one long song, several in the audience hum in unison.

I reflect, nostalgize really, on a story told me seventeen years before by my landlady in Cologne. During the rugged days late in 1944, when there were no bombing alerts, she would sometimes take her children for evening strolls outside the fence by the sprawling, stinking barracks that held Russian women, slaves in the nearby factories. Frau P. and her neighbors would lean against the fences and listen to the prisoners sing sadly and joyfully of love, of disappointment, and of their distant homes. Frau P. recalled vividly the emotions roused by these spontaneous soloists and humming choruses. "Ah, that was beautiful!" she exclaimed.

4

Adventures

"The potential is there."

The optimistic speaker is Max Emery, chief sports organizer for the nation of Malawi. Max is twenty-seven years old and athletic looking himself except for his long, thick eyelashes, which make him look dreamy and prophetic. He and I are part of an excursion heading out of Munich for a drive to the snowcapped Zugspitze in the Bavarian Alps. With us in the olive-drab army bus on this cool, drizzling morning are the two German drivers, a few more persons to be introduced, and fifteen athletes.

Max has borne well a heavy, civic responsibility. His job, which he took only four months ago, was to begin from point zero to produce in one of the smallest and poorest states in Southeast Africa sport as he and I have known it. One might view the scene around us as a sort of early summit of his preparations. The athletes with us make up the very first Malawian Olympic team.

Six months ago Max and his wife were just two more of the short-term diaspora of young Australian adults whom one encounters hiking and being cheerful everywhere in the world. For a year the couple had "done" Europe and were resting in "Jo'burg" (as the capital of South Africa is known to those who love it) when an ad in a newspaper caught Max's attention.

Malawi, a quasi-protectorate of Johannesburg (significantly, the Malawians took no position on the nettlesome Rhodesian question before the Games began), was late in promoting sport the way some other African nations did, most particularly and successfully Kenya. The president, Dr. Hastings Kamuzu Banda, had shortly before created a Department of Sport and was advertising for a director. Max cheekily applied by means of a long, self-praising letter. Someone called him to Blantyre, Malawi's largest city. Max got the job and soon had a budget allowing him to hire some fifty people. He saw his mandate as "to try to get sport going from the bottom, because nothing exists."

Besides the wholesome satisfaction he gets by contributing to "a Peace Corps–type program," Max regularly associates in Blantyre with officials of ministerial rank—a sort of seasoning experience that will increase his leverage when he returns to Australia to realize his distant ambitions to become a sports administrator there.

Like the other whites, Max and I are on hand this morning to observe our cargo of muscular talent under particular circumstances. None of the Malawians have ever seen snow.

When first viewed, the athletes looked more pathetic than inspiring as they ambled late to the bus, burdened with large, plastic shopping bags filled with picnic snacks provided by the Olympic Village food service. Then we all waited for the German drivers.

Max led me about and, as "Dr. Mandell," I was presented to the ladies, Emesia, Missie, and Mabel, and then to the men to get their first names as well. They all stood still until my gesture for contact was an unequivocal offering. Then, smilingly and shyly, they extended their own hands. They did not know that one is supposed to grip.

I have stated my pleasure in being an appraising flaneur at the Olympic Village or at the training sites for the purpose of settling my connoisseur's eyes on the world's most refined physical specimens. The winners of my private beauty contests are, in the pale-skinned classes, the East Germans, the Soviets, and the Americans. The Americans, Jamaicans, and West Africans win in the dark-skinned categories.

The Malawian athletes are from East Africa and only in duskiness are they something like the sassy-skinny, burly-shiny black Somalis, those from the Ivory Coast, or other stunning figures from West Africa who appear in their tribal robes at ceremonies or glistening, near naked at the practice fields. Most of the Malawians are of the browner shades one expects of the American blacks of remotely mixed ancestry. But they lack the size, posture, and noisiness one welcomes in the frizzy-haired Yanks.

The young complexions of the Malawian stalwarts are blotched and pitted—for these people are the easy victims of a number of skin diseases. However, to a man and woman, they all have big, bright, opalescent teeth rooted in clean pink gums. The result, I am told, of a simple diet in which sugar (except for chewed sugarcane) never appears. They are not, however, like field hands or cowed beasts. Left alone, the athletes are boisterous and playful.

We are now riding in the bus. The object of general raillery as we pass through the well-kept pastures and pine forests leading away from the metropolis and to the Alps is Jungle Thangata. It turns out that Jungle is the man I met in the sauna and who impelled me to seek out the Malawian team all together. He is a featherweight boxer whom Max, with supporting pressure from his teammates, successfully returned to his weight class until his bout with a Spaniard. This fight was stopped with one minute to go in the third round. Jungle was then turned loose in the Mensa whereupon he gained seventeen pounds in two days.

I follow only the drift of the athletes' teasing, for it takes place in Chichewa, the lingua franca of a country that, so I am told, has "four or five major languages and fifty or sixty dialects."

A rudimentary amount of conversation with the athletes is possible. They speak some English for their school classes are in that language. As a dutiful journalist I "interview" them to learn that Jungle Thangata works at the Hotel Continental in Blantyre, that the eighteen-year-old cyclist, Langston Grimmon, is a schoolboy at the Catholic Institute in Blantyre, that the sprinter William Msiska is a corporal in the army, and that Raphael Kazembe, a cyclist, is a gardener at a Lutheran church. But all of this information is already in the mimeographed biographical handout that Max prepared ahead of time. Groping for some sort of "insight," I ask them what they think about the action that is going on around us. All giggle, shuffle, and attempt to end by shy pantomime what was never really an interview. I turn to the whites who are brimming over with information.

More than satisfactory to interview (to "direct" might be a better word) is Mike Nicholls, who, at twenty-nine, claims to be "the youngest athletic association chairman in the world." Mike is himself thirty pounds too heavy. He is a red-bearded Englishman who normally teaches his mother tongue at the Polytechnic Institute, a component of the University of Malawi.

Malawi, the former British protectorate of Nyasaland, has been independent since 1964. President Banda, a firm man, is head of the Congress party, which is the only party. Most of the 4,500,000 inhabitants of Malawi are subsistence farmers. Our athletes on the bus are exceptional not only because of their physical skills but also because almost all can read. Less than 10 percent of the Malawian people can read.

The 7,000 "Europeans" (the general term for Caucasians living in Malawi) are mostly contracted technicians who assist in laying down the infrastructure and the technical bases for the growing exports of tobacco, tea, and peanuts. They are also setting up Malawi's educational system.

As a contracted European, Mike earns more than he would in England and is provided a house with servants, including a gardener for his grounds. He is unlike most of the Europeans since he and his wife socialize with native teachers and officials. The older of his two little girls goes to an integrated school in Blantyre, which, incidentally, was named after the birthplace of David Livingstone, the first European explorer in the area.

Mike Nicholls is scornful of those Europeans who, seeking a particular sort of company, remain within the confines of the golf and tennis clubs, still preserves of British colonial society. The whites are protected by the Congress party and live in an atmosphere of race relations that my informers repeatedly stress are in many ways preferable to those in America since there is no violence whatever. Yet the Europeans can be and occasionally are expelled from the country on three days' notice—

usually for "seditious activity." President Banda can be annoyed to vengeance if a car does not move off the road to ease the passage of his official cortege.

When I ask why there are no white athletes on the team, Mike replies, "It wouldn't be fair. Europeans can't be citizens and it would be cheating."

Casually I ask Mike if there are any millionaires in the country. As he reflects, he is interrupted.

"There is a Greek who freezes fish and an old Italian. The Italian exports tea, makes blankets, and sells Fiats. He built a Florentine castle on a hill in the 1930s. There he wanted to welcome Mussolini who would presumably come down for a sweep through Nyasaland after polishing off Ethiopia."

The informant is Paul Martin, a thirty-three-year-old stocky American, also bearded, whose *Wanderjahre* took him to Malawi where he, like Mike, teaches English at the Polytechnic Institute. Paul has no official position with the team. The occasion of the Munich Olympics happily coincided with a period of paid leave. Learning that there were at the time in Munich no plans for bona fide Malawian journalists (Denmark is smaller than Malawi and planned for forty of them), Paul Martin applied to the Press Department of the German Organizing Committee for accreditation and, of course, got it. We had met earlier in transit and, as so often the case with such meetings here, learned a lot about each other quickly.

Paul will file three, 600-word hosannahs to the Malawian team with a Blantyre weekly. The editor will pay the telex charges; nothing more.

"Lots of things I can't write about for the Malawian press might make great stories elsewhere. Can you imagine? Before all the Olympic excitement built up in Malawi, there were only a half dozen pairs of track shoes in the entire country. Few of our sprinters had seen spikes. If Wilfred, our decathlon man, were to win his event, it would make a great story for the *international* press, since he's never even *done* some of the parts of the ten-event program. Were one of our girls to win even a bronze medal, it would be the news of the year in East Africa.

"And the bicyclists! Now, our people are poor. The average worker needs to have a bicycle and will scrimp to save the two months of wages necessary to get one. We even have used bicycle lots. Almost everyone has a bicycle—except the university students, naturally, who refuse to be seen on one. But until a year ago, the only ten-speeds in the country were three old models, owned and polished but scarcely used by members of the Colonial societies. In fact, it was an influential Britisher who corresponded with the Raleigh people in Nottingham and got them to contribute six bikes so we could train our team."

I ask the appropriate version of the question that is almost ritualistic here, "How are the Malawians going to do in the 1972 Olympics?"

"Oh, badly, by Olympic standards. We just hope they don't do disgracefully. The athletes have already been told that they shouldn't expect medals. They're here to learn and to set new Malawian records. And, naturally, they are here to be seen."

"Seen?"

"Sure. People will see the flag of Malawi. They'll see our athletes in their bright red sweat suits with 'MALAWI' across the back. Scoreboards in many places will occasionally have the letters 'MAL' on them, and then people, maybe millions of people, will go home and look in their atlases. There, surrounded by Zambia, Tanzania, and Mozambique, they'll find us, Malawi."

"So the presence of a Malawian team here in Munich in Germany has a lot to do with the prestige of Malawi."

"Yes. To have an Olympic team means you're arrived as a nation. Like Kenya."

The bus enters Garmisch-Partenkirchen, the mountain resort, some of whose fame is a consequence of its designation as the site of the 1936 winter Olympics. During the urgent search for pissoirs, I leave the sightseers to take a small table and chair in a distant *Konditorei* before good coffee and to write some of the above. Upon our assembling an hour later at the bus, I smell cordial spirits.

Mike Nicholls explains: "Never saw a piece of the town. Walked 200 feet and went into this big pastry shop. At once we found ourselves being treated royally by the patron and then by some customers. We were mobbed for autographs and weren't allowed to pay for anything. Great wedges of cake—what do you call 'em? Tortes—oozing strawberries and whipped cream—all topped off with coffee and brandy. We made bloody pigs of ourselves."

As the bus, its heaters whirring now, progresses up and down its many gears to approach the Zugspitze, the Europeans get more excited and the athletes become more somber. Almost no one regards the tidy, chalet-speckled scenery. Though they had eaten breakfast and the laid-on tortes in the café just before, the athletes begin to break out the packed lunches.

Everyone is torpid as we assemble in the lobby of a building to await the pendant gondola cars that take gawkers up the final 2,000 meters to the 2,963-meter highest point in the Federal Republic for vistas of yet more mountains in Germany, Austria, and Switzerland.

The fare, it turns out, is 15 marks (almost $5). Despite their daily allowance of 10 marks of walking-around money that is provided for such eventualities, the athletes balk in varying degrees of intensity. Then, all at once, there is a single ruckus in two separate, churning circles of unequal size. Traveling between the groups are two people: Margie, our until-now quiet hostess, the plainest and least cheerful of all the many I had yet encountered, and Police Inspector Adamson Kamburi, the titular "chef de mission" of the Malawian team.

Central in the upheaval is the claim, maintained by the Europeans, that the evening before, Inspector Kamburi agreed to instruct the athletes that they would pay this fare. Apparently this large, nobly indifferent man, while eating sandwiches and watching television, has cooperated with anyone by nodding assent to every suggestion.

The fifteen athletes, in baggy red sweat suits with "MALAWI" in white letters applied across the back, are indignant and then uproarious in Chichewa. Max, Mike, and Paul are now enraged and, though apparently as unified in their own views as their charges are in theirs, are screaming and gesticulating at one another. Some German day-trippers look on with amazement.

Paul: "They've been spoiled. Been babied all the way and now they'll contribute nothing to an outing provided for them alone."

Mike: "I don't care if any one of 'um ever sees any goddam snow. I'm not going to ride a hundred miles in a stinking army bus and not go to the top of the Zugspitze." A gondola was loading. As he rushes to the ticket office, Max and Paul join him.

Responsibility to my profession as journalist and some guilt at not having gotten much news from the meat of my profession keeps me at the bottom. I return with the Malawian team to the bus, which is indeed stinking, in a big parking lot. Margie has already seen snow and once before has been to the top, so claiming the urgent need to rest from recent parties and the need to store up for coming ones wraps herself in an army blanket and sleeps. The bus drivers stroll on the shores of a pretty lake, the Eibsee.

Shortly before, Paul had suggested which of the athletes would be most open or most revealing to talk to.

I start with Matthews Kambale, a small, smooth-skinned twenty-year-old, who will be running the marathon. As a distance runner he naturally aroused my keen empathetic feelings. I think we liked each other at once. Still, I must press to get much out of him. At home he earns about $30 a month as a clerk for an export firm. He will not pay the $5 fare to the top of the mountain because he could use the money better at home, even though he might someday regret missing the opportunity to see snow, about which he has heard so much.

Matthews began his athletic career as a sprinter and step-by-step increased his distances upon learning that he had more power left after running successively (and not doing very well) the 1,500, 5,000, and 10,000-meter events. When Max Emery sent vans with loudspeakers around in the bush announcing the first twenty-six mile race ever to be held in Malawi, Matthews knew he should enter. There were lots of spectators and nine starters. Matthews was unaccustomed to track shoes, which were giving him blisters, so he ran the last ten miles barefoot. He was first of the three finishers with a time of 3:20, the new (and first) Malawi record for the distance.

Before he went up, Paul had applied the term "sophisticated" to Missie Misomale, like Matthews a clerk with a business firm. Missie has traveled some, having been to Salisbury in Rhodesia. Conversationally we get almost nowhere. She pretends not to hear my questions and looks away. Still, I press on, and she becomes a little lively. I determine that she thinks the most exciting parts of the trip were the first airplane flights and learn (after she giggles and asks for help from her teammates, who are looking on, for the translation from Chichewa) that the name of the Malawian national anthem is, "Oh God, Bless Our Land Malawi."

Under other circumstances my talk with twenty-eight-year-old

Wilfred Mwalwanda would have been more agreeable and more fruitful. The Europeans had respectfully declared several times that, among the athletes, Wilfred is outstanding. He is bigger, older, and far more confident than any of the others. Max Emery's brochure describes Wilfred as "Malawi's best and most experienced athlete." Wilfred had been to the Commonwealth Games in Edinburgh in 1970 where he took fifth in the javelin with a throw of 235 feet 3 inches. His usual employment is in the West Dreifontein gold mine in South Africa. Some part of Wilfred's expenses are being offset by a collection he took up among fellow Malawian miners who worked with him and were eager to send a representative onward. Wilfred looks like and carries himself like guys I had worked with many years ago on the trim lines in the car factories in Detroit. We, the Detroiters and I, got on well.

But now my hoped-for new chum is stubborn and quietly enraged. He, the most Europeanized, had longed to go to the top of the Zugspitze where there is snow. He is distracted and then fatigued by defending himself from his fellows. As kindly as he can in these circumstances, he brushes me off while wrapping himself in an army blanket. Then he opens with his magnificent teeth a plastic bag containing a vacuum-sealed pork chop of the sort that the astronauts took with them.

Other athletes join in, spooning into tiny cups of oversweetened, fruit-flavored yogurt. Some pulverize with their fine teeth sugar-speckled pastries, butter cookies, Suchard chocolate bars with hazelnuts. They move on to plastic bags of milk, apples from Austria, pears from Bavaria, and oranges from Israel. Almost all are in boisterous high spirits. Matthews, the little distance man, quietly leaves the bus to jog in the deep green landscape. The scarfing, teasing, and backslapping continue until the Zugspitze gondola returns late.

Mike confesses sulkily that there was no view at all, since some cloud cover was just below them. He and his colleagues drank beer at a chilly restaurant and chatted with some German engineers.

During the ride back in gathering dusk, everyone is touchy and sullen, but in different ways. One white wants to argue with Inspector Kamburi about just who was guilty in the misunderstanding regarding the expected purchase of the athletes' fares. The older African phlegmatically agrees to everything so he can go back to sleep sooner. Gesticulating, another white explains to Matthews, who is enchanted, just what causes an avalanche. The third of the Malawian white officials sits on a bench seat with one of the female sprinters and desultorily attempts to put the make on her while she likewise resists. Almost everyone else, your chronicler included, attempts to pass the time and prepare for the future by dozing. It has been a bad day at the Zugspitze.

Noon, Sunday, 3 September 1972

Max Emery, the Australian, and Mike Nicholls, the Englishman have beers in their hands as they regard the view from their untidy rooms on the ninth and top floor of their home away from home in the Village. We can see, a mile off, the glistening plastic baldachin, the roof that is the architectural clou of the whole Olympic undertaking.

"Too bad you weren't there for it, Dick. We had a moment of glory this morning," Max announces.

I was astonished that my heart beat so hard at the top of my mouth, for this was physiological evidence that I had begun to "pull" for the Malawian team.

"After Martin Matupi's third and last attempt at the triple jump, the biggest scoreboard at the big stadium showed 16.33 meters after the name Matupi-MAW. This was a personal best, a new Malawi record, and Martin's chance at the medal. Mike and I crashed past some angry and confused guards to get to the pit, primed for rejoicing, only to learn that there had been a much-regretted typing-in error. Martin's actual figure was 13.34, which, it turns out, missed by one centimeter from being the worst completed triple jump of the entire day."

I had earlier decided that Mike Nicholls was probably justified in his claim that he deserved the most recognition for getting Malawi into the Olympics in the first place. He is still full of information.

Shortly after Malawi's independence in 1964, the infant nation began to send track teams to East African meets. In the course of time, a Malawian Athletic Association was formed that eventually sponsored the first appearance of Malawian athletes at the Commonwealth Games in Edinburgh in 1970. They sent Wilfred Mwalwanda and two boxers. As chairman of the Athletic Association, Mike initiated and advanced the correspondence that produced the formal invitation from the German Organizing Committee to send a Malawian team to Munich.

"We knew it was all serious two years ago when they got us to send a *physical* copy of the national flag and the score and a tape recording of the national anthem. They also asked for the score and a tape recording of the *victory* anthem, if different from the national anthem. Only after we arrived did we find out that the Germans were using our flags of their make all over the place. The national anthem was for the welcoming ceremonies when we first entered the Olympic Village.

"We had considered making up some sort of victory anthem and even searched out the original composer of our national anthem, only to learn that he was now selling Coca Cola and wouldn't take an assignment on such short notice. The Germans had been preparing for eventualities that we couldn't envisage.

"We had a problem with the clothes too. Unlike the West African nations that parade in embroidered robes, Malawi has no national costume. We dressed our boys and girls in English school–style uniforms of dark green blazers and gray flannels and skirts—all contributed by merchants in Blantyre. That took a lot of running about and convincing, I'll tell you.

"Another problem was the little enameled lapel pins. We designed a Malawi pin and ordered a lot from London. Somehow we thought that the pins were for *wearing*, and we each duly got one. Our team was hopelessly outclassed by the athletes who brought dozens for exchanging in the shopping arcade. Each Kenyan, for example, got a couple of dozen pins with 'KENYA' on them. Some Yanks had hundreds. Next time we'll do the same."

"Despite the donated materials, wasn't it expensive all the same?" I ask.

"Possibly much less than you expect. The Germans have provided us with a Ford Taunus and a driver for our own exclusive use. The bus for the lamentable Zugspitze trip was free. Dear Margie costs us nothing. The $8 or so for room and board for each of us is a token considering all that we have put away here. We had some money to spend once we arrived. We spent $300 at the shop the Adidas people have to show off their shoes. They were rude because the order was so small and because we as yet had no 'stars.' From now on we're buying Japanese. The big lump was airfare here and back. But we got a discount on that."

"Well, how much do you think the whole adventure will amount to?"

"We did some nicely publicized fund-raising in Malawi the year before the Games—dances, raffles, that sort of thing. Wilfred even collected about $5 or so from all the expatriate miners in South Africa. Obviously, the sums from all these sources were small. The real benefit from these programs among the people will be to increase the attention given to athletics in Malawi. Major contributions were from conscientious members of the British Colonial Society—both in the form of equipment (we already told you about the six Raleigh bicycles) and in cash. But we knew all along that the president would see us through if things got tight."

"Well, then, how much will it cost from beginning to end?" I insist cheekily.

Then, as Max and Mike fetch more beers from a fridge, there ensues a discussion as to whether they should make the estimate in Malawian pounds, British pounds, marks, or dollars. Finally Max replies.

"You can calculate the total budget at about $25,000 of which the exchequer paid half. A lot of people are having a hell of a good time for what really isn't much government money."

"Not to mention," I add, "that President Banda and the Congress party are getting a lot of regime-enhancing publicity both within and outside Malawi's borders. The sum of money is paltry. I'm sure that between $10,000 and $15,000 is far less than the cost of a platoon of soldiers, a light tank, or the Malawian mission in Bonn."

Here I detonate excited discussion. My conferees insist that it is not the ruling party but Malawi as a whole that stands to benefit from the Malawian presence in Munich in 1972.

As I leave the huge apartment building, I spot two of the aforementioned, blue and yellow Raleigh Carltons and see at once that, though they have the rough configuration of the refined $500 precision instruments, they are the sort of road bikes that the Raleigh people are turning out as fast as they can to satisfy the demand of American campus faddists. Weinnemann side-pull brakes and Simplex gears fore and aft. The back tire on one bike is rubbing. Both cycles have rat-trap pedals of steel and no toe clips.

Just yesterday I approached a well-tendoned American cyclist who was pulling away his steed, which had been leaning with some others against a wall in the Village. He was a road racer and his pedals were of titanium.

"Weigh nothing at all," he remarked.

Afternoon, Sunday, 3 September 1972

I am sitting in a lounge, actually a long gallery between halls filled with typewriters. This is the area in the Press Center where the journalists and television technicians can freeload on cloying yogurt and on other dairy products put out by hopeful-for-goodwill German manufacturers. One side of the gallery has a row of telex machines with their waiting operators. In a corner there is a black-and-white television with a sign before it stating that standing is not allowed, for those in back, the telex girls, like to watch too.

The banks of televisions have lots of low lounge chairs in shifting groups in front of them. I remain astonished at the extent to which re-porters from everywhere read each other's papers for news and at the amount of news regarding the sporting events that sports journalists get from watching the various television broadcasts. They spend a lot of time talking with each other.

A usual topic for the African journalists and for the West European journalists, the majority of people in the Press Center, is the still-hot Rhodesian question.

Rhodesia, due to protests of some African leaders supported by countries under pressure from the Soviets, had been banned from com-petition in the 1968 Games. In negotiations lasting years, a bloc of African nations agreed to allow Rhodesian athletes to compete in Munich if they did so as British subjects under the British flag. Accordingly, in early August, a team of forty-four Rhodesian athletes, including six black trackmen, appeared in Munich.

Then, stubbornly employing some technical detail dealing with their passports, a group of smaller African nations protested the presence of the Rhodesians. The independent Africans threatened to boycott. This became frightening on 16 August when two great sports powers, Ethiopia and Kenya, also threatened to boycott. Then, on 18 August, some American athletes signed a statement claiming they would take a "united stand with our African brothers," referring to the Kenyans and others.

On 21 August the IOC met and on 22 August announced that by a vote of 36–31 with 3 abstentions they had barred the Rhodesians. This had been one of the keenest battles of Avery Brundage's life and perhaps his most deeply felt defeat. A galling bitterness was that he himself had to announce this humiliation to the press.

The so-called Rhodesian team hangs around. They are interviewed and are being treated warmly by the people of Munich. The reporters find them colorful. They are telling journalists that all of them would be delighted to compete under the flag of the Knights of Malta or the Boy Scouts.

I am listening to this sort of palaver when an older, important-looking hostess runs in and looks about in anguish. She is followed by a middle-aged man in a well-tailored, striped suit, cut in a style seen among us in 1954. The man moves gracelessly. His face is reddened, and his full lips are puckered to contain his rage.

The hostess searches among the group sucking milk shakes and those torpid before the televisions, which are showing, mostly, some hand ball game. My sympathetic smile falsely communicated a desire to help, for the lady rushes up, running her hands through her hair.

"Please, do you speak Bulgarian?"

"Alas, I don't."

She looks about wildly again and, followed by her monoglot charge, runs into another lounge.

Evening, Sunday, 3 September 1972

The boxing hall is just under the excessively tall, visually inescapable television antenna called now the Olympia Tower. The loaf-shaped boxing hall is the dullest building on the site. It is an ice-skating stadium completed long before any other facility on the Oberwiesenfeld. Now the interior has temporary ranked seating around the walls and four, neat, truncated wedges of "ringside seats" around a raised, regulation platform, making places for a total of 7,200 spectators. The place is not full. Boxing, along with weight lifting, offers some of the less sought-after tickets in the Games. This is my first boxing match ever.

One surprise is that the air in the place is, unlike the Rembrandtesque atmosphere communicated in the boxing paintings of George Bellows or Thomas Eakins, uniformly bright and clear.

Independently of any sympathy on my part as I lean forward or back in my seat the crowd goes through waves of emotion focusing on any sort of action that is noticed. Almost all the noisemakers on hand seem to be locals. This is confirmation that seats are easy to get. If there is not patriotic drama readily at hand for the groups of patriots to focus on, groups coalesce vociferously to cheer on fighters who are scrappy or, conversely, to hoot or whistle at those who are not scrappy. Between fights they disapprove of close decisions. Like crowds in the Roman colosseum, these Olympic spectators want raw action, displays of ultimate physical and emotional spending; extremes, not skill.

A quick knockout. Just minutes ago, in front of me there were two young heavyweights; a secure-looking East German confronted an equally noble-looking socialist comrade, a Bulgarian with good posture. A little bit later (I never even noticed the punch that did it) the Bulgarian dropped to the canvas, bounced an inch, and stayed there twitching like a squirrel I once ran over with my bicycle. He tried almost at once to get up, hanging and shaking his head like an epileptic to dispel the consciousness of his shame. He farted. An all-out calling up of will, detoured somewhere in his damaged brain, brought the boy to his feet, where he lurched about like an old drunk, a dying fool with paresis, a piece of human junk. He took his first sensible or normal step too late, for the referee had counted him out. The young Bulgarian's first and only appearance at the Olympic Games had lasted seven seconds less than one minute. Kindly, gracefully the German lifted the ropes of the ring to ease the loser's passage out and away.

Pieces of equipment at the boxers' corners are orange, plastic funnels with thick white hoses leading from them to buckets. Periodically a trainer holds a funnel before the dumb face of his charge for the expectoration of stringy spit, blood, or, if the spectators are lucky, teeth.

Fights in various weight classes follow one another expeditiously. Each bout is only three rounds long. A lightweight from Colombia, Alfon-

so Perez, leaps hopefully into the ring, dances nimbly during some pre-
liminaries, and then, just before he goes at his Czechoslovakian opponent, in a gesture that causes the whole arena to gasp softly and then
to snicker, he crosses himself—shoulders-head-heart—with his mitted
right hand. For the boxing crowd, this is one of those "merry" (lustig)
touches that give watched sport its impromptu high moments. Perez
goes on to win the fight.

But all this has been a lead-in. Today is Sunday, and Señor Perez's
merry gesture leads me to ponder, at least briefly, the role that Christian-
ity is playing in the XXth Olympics of the modern era.

My motives for going to mass this morning were too mixed to
disentangle here. At one level I wanted to watch an aspect of the Olympic
festival that I expected all other chroniclers to ignore. Like most historians of Europe I am awed by the stupendous momentum of the Roman
Catholic church. Mass, here and now, was scheduled to take place in the
larger of the two Catholic chapels in the Christian Center close to the
chief crossroads of pedestrian traffic in the Olympic Village.

I have stated before that one almost never sees wood surfaces on
this site. The slim, lightweight chair of waxed birch in the chapel was
soothing to feel, and my frazzled sensitivities were eased at once by the
few tones of off-white throughout the interior. There were about forty
people present for the service—a small number considering that the
chapel had about 200 chairs and that this is a community, even if an
artificial and temporary one, of 12,000 people in Catholic Bavaria. Of
those forty, it was quickly clear moreover that among us were three cine-
matographers shooting, four photographers actually clicking shutters
during the service, and a couple of people with whirring tape recorders.
So the intention to immortalize this sacred undertaking was not my idea
alone.

Besides the priest, there was an organist and at least one purported
journalist present—myself. I saw no others scribbling. About fifteen of
the people present appeared as though they might be world-class athletes, and most of these looked like Latin Americans unable to understand the sermon, which was on the necessity for universal tolerance. It
was given in strenuously enunciated, fine French.

Near the close of this loose ceremony, the thin priest asked those assembled to join him in singing, "We Shall Overcome," which he led off loudly in English so heavily accented, garbled really, that he sounded like a movie comic improvisation, a burlesque. The impromptu congregation complied, sort of, and, given the evidence of weak lungs forcing musical tones past timid larynxes, I halved my estimate of the real athletes on hand. And so I have offered one indication of the strength of the Mother Church of our civilization in the midst of the most cunningly contrived pagan festival of our age.

I first employed the Christian Center as part of a large stratagem. I had already learned that I could enter, illegitimately of course, the Olympic Village posing as a Peruvian marathon runner in the last miles of a long workout. Once past the guards, I would then have to move about in sweat-soppy running shorts. So, early on, I tucked a pair of Levi's under my arm. It became necessary to find a place to change.

Close by the places where Adidas, Puma, and Tiger give away free shoes, the athletes' disco, the purple-saried ladies from Ceylon who give away tea, the Mensa, and the heavily trafficked areas of the Helene-Mayer-Ring, is this temporary structure of one high story and a basement. It has a framework of tensed iron members like scaffolding or pieces of an erector set. It has a matte-white fiberboard exterior. Only episodically does anyone enter it or leave it. It took searching to find a sign on the outside identifying the site as the Olympic Village Church Contact Center (Begegnungszentrum der Kristlichen Dienste im Olympischen Dorf).

It contains three chapels—one for Protestants and two, one small, one large, for Catholics (after all, we are in Bavaria!). The furnishings are done in a pared, spare style that is the contrary of the rococo or voluptuous baroque that the art student expects of South German Catholics. Though the larger chapel has one large, old cross holding Jesus, there is no other traditional decoration. Aicher's color dictatorship has been excluded here as in the VIP restaurants. The chapels are all quiet and restful and, for the writing down of stuff possibly worth later employment, nicely located. The place is always open. The meeting rooms (there are no meetings) and men's toilets in the basement are readily at hand for changing from shorts to my street clothes, which while elsewhere I stash in an empty desk drawer. But the entire place inspires assurance and settles my thinking rather than rattling it.

One hears the Olympic hurly-burly nearby and outside, but the ambience immediately at hand is an antidote to the swirling sensuality of glorious, mindless youths strutting about the Village's pedestrian causeways only a few feet away. I am alone and forced to be professionally serious. As I scribble in my little notebook, an occasional peeking-in tourist stares at me. I reciprocate.

A different-looking, rather separately placed group of buildings adjoining the Olympic Village is the German Olympic Center, or Deutsches Olympische Zentrum (DOZ), referred to as "Dots." Occupying perhaps five acres, these buildings are used for the volleyball contests, the labors of some 2,500 radio and television technicians, and the offices of the highest supervising officials here. They have the decorative distinction that, like the U.S. Steel Tower in central Pittsburgh, the structural metal has been left open to the elements to blotch and streak. The rust will give a tone of desperate chic, the sort of controlled accident that is a theme of many contemporary surfaces but that is almost unknown in the architecture of modern Munich.

This architectural complex will have a post-Olympic use that was determined long in advance. After the Games, these buildings will become a college of physical education. Young people learning to be gym teachers will benefit from the practice fields and other fine sporting facilities now being enjoyed by the world. A curious facility, a piece of apparatus close by that serves no function at all right now, is a pretty concrete "mountain" about forty feet high that rises out of rich, green sward. It will be used by classes in Alpinism and has in neatly assembled form all the varieties of overhangs and traverses, wide and narrow ledges, chimneys and grips, that exist in inaccessible nature and that could be designed in advance for the teaching and testing of a would-be technical climber, his nerves, and his Vibram soles. One can guess that the bureaucrats of modern sport might at any time imperialistically seize upon mountain climbing as a fallow-lying form of individualism that, like almost every other sport, should have quadrennial climaxes. Point systems will be devised; impartial judges appointed. To win gold medals, one will have to train mountain climbers. The organizers here have foreseen everything.

One could, if one wished to devote some speculation to it, see this little "mountain," ironically called the Olympiaberg, as ingenious planning ahead, an architectural joke, or a big piece of sculpture. But it now demands our attention for another reason. It is on the bus route of those traversing the distance between the Press Center and the areas of specific Olympic endeavor by athletes. And so, from the beginning, media people were required to notice that on one of the minimountain's "summits," as has been the case so long in the past on so many promontories in Christian territory, there is a large, Latin cross. This one is of timber—a substance one sees only in hidden places at the German Olympics.

There is an easy way, composed of steep stairs at the back, up the Olympiaberg, and I made it for a summit-sit in the customary glorious weather. Once next to the cross, it was clear that it was made of measured and circular-saw-cut four-by-fours. Surely it was assembled by unofficial, Christ-inspired decorator-dissentniks. The first few days here I noticed the casual eyes of fellow bus passengers rest loosely on the cross (it cannot be avoided) and then turn away from it in embarrassment. I have seen no published reference to this unplanned Christian manifestation nor any photographs of it. On the other hand, I saw no trace of vandals' work on the cross or anywhere at all at the churches in the Village. Perhaps Christian symbols will be vandalized in Moscow in 1980.

Marienplatz has been a traditional citizens' gathering place in front of some civic buildings in old Munich. It still is. But now one goes there to buy black-market tickets to desirable sporting events. Last night standing room at the closing ceremonies was available at 100 marks, seats at 300 marks. Boxing remains cheap; dressage costly. Tickets for the imminent U.S./Soviet Union basketball game could not be found.

Usually at Marienplatz one can encounter, and if one wishes observe, some Jesus-hippies. For this great international festival, some also gather in mutually supporting numbers on the grassy slopes along the Luz-Long-Ufer, a crowded spectators' pedestrianway leading from the boxing hall, in front of the Olympic Tower, and to the swimming hall. The groups have from five to a dozen members. A lead guitarist, most often one of several fair-skinned brunettes in fine health, strums three chords to accompany droning voices in one line. The guitarist has a conventional, "joyful," durable rictus. The other kids join in and smile cloyingly to suggest the happiness that lies ahead when we choose Jesus. Their accents and their vitamin-stuffed health indicate that they are middle-class Americans and occasionally middle-class British. Never anything else, though they distribute tracts (that quickly become litter) in

French, German, Spanish, and Russian. The tracts have the Olympic rings on the cover.

Some time has passed for all of us here. These tired yet still-optimistic children now have much in common with the Ceylon tea ladies at the Olympic Village. The latter still wear a lovely variety of saris, but they are now tired of it all and cannot smile spontaneously anymore. Particles of the European crowds, who never linger, regard the Jesus singers with a mixture of nostalgia and amusement.

The mood was otherwise after a recently completed gymnastics competition a couple nights ago. Some of us watched a religious debate. The scene went on at the Coubertinplatz, where the capricious and vast plastic roof swoops so low that one can touch it. The protagonists were lit by distant, mercury vapor lights casting long shadows. On one side was an evangelist, a prophet, screaming Christian warnings in radio-announcer German. His opponent was a boozy Bavarian atheist who bellowed his blasphemous party pieces in dialect. Some respectable folks rushed on to miss the gaucheries and obscenities, but the two held the interest, for a while anyway, of a number of tickled idlers.

The respectful tourist here is, as always, primed in advance to be moved when he steps into the meticulously restored and ravishing old churches in Munich and in the countryside around us. But the cultured assumption is that one goes to pay one's respect to art—to intricate, though comprehensible, music and to uproarious, old decoration. We are supposed to squint or wink at the images of the holy family, the fathers of the Church, or the saints—unless they are starred in the guidebooks. While in these glorious, pompous, clean churches one may notice a few old women praying in their brown wool coats. We know we are supposed to disregard them as one does well-behaved pets in good neighborhoods.

5

High Spirits

Sunday and Monday, 3 and 4 September 1972

Here on the site I (or we) often have companions. One cannot use the term "friend" because in this atmosphere we have abandoned our histories. The friends of our past are impossibly distant. I am just about impossible to reach by phone, and international mail is not getting through. We are intimate with whole rows of new persons picked up with happy nonchalance. And when we drop them for others, no one minds. Substitutes, equally confiding, funny, and appreciative, are at hand, smiling invitations.

The little journalist from Helsinki who, as the green Olympic ring of Europe, was a coparticipant on that television program in Bonn comes and goes. She looks and moves like a caricature of Sonja Henie except that she smokes furiously and has dark curtains under easily wetted eyes. In Bonn she leaned against me and told me how she needed protection.

Here she usually needs a drink as well. The drink provided, she offers me in exchange rather remarkable personal confidences in connection with named personages (all unknown to me) in Finnish politics and the arts. When there were no cabinet ministers or television producers about, we were chummy in Bonn. During the Lufthansa flight back to Munich, she assured me with nods of her pretty head that she could promote a Finnish translation of my book on the 1936 Olympics. We agreed that we deserved a leisurely supper together soon. Somehow, after we arrived at the Munich airport, we split at once (but I was neither astonished nor downcast). Still, when we meet in the Press Center, we hold hands. Once at the busy bar, she kissed me full-face-on when I interrupted her tête-à-tête with a Norwegian twice my size. The giant grinned tolerantly.

A different pickup. In my room she dawdled, looking about for whole minutes as I observed keenly, waiting for an unequivocal sign. But suddenly, she was all business, unpacking her tape recorder and a pad of yellow, lined paper. Only then was it certain that the choice piece was there on a quite legitimate expedition arranged earlier by telephone—in this case to interview for a Munich paper an avowed pessimist about the Olympic Games. She was high-cheeked and dark, with rich oily skin best observed about the loosely held cleavage in her knit, ribbed sweater. She was conversationally deft. I spoke, it seemed, with facility and wit under the impulses of her quick, professional, yet mockingly affectionate questions. Was she *that* skilled, or was there again under construction an adventurous relationship between us that was fundamentally based on an exciting conjunction of our respective hormonal systems? We were giggling like cousins who had been in love for decades. At the good-bye handshake, I held on.

"This has been entirely delightful. We must meet again under less dutiful circumstances," I offered and she agreed. But, of course, we did not.

The next day, her buddy and coworker, a photographer, appeared, declaring that she had been most particularly eager to meet me. This second one was older and tougher, yet more merry and voluptuous. Though German, too, she gesticulated like a Sicilian. Laughing, I lolled back in an easy chair and then walked about my room as she alternatively framed me in a black Contax rubbed through to the brass and a heavy new Nikon with a long lens. She chattered of her many adventures. She had wandered for a year in the United States. Even worked for several months in a bar in New Orleans.

We went outside for some snaps of the American professor who is a long-distance runner. Her stories, the teasing and shoves to move this way and that, roused a jolly performance as I jogged in place in blue nylon shorts. She went through four rolls of tri-X. Some of the shots had to be good.

"Could I have the negatives after you have printed the pictures you want? I might use one for a dust jacket on my book on these Olympics. It goes without saying that I would give you the credit."

She laughed my request away, "No. We don't do that. We always keep our negatives. Who knows? Tomorrow you might shoot the queen of England [Elizabeth II's arrival was imminent], and I would want my pictures on hand. I'm sure you understand."

Then, too, there are the hostesses, sometimes in flocks, wherever the journalists or technicians must gather. Except for the annoyance that they apply heavy eye make-up, they recall recent college grads whom no one would be ashamed to take just about anywhere. Even the homely girls look like those pleasant kids everyone fooled around with and who eventually, to everyone's astonishment, married well and stayed that way.

The girls leap to do favors. It is their job after all. They like my German, an uncommon accomplishment here, which I overpronounce in their presence. When idly looking about the Press Center I sometimes mischievously hold a gaze on them, and, on the basis of my samples, I would say that about one in six (of those not already taken by another journalist, that is) answers my count-of-four stare with the tiniest smile that is a provisional promise to consider. With those hostesses with whom there is some business contact—at the motor pool, helping with the German yellow pages, at a computer printout—my scientific probing of the possibility of further investigations is answered by a bigger smile of understanding by about one in three women, maybe more.

Little deeper fraternization takes place in the open. But there are plenty of places to meet in the Press Center where one can exchange minimal biographical and professional data, dally, play light slap-and-tickle, exchange crucial numbers, and arrange a rendezvous. We all have private rooms or apartments. Our soldier-concierges have been told—indeed commanded—not to record who comes and who goes.

Our pickups are not all cross-sexual.

An appearing and disappearing companion is Ell, whom I rescued from a scholarly congress on sport about ten days ago. He is a very large adult but was dressed like a child in a bright Hawaiian shirt, fringed cutoffs, and flip-flops. Though far from shy looking he was self-consciously out-of-place among all those people in professorial suits. I was headed for a gymnastics practice and asked him to come along in my soldier-driven car.

Ell was recently one of several reigning "Mr. Americas," each of whom is chosen by a different organization of bodybuilders. He is in the heavyweight class. He has tanned skin, even teeth, and waved and streaked blonde hair. His thin hide exposes the striations of his prize-winning musculature. Though stupendous in the upper arms and calves, he has the small hips and delicate knees, ankles, and wrists favored by the judges in the male beauty contests.

My new companion is a demonstration of the Lord's injustice in the distribution of gifts. Handsome by most standards and exquisite by some, Ell also has a doctorate in physical education. His research is about positive and negative work. His dissertation required monitoring and calibrating with attached electrodes the undertakings of human subjects doing strenuous things in a vat of mud.

"What kind of mud?"

"Just plain ol' Texas river bottom mud. You make it thicker or thinner by adding mud or water."

Ell wrote an anecdotal article based upon his research that has photos of him wallowing with a statuesque coed in the mud.

"*Sports Illustrated* almost took it. Then it was turned down by nine more magazines. Maybe I should have spiced it up instead of talking so much about my scientific research. Mud is interesting though. You can do all sorts of experiments in it. If I could invent something like it that didn't stink and didn't stick to you, I could make a fortune."

SI favors its staffers and is a tough nut to crack for a free-lancer. However, Ell has no trouble getting his research articles on training routines or nutrition published in the physique mags. He himself is sometimes displayed near-nude in the ritualistic positions. He has just recently been on the cover of *Strength and Health* and has copies of that issue with him.

His declared mission in Munich is to interview athletes about food. But the desired subjects are stashed away in the Village, so Munich has been a disappointment as far as research is concerned.

In other respects, we are disparate, but here we are often in harmony. As we watched some women gymnasts, I looked away from time to time to coach him in the stance to take when presenting his doctoral diploma, his physique pictures, and his magazine articles to Hans Klein's office in order to get impromptu press privileges.

Sure enough, a day later, this "Mr. America" got a pass letting him into the weight-lifting competitions. But soon, suitably coached by me and others, he was sneaking into lots of forbidden areas.

He helps me, and I help him. He loiters at the moneyless Olympic Village, schnorring meals, playing Ping-Pong while stripped to the waist, and talking about food with Soviet and Japanese athletes. Though I balk, he cons others into serving as his translator. Ell knows no word of German. He calls the coin of this realm "dootch marks." Hand to the side of his mouth, he tells me of the reputations of certain saunas and more than I want to know of the diets and drugs of the weight lifters. There is useless gossip about Mark Spitz and the big American sprinters. He confides the lies employed in order to obtain free shoes as well as training suits, scuffs, and luggage from the Adidas and Puma people. There are no conversational lacunae. His voice is not well modulated, and I miss a lot. He has found twin female Canadian gymnasts and is eager to immortalize his presence here by means of some sun-lit oiled physique photos with the girls at his splendidly flared sides and the Olympic clou, the great roof, in the background.

Though domestically compulsive regarding punctuality, I stood him up a couple of times. Yet we are pleased each time we encounter one another. Our mutually appreciated relationship is more than merely convenient, but it is unimaginable either in his customary location or in mine.

We are all having a marvelous time. But so much of our high spirits seems to be current only and to depend upon our providential presence at this time at this place. I feel this most keenly off the site. Disturbed that my judgment was slipping by steady immersion in this narrowly enchanting, temporary, artificial atmosphere, I ordered a driver to take me late one night to the hashish bar on the Elizabethplatz that I had visited in May. The Piper Club once must have been a toney place with "oriental" decor. It was again (still?) packed with dirty young adults casually greeting one another and moving lethargically to smashingly oppressive rock music. Some seemed to be tripping in murky areas. The air was hot and smelled more of chemically flavored soft drinks and Gauloises than it did of hashish, which one perceived only in whiffs. I dutifully purchased five grams of some light stuff from a flabby boy in a new, black leather overcoat. On the spot I had no pipe to smoke it in.

There was no theme, no focus. I decided I did not want to be where the air was unfriendly, unsortable, antilogical, and where there were no schedules of pleasurable spectacles ahead. There were no affirmative symbols leading to meaning. The sickly children (all German as well as I could determine) were not seeking indications of deeper, unifying pulses in the universe but were irresponsibly fragmenting their perceptions and their pleasures. The sensuously strong and sensuously repellent atmosphere was unathletic, un-Olympic. I fled in a taxi.

Other sorties into Munich—to ship books, to seek experts not on the sites—seem vaguely dangerous or disloyal tasks worth struggling to end quickly. The feelings of traitorous uneasiness are dissipated once in a location that is designated as "Olympic," for example, the isolated regatta site, the grounds of the palace at Nymphenburg for dressage, and the protected halls for weight lifting, wrestling, and some other sports that are bus rides (in "Olympic" buses) away from the main site. And I feel relatively snug at the special exhibitions such as the one on the German excavations at ancient Olympia. But I am avoiding the city's nontemporary art museums.

The intensifying assumption that one is a vital element in a grand, symbolically rich undertaking must be yet more secure among those having more rigidly defined functions within the sacred circle. When moving about Munich, one rarely sees people in the readily identifiable official uniforms. The tourists one sees (and the city is not especially crowded) could as well be gawkers in Belgrade or Copenhagen. The athletes display themselves and train in or near the Olympic Village or at the facilities of closed-off sports clubs in the area. Except as remote, magic figures, they are only seldom seen other than (with auras it is true) at their applicable sites. Compliant as always, the athletes have helped the organizers' attempts to isolate and cherish the fleshy substance of Olympic celebration.

The residents of the Press City spend most of their time with each other, seeking hard news, attempting to verify rumors. They spend a very great deal of time keenly observant before the banks of many television sets. They type, telex, develop film, talk, eat, and drink at the center. It should be indicative of general organizational success that the bars and restaurants of old Munich are far less crowded than during the Oktoberfest and Fasching. This relative spaciousness and the police-enforced normal prices are causing the merchants to complain, the newspapers report. Those of us who are "Olympians" or are Olympic hangers-on are living in a magic world superior to that outside the fences and the checkers of our identification badges. We participants are doing our best to live gracefully our Olympic lives, which are busy, joyous, artificial, subsidized, and therefore cheap.

Besides the private quarters, the vulgar lavishness of our food, our cars and drivers, an insurance policy, the free photography, the stewards, the banks of communications equipment, the hostesses, we get other things.

There are lots of little samples of merchandise. An Italian vintner distributes samples of a bitter white wine. My steward placed a bottle on my desk one day. The Gillette people gave us a kit containing their new shaving system featuring little black cartridges holding two peeking blades. I used the system at once and became an instant convert. I received two portfolios and a large shoulder bag—this last a present of the Fiat company.

The amount of printed material placed in our mailboxes or offered for the picking up is too much to be treated with respect. Much of it is pamphlets or whole books with much-too-detailed descriptions of the sports progress of individual nations. There are biographical dictionaries of the national teams. The Federal Republic produces literature that is most expensively printed. The Democratic Republic produces the most in volume. The Americans tossed off a mimeographed tract of some forty pages, and I only saw a couple of them. We are perhaps overinformed with free materials.

The incessantly busy newspaper store (reporters read each other's papers) in the Press Center has on display a 100-page picture book of hagiography called *Kenya's World-Beating Athletes*. The price is $5. I want it. I am annoyed as I hand over the money, for now I feel that because of my elevated position anything I desire here I should have for the taking. Some expensively dressed, overfed, Western journalists complained when some mistake in scheduling caused them to give out cash for a shared taxi.

The object, usually more implicit than explicit, of a sports organizer is to offer the feeling or the pleasure to his clientele that they are participants in a magic circle. Sport, with its iconography still in the process of formation, its shifting and uncertain divinities and attractive, though as yet unspecified, ideology, has been gathering mythic significance. Our genial hosts here have provided an inconceivably (literally) magic occurrence in a somber, serious, surrounding world in which traditional rites have deteriorated and the old symbols are exposed and held up for general ridicule. If we think about it, we know that here in Munich cunning theatrical engineers are able to invent festivity from nothing and that we will love it.

My presence here is due to my professional stance that this festival is the result of the application of exceptional insight and heaps of treasure to accomplish particular ideological or political objects. In my diary I keep proving this to myself. I know that these objects have nothing to do with pure play or sport. That is the XXth Olympiad I came here to expose, and in my notebook I have been a dutiful little cynic. But as a participant, I have given myself up to good times. Happily, I revel in a richer life on a piece of temporarily hallowed ground. Some about me believe that their enchantment began with the opening ceremonies. Mine began earlier—perhaps in the cycling stadium.

Some confessions about to be recorded will surely seem senseless when I am again immersed in the quotidian existence, but I feel I must chronicle while hot some aspects of the febrile suggestibility. But many here feel that their alertness to symbols and their impulsive trust are indicative of deeper pulses in the universe that this opportunity providentially has offered.

I. The deferential soldier from Mannheim who makes my bed in the morning and who brings on request to my room cups of fine coffee and bottles of water from the Kaiser-Friedrich Quelle has the same name, Mandel, but with the difference of one letter. This piece of news came out recently in the course of yet another attempt at a conversation that deteriorated because of his abject manners and his unwillingness or inability to speak high German.

The name is not rare. Elsewhere I have met Mandels with one or two ls. Somehow in these circumstances the presence of this relative who is not a relative seemed indicative of deeper things. I was full of wonder.

An occasional companion of my new chum, "Mr. America," and therefore of mine, and a recent contributing guide through an evening at the weight-lifting contests is a slow-speaking, young Australian with a drooping nose and big pores. He writes for some power-lifting magazines and runs a small mail-order business for bodybuilders. I listened with partial interest to his expert dilation on the drugs, the anabolic steroids, that weight lifters take and on what these drugs do to their remarkable bodies. He sells physique photos and makes his own movies of great weight lifters, some of whom he actually films as we chat. One of the boy's assignments here in Munich is to satisfy a man in Florida who adores, remotely, muscular women. Facilitated by long lenses, the compliant Australian was amassing several hundred feet of frames of the legs of the lady shot-putters and discus throwers who were in action at the practice fields. He would be nicely recompensed by turning over to his client the product of this work.

We offered our full names late, which often does not happen at all, and I learned with joy that the Australian's name was Wayne Gallasch. I was born in Wayne County in Michigan. My mother's family name was Gellasch. I had never encountered this name outside Detroit, which is oversupplied with my relatives. True, there is a difference in our names of one letter (as there was with my steward), but rapid and subsequent talk (accompanied by happy amazement by both of us) revealed that our ancestors had left East Prussia at about the same time more than a hundred years ago and that, yes, we were kin. I felt intimate with this man who anywhere else, name or no name, would be for me a piece of curiosa.

Again and again one hears of people who have felt blessed to encounter beloved, lost friends. Several times, most particularly in the last few days, I have heard distant shouts behind me of "Dick!" or "Mandell!" When I turn to look, there is no source for these eager greetings. The déjà vu shiver occurs so often I no longer ponder it but stop what I am doing and wait for it to pass.

II. The Australian journalist who was the blue ring on the Bonn television broadcast introduced me to a Californian who arrived ten days ago without tickets or reservations. The youth yearned to see the pentathlon competitions, which he himself plans to enter in 1976. Though big, he is not handsome or remarkably charming. By merely hanging around the television sets in the Press Center, he found himself the receiver of meal tickets, spare rooms to sleep in, and presents of the scarce passes for the very events he had only hopes of seeing. His fencing coach, who is on the site, got him a free pair of specialized Adidas shoes. He has saved enough money out of his anticipated small budget to buy a $100 wristwatch for his girlfriend at home. He has just got the news that his father has been nominated for a Nobel Prize. He feels (and he regrets admitting such things) that this Olympic festival is somehow being run for his benefit and, by extension, that just now the world is being run for his benefit as well.

There are ever more freeloaders on the spot. Most are Americans. They learned by retold tales of Woodstock or by experience that at a large festivity they can safely make their way. They arrive in $150 Volkswagens or with $50 Kelty packs. They forge gate passes, eat in the Mensa, and sleep in their down bags in already crowded rooms in the Village. When challenged as gate-crashers, they pull the "dumb American" routine, "What? Huh? I don't understand. What? Huh?" and they push their way through. The guards are unarmed, and they do not chase.

This sort of success cannot be entirely unexpected. The organizers did not plan for the chutzpah of young Californians. But the kids are so breezy about it all, and they so easily con all on hand. Myself included. I eagerly believe liars, treat entertaining beggars to meals, take people places. To acquaintances of five minutes I offer confidences and get astonishing insights in return. We pick up and drop people. We make promises we will not keep.

III. Modern usage and conventional categories of description are lacking to explain neatly what is meant. I am frighteningly alert to symbolic indications that have suggestive origins. Some signs have given me glimpses into the future.

A. Many at the opening ceremonies on Saturday more than a week ago observed that late in the piled rituals, the doves were released to swirl upward. These symbols of peace are posited to spread this desirable condition from the happy stadium to their symbolic destination, the world.

It was an inspiring sight. Yet, it provided a rugged moment, for, as with many complex pieces of engineering, a little thing went wrong. No birds got caught in the dubious roof, which would surely have damaged our expectations for peace in Munich. The thousands of birds rose, making thousands of graceful curves into a haze of disappearing flickers. With an exception. One individual valiantly imitated his fellows, flapped alone for a while, and then plunged into the Brazilian team. Some in the stadium tittered; many did not.

For some in the latter category, this incident established a miasma of fearful premonition about the Brazilian athletes—and by metaphoric extension, the Brazilian nation. I relived atavistic memories of a solitary bird being a harbinger of death. Some childhood incident, perhaps when a sparrow flew down a chimney and threw an ancient Prussian aunt into yelling terrors. It was an emissary of God warning us of calamity, death. I cannot now recall any ensuing calamity, but the symbol stuck and was brought forth to me decades later by that falling dove.

This lurking feeling of possessing evil advance notice continued. At a dressage performance in Nymphenburg, I was drawn to, indeed almost enchanted by, a dark, magnificently handsome woman, outstanding in a riding outfit, whom I had already observed, as a voyeur, after returning from Bonn at the Munich airport as she chatted with a sportswriter. Providentially, the same journalist was at Nymphenburg. I asked him to identify her and he did, giving me a name with many parts and the final announcement that the fate-carrying woman was a Brazilian. I was shaken and felt I should warn the Brazilian team of some impending horror. The prophecy struggled to get out of me. But what words would I choose? Would anyone listen?

B. A maddening premonition. As a good bourgeois, I have exposed the generous German hosts as immoderately wasteful. For the bourgeoisie, prodigality is sinful and invites punishment. In May I suggested that some aspects of this modern celebration can usefully be observed as a potlatch. All of us here are now living in a volatile state of heightened suggestibility and irresponsible euphoria. Will we go on? Will we loosen yet more our cherished control? Do a lot of us want to transcend the present indulgences and move to greater excesses, an orgy to wreck all restraints?

I anticipate (not the correct word for I am ashamed of the anticipation) with fear and pleasure that a week from now, at the conclusion of the XXth Olympics, the athletes and the surrounding human apparatus, your writer included, will be entirely jaded, yet packed with energy. We will all begin our own unplanned festival of waste and destruction. The outlines of the impending wreckage are deep within and cannot be recalled for conventional description. They are like confused dreams. The images are in semidarkness. There is orange light from the side. Mobs of small-toothed, pink-gummed, screaming women, their hanging breasts swinging as they run, sweating in the moist heat, attack horses to suck blood from their ripped necks. The women are bigger than I am.

Hundreds of naked men, athletes, swing studded clubs to wreck plastic surfaces and smash glass. It gets darker and the churning tableaus are lit not by the inescapable fluorescents of our lives here but by licking flames. There are big drums, little fifes, whips. Gustav von Aschenbach had such dreams in *Death in Venice*.

These premonitions are not at all saddening. I am choking with impatience for action. Were the mobs of revelers to rampage through the Olympic Village smashing the place up, pissing from balconies, and screaming in circle dances around a hideous giant rutting a ravishingly lovely gymnast, I would slide in among the other sweaty participators to be there. Would I wait to waved on as next? I could shout louder than the others to urge new outrages. What outrages? I cannot even guess.

It does not seem paradoxical but crazily fitting that we, the beneficiaries of this seducing festival, should reward the generosity of our hosts by obliterating all they have offered us. Perhaps then their victory over us would be total.

Morning, Monday, 4 September 1972

The Crystal Palace Exhibition of 1851 inaugurated the grand series of modern international festivals of which the Olympic Games of the present are the most vigorous and still-evolving part. An overarching fear of the vocal opponents of that striking innovation was that the mere presence of the projected millions of visitors—crowds with no proper-tied leaders—might cause the unrestrained people unpredictably to co-alesce into whirling mobs of rioting strikers who could well slaughter Queen Victoria, expel the aristocracy, and declare a Red republic.

There were, it turned out, no riots, no strikes. Everyone in London, foreigners included, had a marvelous time, and there were no acts of violence at all in London during the summer of 1851 that could be blamed on the great exhibition.

A similar observation about what we might call a "festival of peace" could be made about the colossal concert-happening at Woodstock on farmland in the summer of 1969. There the crowds on hand numbered 300,000 or even more. The concentration of people was denser and ev-erything was far more disorganized than at all the sites combined at any Olympic Games, including these. At Woodstock, there were accidents due to individual irresponsibility, but there were no coalescing riots or violence of a political kind.

Here in Munich crowds that have only standing room at the end sections of the stadium must be pushed beyond the levels of expectable endurance by their packed, noisy fellows, but one neither sees nor hears of scuffles.

We, the seekers of news on the spot, have been maddened by igno-rant guards obeying foolish orders. We are not violent. We glare and then walk away to connive getting past them. My reveries of violence churn, very likely pleasurably, at some suppressible level. All of us in Munich are well kept in check by both external and internal mechanisms at our sacred celebration.

Afternoon, Monday, 4 September 1972

The sauna near the Soviet dorms has a reputation. When I had looked in at other times, it was somber with the sufferings of weight lifters and boxers oozing scarce internal water to stay in their registered weight classes. This time, when I pulled at the tight-fitting door to get into the 10' x 5' x 6' cubicle, I was astonished and backed out. The room was full of cooking flesh. No space for another. Soon three big men rushed out. I got in to settle in a corner and perceived at once the attraction.

On a low bench, hunkered with forehead on knees and heels drawn up to her bottom, was a glistening female. The dozen or so males on hand were not talking, though a couple of large Orientals gave each other grins and knowing looks. Our guest raised her head a couple of times to look around vacantly. She took good-naturedly the putatively accidental jostling. She left the sweatbox, and then so did I (earlier than I might otherwise have), to douse in a strong cold shower.

Under the tan she was a fair Teuton. Her German (she answered questions briefly, politely, but not willingly) was tinged with Bavarian dialect. Her clean hair was back in a stable bun, and she wore large gold hoops in her reddened ears. Several years past being a teenager, she lacked the compact correctness of an athlete. *Softig* with fetching dimples above each flaring buttock. Her skimpy crotch hair was a cute, beige tuft. The large pink nipples were snubbed, having no definite points, and her heavy breasts hung some. A few shades in the direction of voluptuousness and off the *Playboy* ideal.

She slowly dried with a beach towel and, with many shakes and adjustments, put on a purple velvet bikini. Some sauna-door Johnnies with towels around their middles also watched. The whole undertaking was oddly quiet.

Amid general regret the star of the sauna descended for a swim in the pool downstairs and then, to suppressed rejoicing, returned for the slow peeling of the purple bikini and a long sweat before the quiet, appreciative audience. Some Russians and some Mongolians with cauliflower ears were overjoyed and could scarcely believe their eyes. I had heard that girls were often in this sauna and was delighted with an actual and superior sighting. "Good, clean fun," I thought and meandered my way past a row of massaging rooms to an adjoining sun deck.

With the ease one expects here, I became immersed in a conversation with two American gymnasts. They were naked like myself. Both were coincidentally named Jim. One wore braces on his teeth; the other did not. I had seen them and their teammates in an American national competition two years before. They agreed that their team performances here were not what they had hoped for.

I commented on what many observers had remarked about the

American teams. The gymnasts I had observed in practice and competition lounged about in their straight chairs or did impromptu stretching exercises almost anywhere. When one of their fellows did well, they gave him generous fanny slaps; when one did badly, they stroked him and whispered boosting clichés. This was a contrast to the public behavior of the other high-level teams—and most particularly to the chilly demeanor of the Soviet gymnasts who revealed disappointment or joy only long after their performances were over—on the victory podium, for example.

They agreed that many American athletes were accused of not being "icy" enough.

An annoyance for them was the behavior of the German audiences at the competitions. They whistled disapproval and rang cowbells at *every* decision affecting a German gymnast and were treating like a rock star the white-haired Bernd Effing.

One Jim said that a couple of these German gymnasts were becoming horses asses in the light of all this media adulation and that the noise in the sports hall where the competitions were being held was influencing the judges to give unjustly high awards to the host team.

The general amiability (a couple of other sunbathers had joined us by now) was loosening. I wanted to try hypothetical projects for their comment. Would it not be nobler simply to drop the long horse? Even with the supreme performers, the critical issue in the all-too-rapid maneuver, the positioning of the feet at landing, due to the strenuousness of the undertaking, is, to an irreducible extent, the result of hazard. And in this event, especially, no further improvement was possible.

A couple of coaches had joined us. We talked of other gymnastic events. All were so tolerant! I said I was an "esthete." I talked of the bittersweet pleasure that comes when one watches while something that a stern youth should not be able to do at all is done beautifully. Then it is over before one can savor what transpired. All agreed that at a high-stakes gymnastic competition, the buzzers, bells, announcers, and flashing lights on scoreboards detract from a happy impression.

I was employing the word "esthetics" and the dangerous one "beauty" repetitively, but still, when some skeptics left our little group of six or so, a couple more came by to replace them.

Was it not possible that the limits for creative work in all the standard events—save one, the floor exercises—had been reached and that perhaps it was time to rethink top-level gymnastics from the beginning? They balked at the word "creative" as they earlier objected to the words "original" and "beauty." One Yank, a coach, flared with anger when I said that humans were never going to be more "beautiful" than the supremely accomplished and supremely cool Mikhail Voronin, a twenty-seven-year-old, aloof Soviet gymnast. He almost shouted that Voronin was a conceited, self-centered asshole.

I was into it. I felt I was given permission here to project yet another mental construction that might conceivably lead to some mutual use of high-performance sport and ambitious, original art. In discussions of Effing and Voronin, I had perceived that the use of the word "beauty" with any suggestion of the erotic among these disciplined (despite the sprawling in public) Americans was likely to be viewed as equivocal or worse. Yet I plunged ahead.

The only creative possibilities left are in the floor exercises. And before real esthetic progress can be made, certain arid notions of chaste masculinity and winning have to be gotten rid of. How ravishing, how close, perhaps, to an ultimate art performance, a *Gesamtkunstwerk*, it would be to watch the best floor-exercise gymnasts perform in set pieces much longer than the obligatory seventy seconds. We could have them perform discontinuously, in groups, with pauses, to the accompaniment of music in varying tempos—like the movements of a classical suite. Why not men and women? I had for days been fantasizing (and may envisage episodically forever) a pas de deux by Voronin and Ludmilla Turishcheva, a Soviet gymnast of partly Asian ancestry and of disturbing loveliness.

I was waving my hands now. Body water beaded my face and ran in rivulets down my sides. Then I went too far. I proposed the project only offered by the very brave—Leni Riefenstahl, the titan cinematographer, for example: to have the most beautiful men (they owed it to us!) perform naked—just as we were, I pointed out. And I screwed up further by commenting that gymnasts might not stimulate as intensely as the big sprinters and big wrestlers favored by the classical Greeks because, though often surpassing pretty (as both Effing and Voronin incontrovertibly were), gymnasts were often skimpy in the behind.

One of the Jims had left and the two remaining attendants were uneasy with my gesticulation and vocal modulations. All were reluctant to admit that the object of the gymnast was to approach "beauty." "Perfection" was the word that was employed all around them, the one they used and that they thought was apt. They were in fact all kindly, listening far more than they spoke. We chattered on in the sunlight. Some others, also naked, came by to listen and add remarks. And then I saw that I would be late for a much-desired appointment.

Returning from a fast, cold shower, I saw a group around the door of a fluorescent-lit room. A couple of the amiable gentlemen were recognizable from the sauna an hour or so before. No one protested as I slid through the sweaty skin of men like me to see that the star of the sauna was now on her stomach on a padded, black plastic table. Pummeling her was a hairy, middle-aged, dark man, who looked worldly though he was sopping with perspiration and wore only a towel about his large middle. He stroked her thighs with the aid of a slippery soap solution. This went on for a while. On a dare, a thin boy mumbling something in South American Spanish reached way out to slide his wet hand between her fine body and her plump arm at her side. Neither the massager nor the massagee minded at all. There were giggles and some low speculation in Spanish and some Slavic tongues.

The tone of the company had now shifted to one of mumbled and indefinite but eager waiting. All the spectators had been wearing towels about their middles, but they began fidgeting their hands around and above their balls. Still, it was all going so slowly! I was all sweaty again. The confluence of anticipating tension and compulsive punctuality were giving me a sharp headache. And just as I turned a corner outside, I heard a little click. A look revealed that they had at last turned the light out.

Evening, Monday, 4 September 1972

Once again I am in the hall for the weight lifters. And again, I am buttressed with company by two who are much more knowledgeable than I. The competitors this time are the heavyweights who are just under 110 kilograms or 220 pounds. (There is yet another classification—that for the "superheavyweights" who weigh more than 110 kilograms.)

By now I have become a stricter critic of the theater in the many events that I have observed. My companions are bodybuilders—one American, the other Australian. Both are enchanted onlookers but are critical, though in a much narrower sense than I am. They are observant of technique. But still, as has regularly been the case here, they educate with alacrity those who are ignorant. I ask many questions:

"That Hungarian just sniffed hard from some shiny tube his trainer held out to him before he went on the stage. I assumed that any sort of drugs were illegal here. What's going on?"

"Sure it's illegal. But inhaled Benzedrine (that's probably what it is) can't be detected in the piss after the lift. They are all loaded on drugs, but the smart ones from countries where the stakes are big and the chemists are clever will not have them using drugs that can be found out. What most have used are the anabolic steroids. Long programs to give them muscular bulk. Bulk in some places and shrinkage in others."

"What d'you mean 'shrinkage'?"

"That guy will win—the Russian, Talts. If you saw him in the shower you would see that he couldn't win a gold medal in a certain category. He's like a baby down there. None of these guys, I bet, could screw more than once a month."

And it is distracting during the lifts of these big men, the strongest in the world, to observe, as one ought not, the curious aside of their trembling little peckers and balls immediately behind their thin jersies. Such a pathetic, childish contrast with the evocative, supermacho, six-inches-wide leather belts with massive buckles that they carry about their middles.

"Why don't they wear some kind of jock?"

"It seems like they would wear some kind of padding like the bullfighters do. Jack Johnson used to wear a rolled-up sock in his boxing tights in order to rile the rednecks even more. It seems curious that they expose those little things, since they're showmen just like we are."

"How so?"

"Well, that dance performance they go through for three minutes has been strictly limited to just that period of time. If the judges didn't hold over them the threat of disqualification, they'd be up there entertaining the audience all night. It might be exciting with the sometimes nicely proportioned middleweights or even the lightweights, but almost all of these guys are *ugly* prima donnas."

I remarked, "I haven't seen any handsome power lifters. They all, even the smaller guys, seem sort of gross, bulbous, and hairy. Not the kind of picture you guys like, right?"

"We like to watch them. They do not respect us bodybuilders. We cannot do what they do. Perhaps they claim and we acknowledge their superiority. They are entirely focused on statistical performance. We don't use the word 'beauty'—the boys around us get nervous if you talk that way, but that is what is really on our minds. By the way, though there are steady attempts to get bodybuilding into the Olympic program—it is practiced at the highest levels in much of the world—the Soviets are absolutely opposed to it for philosophical, most particularly Marxist, reasons."

The Soviets kept coming up. At meets it is not uncommon for a power lifter from anywhere to come out on the carpeted dais, stare in horror at the weight, and be ordered away after the three minutes are up. This evening, the talk is of the performance last night of the Soviet middleweight and world-record holder in all his events, a star, twenty-five-year-old David Rigert. Portentuously distraught from the outset, the hero began with weights far below his record lifts. Rigert went off balance with his first two tries. Then Rigert could not even grip the bar on his last attempt. He stared in a puzzled fashion at the weight, then, as though stunned, at the spectators. He pounded his fists against his forehead and with streaming tears ran from the stage.

Tonight, as my companions predicted, Talts is the winner with a total of 580 kilograms.

6

Interruption

9:40 A.M., Tuesday, 5 September 1972

"That's big news, isn't it?" The speaker is Ian Woolridge. Shaking my head to dispel the incredulity, my remark as I begin to believe is, "The Jews again! And here too!"

Ten minutes late, Woolridge, a sportswriter for the *London Daily Mail* and broadcaster for the BBC, had knocked at my door. We were to arrange for some television interview that now cannot take place. He knows only that during the night some Palestinian guerrillas armed with rapid-fire automatic rifles broke into the Israeli building in the Olympic Village. They are holding hostages. One, perhaps two, Israelis are dead. Still yearning to disbelieve, I keep pressing him for details. He can furnish no more. He waits around until it is apparent that I am going to accept and adjust to the "big news" that he has come with and that he must pursue. Having nothing more to talk about, he tells me of his recent visits to the Rhodesian athletes (until just now *this* had been the prime political issue on the site) who have found rather striking sympathy in the hearts of the Bavarians. He was also at that memorial ceremony arranged by Willi Daume at Dachau on 25 August. He found the ceremony "moving" but "inadequate." I know now that I have not been as diligent a critic as I had intended to be at the outset and that my diary will have a major division.

Knowing that I am on the scene of a soon-to-be-historic event and hoping desperately that I might somehow help to turn horror around, I put on the Peruvian distance-runner costume. Disingenuously, I hurl myself at previously crashed entrances to the Village. No go. The alerted guards have closed all gates and now examine the press pass ("only a press pass") with proper care and turn me back. Jogging somberly I return to my room, aching in every aspect of my body and soul, and change to drab clothing. I become a participant, a partaker—one of many millions—in a freak, impromptu festival of disappointment.

The fences of the sprawling Olympic Village are watched by large numbers of already bored-looking troops. Nearby there are dozens of military vehicles—gun and troop carriers—which are labeled as belonging to the police. The most admonitory sights are the pairs or trios of soldiers in heavy overcoats with automatic rifles slung around their shoulders who stroll the landscaped hillocks above us. The buildings of the Village are in the background.

There are lots of people on the site. The groups are small, but there are many of them. They huddle around portable radios. The infestation of spectators is especially thick around the fences near the athletes' apartments where one can see, point to, or photograph the dormitory in question, Number 31, near the television broadcasting center.

Rumor (later proven true) has it that the first announcement of the upset came in the form of a stray bullet that entered the cafeteria of the nearby DOZ at 4:30 this morning.

Adults have long faces as is proper in these circumstances. It is jarring to see accompanying children playing. Some older boys are still collecting autographs. Groups of a dozen or more people are staying around the radios, though they offer ever more music and give less news. One sees the same long lenses attached to the same clicking fine cameras that earlier one saw trying to immobilize long jumpers. The mood has changed. We are now sad and all disillusioned, but oddly, we are still together. So the whole territory is still magic ground, and I am still at a festival. Politics and terror have become spectator sports.

Still, I am bitter that strangers have whisked away my distinction as a special observer. In efforts to shake this feeling of loss, or in an attempt to restore something that may be only misplaced, I move about to make observations that will not be those of a mob. Can I do it?

I. The bare bones of the drama seemed incomprehensible for about an hour. Then I found it easy to imagine a group of a half dozen or so intelligent individuals (I envisaged them meeting often long before in a large, clean kitchen) who did not share the European, liberal-repressive social ideology. They would use the Olympic Games in order to dramatize a great injustice and promote their particular, reckless kind of politics. I would not be too astonished just now to learn that the symbol of their movement is the five Olympic rings. Considering that Avery Brundage, the president of Malawi, and the Communist children all favored the political use of the Olympic Games, there was no compelling reason to think that some little group of fluid ideologues would pass them up. They took a handy opportunity to appropriate an audience of a billion that was thoughtlessly and generously provided for the use of all.

What the guerrillas did was to reject our festival. We wanted everybody to play our game, and they refused. They did not agree to our rules and therefore cannot be fulsomely accused of not "playing fair." The guerrillas did not, of course, break the rules of the game they were playing.

II. I see big Germans aged fifty-four or older strolling the site and pointing at dormitory Number 31 with gnarled walking sticks. Some must be former Jew-killers. Then all sorts of emotions touching my Jewishness compel attention. Should we be declared an endangered species? Will Golda Meir (now under pressure to release 200 Arab prisoners so that the Games can continue) take the public position that being Jewish carries with it an ineradicable, special hazard and write the hostages off? Might I someday be written off?

Bitterly the realization becomes solid that, as with every previous stay in Germany, I have avoided the social dismemberment that sets in here whenever I have tried to consider what connection I might have with the historic Jewish problem. In Cologne as a youth I tossed the Auschwitz books I had brought with me for vivid reading. Typically here I am introduced around as a German-speaking American of German ancestry and have not bothered to alter this partially true statement. I recall now that when the Israeli team marched into the stadium in the opening ceremonies, my quiet, prayerful desire was that they would be welcomed and made happy in Germany, just as I have been.

I recall a rhetorical question posed to me shortly after I first arrived in Germany seventeen years before and then employed by me many times afterward: "Wer hat am meisten die deutsche Kultur geliebt?" ("Who always loved German culture the most?"). And the answer—everyone knows it—is, "the Jews."

High on my list of projects here was to spend time questioning members of the Israeli team. Malawi (safe, distant, bloodless) intervened. I kept postponing the approaches. I wanted the Yank, Mark Spitz, to win all the gold medals. The fact that I wanted him to win here, as a Jew, I kept secret.

The worst lapse was the missing of that memorial observance that took place at the old death camp near Dachau on the Friday morning before the opening day. I could have returned from Bonn on an evening flight on Thursday. I knew in advance that, though new and synthetic, this would be a ceremony that would have a valid, historical basis. It was necessary. As a German, a Jew, and a critic, I would be a needed, especially alert participant. Instead, I avoided painful, unpredictable emotions to booze and sleep. The singularly necessary observance at Dachau had passed when the plane landed in happy Munich—an improved Munich because that ceremony had taken place. I would have to shudder with self-mistrust as I sought detailed accounts of repairs made at Dachau.

III. An undercurrent here is the assumption, whispered and not made public anywhere, that the Olympic Games of 1980 will take place in Moscow. For many years, Avery Brundage, authoritarian that he is, has been lied to and flattered to the point of submission by Soviet and East German sports bureaucrats. That the Olympics in Moscow of 1980 will be a forceful and crude demonstration of Soviet power goes without saying. As a critic I oppose the Soviet Games because they will be too coarsely ideological and not loose enough. But perhaps now Moscow is the only place to hold safe Olympic Games.

IV. My mind fashions successive clever schemes to save the lives of all hands. I soon learn that I am one of dozens here, and by extension millions the world over, who have analogous heroic reveries. And this revelation shrinks yet further my confidence that I am in a particular position with a particular point of view.

My own plan would be to get the lot in dormitory Number 31 into an airplane that had been previously fitted to release jets of an instantly immobilizing gas. Later I learn that several original thinkers had equally cunning imaginations that came up with the same scheme. By extension again, millions are synchronistically chiming in. We all shrink. The sadness intensifies.

A peculiar difficulty of the dilemma (by this I mean the efforts to solve the impasse in dormitory Number 31) is that *the Germans cannot kill another Jew*. Many of the silly, sentimental, and frantic accusations, projects, and expressions of despair in our planning imaginations are based on this assumption. And this assumption is everywhere in Munich just now.

4:45 P.M., Tuesday, 5 September 1972

The organizers invited me here as a sort of sourpuss-in-residence. That they did so is an indication of their confidence that all would turn out well; that, as an object for convincing, I would be convinced.

It was an agreeable public role. Hans Klein sent people over. I was a basis for journalistic copy before the shootings as a skeptical "anti-Olympist." Much of my growing pleasure I kept secret; some I could not hide.

And as a pessimist, almost as a discovered prophet, I am sought after now. For an aspect of the upset is that there is, in fact, little news. The "terrorists" (this word rather than "guerrillas" got currency after midafternoon) keep issuing successive ultimatums. The world is aroused. More big shots keep flying into Munich. A reporter I trust says he saw Moshe Dayan at the airport. We hear lots of stuff like this. The situation may be changing in many ways. But there is no real news.

In heavy traffic on the way to a hastily arranged national television program, an old, burly taxi driver with hairy arms raves: "Shit! Filth! Capitalism! Politics! It's the politicians who made this damn mess. They were the ones who made me so jubilant when we went off to war against the

French—a nice sort of people, who were and are, I know now, no differ-ent than myself. They made this mess! They, the crazy politicians, should all be lined up against the wall and shot—tat-tat-tat-tat-tat! Like that!"

"What should we do now?"

"Free the 200 prisoners in Israel, naturally, so the Olympic Games can go on."

"Do you think that is what the people [Bevölkerung] of Munich would like to see?"

"Yes, of course."

More "Crap! Crazy! Politics!" as we listen to a radio announcer who repeats those few pieces of substantial information and circumstances we already know. He tells us that another deadline for preventing the slaugh-ter of all the hostages, that of 5:00 P.M., has been extended indefinitely.

Just then, five brightly jersied road cyclists, hopeful for the future, their noses near their front wheels, their behinds wagging in the air, pass us at some speed going in the opposite direction.

"Ah! Look at that! Doesn't that look peaceful [friedlich] now!" the driver exclaims.

As was usual during the day, the radio switches to sweet mood music ("In order not to make the terrorists nervous," someone in the Press Center had remarked). The driver begins to hum along as he makes his way in rush-hour traffic.

11:00 P.M., Tuesday, 5 September 1972

A hustling producer for the Bavarian state television network has improvised a two-hour program for national distribution. The broadcast will, he posits, thoroughly and responsibly give all the Germans a basis for understanding what has happened. An eager news hound, the pro-ducer had called on me earlier in the morning and was one of the first to demonstrate that as an official pessimist, and a "journalist" and "profes-sor" to boot, I am, faute de mieux, a mine for news.

However, once electronically presented, I accomplished little in the way of entertainment or clarifications. Several classy, authentic German journalists also had no news to report but were incomparably slicker scene-stealers. The technique, which I had also encountered in German scholarly congresses at the conference table, goes something like this:

"As I myself see this problem, most assuredly, a very serious one, it has three sides, all of which merit careful examination. The first of these has four aspects, all of which are most complex. Now I always . . ."

As the talkers talked and others fidgeted, rumors, which went on the air, flowed about us. There were claims that there had been earlier warnings of an imminent attack on the Israeli team; that the Israelis had requested special protection and had been refused. (One might ask, "Why not grant special protection to North Korea, Uganda, the United States, Great Britain, and other historic committers of atrocities against other peoples?")

But discussion centered on the problem that was obsessing dilettantish circles in Germany. This was the question of security at the Olympic Village—a question I knew was idle because of the relative ease with which I and other connivers had been able to pass in and out.

A star of the television show—a personage who contrasted sharply with the rest of us in our shoulder-padded suits and shaven cheeks—was an Israeli official. He was the friend of Moshe Weinberg, who was the first Israeli to die; Weinberg was, in fact, shot almost in half before his body was thrown out of dormitory Number 31. In ordinary circumstances, this man might have looked athletic, but now his eyes were red from weeping. He had evidently dressed quickly some time ago, for his wrinkled yellow trousers lacked a belt through the loops, and his cheap, short-sleeved shirt had never had the tabs of the collar buttoned down.

This poor creature was ghoulishly pressed to tell us stories, shocking in their ordinariness, about the dead man. One fact caused me to gasp and sob: Weinberg had had his first child just three weeks ago.

Another difficult moment in the show was produced by the inclusion of a hastily assembled documentary of previous terrorist acts by Palestinian extremists. It included footage of the cleaning-up operation after a slaughtering explosion somewhere or other. The broadcast was in color. A squeegee at the end of a long pole pushed Jewish blood with some Jewish flesh particles in it toward a sewer drain. The image stayed.

Another snippet for the show was a tape of Chancellor Willy Brandt, winner of the Nobel Peace Prize, looking even worse than he had appeared at earlier sightings in the Press Center. The leader of Germany could produce from his fund of intelligence nothing better to talk about than how splendid the "Olympic idea" was; how the "Olympic idea" had been damaged. Brandt felt that we all had a yet greater obligation to strengthen the "Olympic idea."

Some master of ceremonies attempted to determine if we political experts and journalists believed that the Olympic Games should be ended entirely, called off until 1976, or merely interrupted until authorities "reached an agreement" with the terrorists or the affair was otherwise concluded. No one wanted the Olympic Games to end. The general expressed wish was, "Wait and see."

Later, a German journalist, one of the long talkers, an expert on the American South and, on the other hand, Africa, drove me to the Marienplatz the central square in the old town. He kept telling me, a captive in his front seat, in loud British English, what a ghastly thing the American handling of the Indo-China situation was. He intended that I feel wretched, and he succeeded. I had an uncanny certainty that in 1936 in Germany there were comparable scenes, with American visitors taking part. I could imagine myself retrospectively, a knowledgeable southerner telling a German who was investigating lynching that Hitler was a dangerous man. The German in 1936 could do nothing. I can do nothing.

At the Marienplatz there were happy crowds. The Jesus-singers were especially fake-joyous.

Back at the Press Center at about 10:00 P.M. a big press conference was under way. The *release* of news was tightly restricted, and the efficiency with which it was released (if not its gathering) was rather a tribute to the organizers' control of their operation. The Press Center was indeed the place where news, good and bad, first appeared.

At the moment of my entering, there was the thickest concentration of reporters I had yet seen. Willi Daume was on stage. So heavy was the crowding that some journalists despaired of hearing, much less seeing, the boss and were holding the mikes of their tape recorders up to loudspeakers.

This was also a time when the obligatory offering of the German talk in English and then French versions broke down. Near-majorities were attentive to German and then English. Then almost all became

noisy, chattering or doing other things during the excellent French. The
few French speakers about were then themselves disruptive as they
roughly demanded respect—"S'il vous plaît, messieurs!"

In any case, Daume, while trying to cover any decision that might
be made without his consent, said that he did not believe that the Olympic Games as he had planned them could continue under these new
circumstances. This could be an announcement of the end of our party.

I circled about a bit listening to people posing as knowledgeable. A
rampant rumor had it that ranking big German and Israeli politicians
were on the verge of an "agreement" with the terrorists.

Our mailboxes had a press release outlining a mourning ceremony
to take place the next day at 10:00 A.M. in the Olympic Stadium. The
program is of interest for more than idle reasons:

> "The Creatures of Prometheus" played by the Munich
> Philharmonic
> Speech by International Olympic Committee President,
> Avery Brundage
> Speech by the Organization Committee President, Willi
> Daume
> Speech by the Israeli Chef de Mission, Shmuel Lalkin
> Speech by the Federal President, Gustav Heinemann
> Funeral March from Beethoven's "Eroica" played by the
> Munich Philharmonic

The order of events seemed clear. So strategically placed had been
the death of one Jew, perhaps two Jews, that the organizers had seen fit
to call off the Olympic Games. I assented. While sorrowful about the
unwished-for ending of a fine party, a high point in my life, I felt I should
list or distribute the blame for this accident:

> I. The communications system available for the use of
> anyone in 1972.
> II. Some Germans, most of them now dead, for placing
> the Jewish problem in its present prominence.
> III. The terrorists.

6:00 A.M., Wednesday, 6 September 1972

All dead!

The steward-clad soldier has been listening to the radio and wakes me, "Our people wanted to let them fly out of the country, but the Israelis and the International Olympic Committee demanded that they be captured in Germany." This was the first time I witnessed the necessity to affix the guilt.

In a botched shoot-out at the Fürstenfeldbruck military airport, besides the two Israelis murdered in the dormitory, nine more Israelis died. So did five of the eight terrorists and a German policeman.

10:00 A.M., Wednesday, 6 September 1972

Having no responsibility to an audience craving news and knowing that the process of shifting guilt would obscure the facts in this bungle, this catastrophe, I would stand by and record how the modern Olympic Games ended. Therefore, I am on hand early for the providentially arranged mourning ceremony (originally for only one or two Jews, we recall) at the stadium. I save a corner of my mind for the problem of deciding whether I should leave Munich quickly or hang around to chronicle the cleaning-up operation.

The stadium fills slowly. The weather is perfect—as it has been since the Games began eleven days ago. Cool air, bright sunlight through a slight, mystifying haze. I am seated at a table in the press section, close to the infield and the VIP section of the stands. Foldable chairs are in a large rectangle on the grass infield before us. This section of some 2,000 seats gradually fills with a stream of persons coming from the Marathon tunnel. Their costumes are more colorful than those in the stands. Many of us are in dark suits. We assume those before us are all athletes.

Before I record some important incidents in the history of the modern Olympic Games, I must offer caveats:

I. I and my nearest companions, a middle-aged American on my left, a young Danish Marxist on my right, did not know that the many thousands slowly filling the usual seats around the rest of the stadium were ticket holders, hoping, very likely, to see the first parts of the decathlon, scheduled for that morning. We assumed that this was a sponta-neous grouping of dutiful mourners, like ourselves.

Nor could we distinguish the nationalities of the athletes gathering on the field. We could not know that the Soviet and East German athletes were commanded not to appear.

II. Neither I nor those around me expected anything but an ending of the Games. The program in our hands and Willi Daume's announce-ment the night before, all sealed by the new scarcely absorbable disaster, suggested only this.

III. We knew almost nothing of what took place at the Fürstenfeld-bruck airport early that morning. We had only a statistic: "All dead."

IV. As at all ceremonies I and (I assume) others were in a state of symbolically tuned alertness. What might be passed off as inconsequen-tial in more casual circumstances could appear to any of us to be an indicative aspect of an organic, hidden fabric of immense significance.

V. I am aware that my picture of the meeting will be different from those given by others. Many on hand surely shared my expectations as the ceremony began but very likely felt guilty about their relief in the subsequent outcome. They may have then felt that they had to present a nicer picture of what took place.

The program begins with the slow-tempoed and long so-called "Funeral March," the second movement of Beethoven's Seventh Sympho-ny, which I had expected to end the occasion. The amplifying system, which had been loud and faultless throughout the Games, is working irregularly. As the conductor thrashes through this monument to prepo-litical German humanism, the television cameramen and the paparazzi aim at the queens and princes in the VIP stands, perhaps frantically focus-ing on the moribund, though still usable, symbols of another system of political stability while the "Olympic idea" is being laid low.

The Israeli chef de mission, scheduled to speak third, speaks first. Shmuel Lalkin employs Hebrew in Munich for all the world to hear. Gradually we understand what is taking place in part of his speech. He is reciting in Hebrew the names of the Jews killed. This brings all those in the stadium to their feet—the first and early opportunity for the 80,000 on hand to participate. The German translation (mercifully the names are omitted in the German, English, and French versions) of this sports bu-reaucrat reveals that, though his team would be leaving at once, at the next meeting of the modern Olympians, one of the participating nations would be Israel. My Danish companion and I stare at each other. Scattered parts of the spectator crowd applaud lightly. We shudder. One does not applaud at a funeral.

A curious event during the translations is the hailing and fetching of a stretcher for an individual in the VIP stands who is then carried out. This action, seen by all and not reported, gives yet another symbolic overlay to our ceremony. It suggests more deaths ahead.

Willi Daume, scheduled to appear after Avery Brundage, is the second speaker. Curt, terse, predictable grief—except for the extraordinary sentence at the end, which for me, despite everything, will establish Daume as my hero at the last modern Olympics: "We can have only the faith that we alone do not form our destiny, but that our past and our future lie in some higher hand." This is the first suggestion at any time in the course of this long and bold display of structured power and inspired paganism that the horrors of existence might be due not to faults in human planning but to elements in the cosmos that test and punish and are not alterable by focused human pride, however grand and organized.

An unscheduled speaker is the Israeli ambassador to Bonn, Ben Horin, whose use of Hebrew, comprehensible to few, permits us to reflect that something underneath is going on. Is there a new drift? Everyone is extremely restless during the translations that display predictable grief expressed predictably.

The Dane, a serious, skeptical youth with thick glasses and with wiry yellow hair sprouting randomly from face and head, leans over to ask me, "Why is this such bad theater?" And at the moment of this last word, Ben Horin's English translator notes that "the assassins chose for the scene of their senseless crime the theater of the Olympic Games." At the word "theater" this time the Danish man and I shouted in unison with the laughter of irony.

Gustav Heinemann, president of the Federal Republic, is next—clearly leaving the field to Avery Brundage. Heinemann's approach to the podium is greeted by German applause (more applause!).

At the first enthusiastic reaction to Heinemann's speech, I am agitated by the scornful vulgarity (this is after all a funeral ceremony just after a lot of particularly horrible, strategic, and significant deaths) and so leave my seat to move among a crowd that I will be no part of. As the nicely

enunciated clichés of grief and outrage proceed, I am suddenly clairvoy-
ant and know that the meat will be in Avery Brundage's speech, so long
postponed.

Moving quickly about in bright, cool sunlight around the top rim of
the stadium, I notice that the flags of all the nations are at half-mast and
that a bouquet of red, yellow, and orange roses lies at the base of the slim
tower holding the hissing and heat-radiating "Olympic" flame. Cheers
become more frequent and less restrained as Heinemann's speech, a
long one, goes on.

Cheekily: "The Olympic idea is not defeated! We all owe it stronger
allegiance than before!" At the conclusion of this, the participator might
think he is at a really big rally, perhaps at a Woodrow Wilson Fan Club
assembly. Or, shutting one's eyes and blocking the horror, that the cheering is for a football goal. It becomes more apparent that the Munich
crowds want this party to go on. Grateful for their opportunity to participate, some different sections of the crowd applaud his English translator.

Though he can be seen only as a speck by most of the 80,000 people
on hand, Avery Brundage as usual gives a ponderous, dignified impression. Returning to my seat, I nod vigorous assent at his correct summary
(I write now what I heard at that moment): "The bigger the Games, the
more they are subject to commercial, political, and now criminal activity."
But then I am jolted by the selfish insertion, "The Games of the XXth
Olympiad have been subjected to two savage attacks. We lost the Rhodesian battle against naked political blackmail." This piece of grotesque self-
indulgence, referring to the Rhodesian problem that had been obsessing
him for months now—a battle he took personally and one of the few
political battles he ever lost—raises shivers of embarrassment and some
sour smiles in many places in the press section.

Then I hear it. We all hear it. Brundage declared, "The Games must
go on!"

This is greeted as a joyous release by the overwhelming mass of the
people on hand.

In the light of Brundage's remark about commercial, political, and
criminal exploiters, this short speech is the crudest evidence yet of the
destructive schizophrenia that is the slippery kernel of the "Olympic
idea" and its physical emanation, the "Olympic movement."

The reporters are tensed for action. Then Brundage lays down the confirming statement, "We declare today a day of mourning and will continue all the events one day later than scheduled." Released, the press people run for the telephones and telexes.

I knew that what I had been a participant in was the transformation of a funeral into an affirmative theatrical undertaking, a sporting contest with a victor, for spectators to cheer at.

It was late. And now the fans were behaving as though in the last quarter of a game, the score of which, a victory for the home team, was a foregone conclusion. Thousands were leaving the stadium as a disembodied announcer told them the orchestra would play the overture to "Egmont."

This was not on the program distributed in advance—possibly with good reason. The piece does not have the popular appeal of some of Beethoven's other short orchestral pieces because so much of it is so stern and somber—almost like sepulchral music. The beginning is anguished and foreboding. There are some agitated and heroic development sections. And then, almost astonishingly, the overture ends in a long, bombastic and ecstatically joyous coda.

All of this indicated that (as later was verified) despite the original program keyed for cessation and then the additional fifteen deaths at the Munich airport, commercial, political, and professional interests (three of the five speakers of the day were sports bureaucrats—the other two were political bureaucrats) had determined that, although some blood was spilled along the way, an unavoidable interruption was all that could be allowed for the grandest athletic games of all time.

So it was good theater, not bad theater. I recall that the translations of Heinemann's speech were accompanied by lots of note-passing around the main microphone at the VIP stands. I believe they were written gauges of the new order of events, more impromptu than those on our original program, now a curious document, which I have preserved.

The most focused-upon little objects or symbols during this hastily arranged, then hastily altered, festive climax in Munich were the yarmulkes, the traditional skullcaps worn by men during prayers in Jewish ceremonies to indicate that someone, God, is above them. Shmuel Lalkin and Ben Horin wore the caps, and so did a rather large proportion of those in the VIP section. Seated in the middle-front of the rectangle of the 2,000 to 3,000 seats for putative athletes on the playing field were a group of twenty or thirty persons, the males of whom wore yarmulkes. They were directly in front of the speakers. Several times during the ceremony they were pointed out to me as the remnants of the "Israeli team." It turned out that most of these mourners were Jewish kids fetched for the occasion from a nearby youth camp.

The Dane and I happen to be leaving the stadium in the same stream as the Israeli youths. I cannot prevent myself from reaching for the sleeve of a tall girl to get her attention. I wish to express some sort of condolence. I feel I must say something even if it is a meaningful cliché. She turns on me with a glare so astonishingly vicious, I am dizzy with shame. I look like and am made to feel more like a German coach than a sharer of her blood and the blood of the murdered ones.

The Dane steadies and reassures me: "They're under strict orders to speak to no one."

Thursday, 7 September 1972

It seems certain now that the sentiment here on the site is almost universally in favor of continuing the Games just as Avery Brundage declared. The opposition to this notion, what there is of it, is on the part of a few young sports critics who can scarcely be heard. The young Dane who was my sympathetic companion at the funeral ceremony saw the resumption as a demonstration of the power of irresponsible, monopoly capitalism.

One of the common rationalizations for resumption is that Israel "requested" that the Games continue. I have not seen evidence of this in any official announcements. In fact, given that Israel wrote the lives of the hostages off early and that the Israeli politicians would like to gather as big an ideological harvest as possible from any new developments, it seems that Israel could gain most from a *discontinuance* of the Games, forcing the whole world to grieve.

What did happen in the course of the funeral ceremony was that a prominent sports bureaucrat, who happened to be a grieving Jew, declared himself in favor of having an Israeli team at some future Olympics.

Another explanation, the one usually smartly spoken into the tape recorders of journalists prowling for athletes who will speak on this issue, is that to stop the Olympic Games would be to "give in" to terrorism. This is based on a false assumption. If those who so effectively initiated the performed atrocity wished to stop the Olympic Games, they would have done so ten days before. The thugs knew they could use the same stage exploited by so many other political ideologues, sanctioned and unsanctioned, for special politics of their own choosing. The idealistic, cunning desperadoes misjudged the tough opportunism of the Israeli politicians that resulted in the death of five of their number and a laissez-passer to punish granted by world opinion to the enemies of the Palestinians.

Like Julien Sorel shooting Madame Reynal in the red-draped church, the Palestinians committed a crime, horrible in any circumstances, in a cathedral. They went beyond the reveries of Gimpel the fool to rupture the sacred by pissing in the bread dough. We had endured and were surviving from blasphemy. The terrorists broke some rules (our rules, let it be remembered), but it was stunning theater.

As with my shock after hearing of the first atrocities (the ghastly, ironic phrase, "only one or two murders," haunts a lot of us), my astonishment at the action to continue the Games was brief. Just as I imagined the preparatory meetings of the Arabs taking place in a kitchen, my imaginatively reconstructed meetings of the IOC millionaires and West German cabinet ministers took place in a tasseled suite in the Vier Jahreszeiten hotel. I guessed that Willi Daume had been excluded. He told me later that he had indeed been excluded.

Before the recent unforeseeable development, the big German politicians had been shouldering one another aside in their efforts to reap the harvest of publicity that resulted from their paparazzi-accompanied appearances on the Olympic site. The newspapers have kept us informed of the continuous performances of Rainer Barzel before the cameras, arm in arm with any available or makeable day-tripping celebrity.

A neat, really a fabulous ploy, which put all the national and local politicians briefly aside, was the stagy offer of Walter Scheel, the foreign minister, to replace the Israeli hostages with his own person. One person who has tended to business in these three weeks is Helmut Schmidt. I had no way of checking then, but I assumed that he, like Daume, opposed continuation and then grudgingly chimed in with the overwhelming consensus. Willy Brandt has before and after the atrocity stupidly and ceaselessly reiterated the sacredness of some "Olympic idea" that along the way was demonstrating the power of his new Germany.

A newspaper reports that the International Olympic Committee's executive board voted "overwhelmingly" to continue the Games. A nice game for the morbid imagination is to construe a catastrophe sufficiently grandiose to convince Avery Brundage and his sympathizers in the IOC that they should destroy or even diminish the basis for the existence of that body. How many deaths? Thousands? Millions? How many millions? The lamenting sports bureaucrats of Israel who supported the continuance of the Games are like other sports bureaucrats. Should we have expected them to favor the wiping out of the quadrennial summits of their professional lives?

An article in a Munich daily, the *Abendpost*, should have given rise to some essayists' attention but did not. It was the public announcement by Professor Dr. Josef Nöcker, chef de mission of the West German team, that he would not be prejudiced against (verurteilen) any athlete who wished to refrain from competing out of sympathy with the suffering Israelis. From the beginning it seems extraordinary that a chef de mission or any of his subalterns have it in their power to get any amateur athlete to do anything whatever. We are supposed to assume that athletes are neither employees nor slaves. Then, on second thought, the very notion that athletes in large numbers might make some symbolic or decisive demonstration against the orders of their trainers appears at once ridiculous, tragic, and symptomatic of a moral basis of high-performance sport. An American reporter who specializes in apocrypha tells me that some self-impelled Dutch and Norwegian athletes have gone home in protest. One might first expect such gestures from people—even athletes perhaps—from these nations, but still, it now seems unlikely.

Here in Munich and at the Olympic sites the opportunism of the picture-snappers and prose-makers of the daily press have come to boundaries that will not be transgressed. The atrocity is being moved already into the realm of a nonatrocity. Identical pictures, testing the capabilities of the big, long-distance lenses, show fuzzy snaps of a helicopter with its top blown away. We see television footage of streaking tracer bullets at the airport during the grand evening in question, but they illuminate nothing. Some photos of weeping relatives but no snaps of mangled corpses. No blood-pushing squeegees. We are starting to smooth over.

In the cafeteria I encounter one of my fellow television panelists of Tuesday evening. He is prominent in Bonn and has a coterie. He says the prospect of interrupting the Games was too much for the officials to face. "The economic interests. . . . Why it would have required a year of work on the part of all the lawyers in Bavaria to reach settlements over unfulfilled contracts. No, the Games had to go on and I'm pleased." We chatted listlessly about ourselves for a while. Then he became offended when I presumptuously said that I intended to publish an Olympic diary. The prominent German will do the same.

Evening, Thursday, 7 September 1972

The following is part of a press release in English from the German Organizing Committee. The date is 7 September 1972. "In the already printed starting lists, the names of some of the Israeli athletes who lost their lives are included. For the by the computer [sic] electronically recorded result lists, there is no other possibility than to note the names of these athletes with the remark 'not present' [nicht angetreten]. We ask you to accept this as a technical necessity and not as a lack of reverence."

Here and there around the site one hears of proposals to make some symbolic recognitions that the ongoing summer Olympic Games of 1972 are not as they were when they began. I and others suggest the elimination of the victory ceremonies with their provocative clanging of national anthems and the hoisting of patriotic flags, many of them redolent of mutually antagonistic ambitions or of outright wickedness. We get nowhere.

The only adjusting action taken, aside from the postponement of one day, has been the cancellation of Press Chief Klein's Bavarian Press Festival for Journalists at the End of the Games, scheduled for Monday, 11 September, a day that will now be taken up by the closing ceremonies. I must quote from this document in order to illustrate the cute, precalamity, Press Department style:

You will be entertained with plenty of music, pretty "Dirndl" (Bavarian costumes) groups of "Schuhplattler" dancers and Bavarian folk singers in a festive tent with a capacity of 3,000 persons, were [sic] you will be served with choice culinary dishes: three whole muttons (roasted on a spit), 40 porklings from a charcoal grill, 300 legs of veal and pork, 2,000 chickens, Steckerfisch (Munich specialty—fish roasted on a spit), 1,000 pork sausages with sauerkraut, 1,000 Regensburg and Viennese sausages, a cold country-buffet, 10,000 rolls and Bretzels and so on, and of course umteen barrels of Bavarian festival beer.

Of course, surprises have also been arranged. But we won't reveal what they are; otherwise they wouldn't be surprises any longer.

Embarked on employing the writing of others, I include a couple more bits in order to give concrete form to some currents around here. The first is a photocopied letter written to Willi Daume from an esteemed colleague, a Bonn professor who has written courageously about sport in the Nazi regime. His exposures of the use that the Nazis made of physical education and high-performance athletes are monuments of postwar German scholarship:

6 September 1972

Mr. Willi Daume
Organization Committee of the XXth Summer Olympiad
Munich

Dear Mr. Daume
The barbaric decision of the International Olympic Committee to continue the Munich Games fills me with shame.

Henceforth as I discuss the IOC in the course of my academic career, I shall demonstrate that the IOC, as was shown in Munich in 1972, is a club of characterless opportunists (I will, however, treat you as an exception).

As a personal protest, I will never again enter any of the various arenas in Munich.

With best wishes [verbindlichen Grüssen],

Prof. Dr. Hajo Bernett
Sports-scientific Institute of the University of Bonn

P.S. I am sure you understand that I intend to offer this letter for publication.

Following are some sections of the lead editorial in today's *Süddeutsche Zeitung*, acknowledged to be one of the two or three most complete and responsible German newspapers. The *Süddeutsche* is published in Munich.

> There are in the world some big cities which, once having acquired reputations, are unable to get rid of them. Chicago, for example—capital of gangsterism; Shanghai—center of the opium trade and of every sort of depravity; Paris—light-hearted lasciviousness. Now, in actuality, the truth is often otherwise, possibly even the contrary. Still, the cliché overshadows reality. Munich is one of these cities.

> There may not exist a great city whose people are less imperialistic, less aggressive, more peaceable, more full of simple human qualities than those of the Bavarian metropolis. However, various slogans have stuck to the name "Munich." Capital of the [Nazi] "movement" [die Bewegung]. Originator of politically ideological lawlessness. Site of the capitulation of the law before naked power. "Brown" Munich. Bulwark of vengeance [Revanchismus]. However contourless and emotional these notions have seemed to us, they now appear to have been confirmed.

> There has hardly been a press reaction in the world that has not spoken of these [historical] connections. It will be many years yet before one will be able to think of Dallas without remembering at once Kennedy's violent death. To the outside world it seems almost as though this city in Texas brought the assassination upon itself. Since yesterday, we may have to live with the analogous, lingering opinions of half the world.

7

Cleaning Up

Friday, 8 September 1972

Early this morning the bulletin board for English readers at the Press Center held the following "Press Release":

After the insulting display of the two American athletes given in the stadium on 7th September, when they were awarded their gold and silver medals for the 400m. event, the Executive Board decided that, being the second time that the USOC had permitted such occurrences on the athletic field, these two athletes had broken rule 26, paragraph 1, in respect of the traditional Olympic spirit and ethics and would, therefore, be eliminated from taking part in any future Olympic competition. If such performance would happen in the future, the medals would be withheld from the athletes in question. The United States NOC [National Olympic Committee] has apologized and has been cautioned about future competitors.

I both regretted not witnessing the powerful display and was relieved not to have been forced by my presence to partake in the blasphemy. The language of this extraordinary communiqué suggested to the imagination that persons still unknown to me turned about, lowered their shorts, bent, and "mooned" black asses into the old white face of Avery Brundage. For this, Brundage would punish the American nation.

After chasing down the morning papers, I learned that Vincent Matthews and Wayne Collett had given a "Black Power demonstration" during their victory ceremony. Sections of the crowd had become irritated and whistled as they left the stadium. Nothing about the action of the IOC was in the papers.

At the headquarters of the American Olympic Committee, a polyglot crowd of reporters and photographers were seeking pictures or films of what had taken place. There were none. As we churned about, I chatted with an American physician, one of several contemporaneously being saddled with blame in a contentious doping case, the disqualification of sixteen-year-old 1,500-meter freestyler, Rick Demont. Demont had been taking a prescription asthma drug, and American officials had neglected to clear it with international Olympic officials.

The physician told me that the USOC, rather than apologizing, had decided to defend the sprinters and to attempt to reverse the IOC's ruling.

Late in the afternoon, a German paper printed four photos of Matthews and Collett. Both were on the platform reserved for the victor, Matthews. Their demeanor contrasted with that of the bronze medal winner, a Kenyan, who was respectfully at attention, presumably for "The Star-Spangled Banner." One American yawned and blinked; the other scratched himself and toyed with his medal.

A later viewing of film of the ceremony showed that the newspaper photographer had selected, out of the strip of negatives from his motor-driven single-lens reflex with a long lens, those photos that would most nearly make the victors of the 400-meter event look like sassy apes. The "display," then, was only an incident of desultory selfishness. It was half-hearted, slovenly fooling around. I have never seen a photograph or anything else that might have been clearly interpreted as a manifestation of "Black Power." Matthews, however, has in the past made some clumsy statements about racism in America.

All on hand here are symbolically tuned and have given their own views of the deeper meanings of this event, and so I give mine:

I. "The Star-Spangled Banner" has nothing to do with the 400-meter dash.

II. To continue these pandering victory ceremonies, especially after the calamity of three days ago, is in bad taste, possibly a deliberate provocation on the part of the pagans who have prescribed moral tone at the Olympic Games.

III. Avery Brundage (no one doubts who is behind the press release) views all athletes as figurative, old-style "niggers." Impulsively he grasped the chance to punish the American nation for supposedly allowing the public parade of a couple of authentic, but only slightly bad, "niggers."

IV. Everyone here knows that the Olympic movement as a colossal toy for the IOC is falling to bits. Here no corrective for the larger dissolution is possible. In small affairs, symbolic reforms are, as we have seen, still possible.

This little exercise of administrative power, in addition to suggesting a certain despair at the top, revealed the repressive political views of those who run the Olympic Games. The symbols—rings, spirals, doves, and flaming torches, as well as national anthems, flags, and medals—have been exposed as ersatz and possibly contemptible. The act of Brundage's executive board affirmed political hierarchies that stifle and depersonalize athletes. Furthermore, Brundage demonstrated the subordination of American sports bureaucrats to some frightened, international aristocrats.

Throughout the course of these Games, numerous rule or judgment disputes, many of which were over decisions that were flatly wrong or even dishonest, have been handed to the IOC as a final board of appeal. In every case, the IOC supported lower bodies of jurors. The implications of the Matthews-Collett case, however, are especially threatening to nonconforming athletes and their sponsoring nations and mark a step in the further deindividualization of world-class athletes.

An immediate consequence of this coup de theatre was that two sports heroes, American heroes, black heroes, were barred from their places in the 4 × 400-meter relay scheduled for the last day of competition. It is indicative of the narrowness of the American journalists on the scene that they viewed the loss of the gold medal in this relay (a moot point) as a greater loss than the exposed political basis of the Olympic Games and the cruelty to two fellow Americans.

There is some available anecdotal spice in the form of an anticipatory vignette here. The program for the closing ceremonies has just been distributed and reveals that Avery Brundage, as retiring president of the IOC, will play a larger role by far than any other individual as this festival, possibly the last of the Olympic Games, ceremoniously ends. He alone is to ascend a podium while the national anthems of Greece, the Federal Republic, and Canada play, and the flags of these nations are hoisted in a larger approximation of the usual "victory ceremonies." He is then to give a prescribed invitation to all of us to assemble in Montreal four years hence. And then my program has the following section:

Standing Ovation
As Mr. Brundage retires to the VIP stands, the words "Thank you Mr. Brundage" will appear on the scoreboards. The Armed Forces Band will play "For He's a Jolly Good Fellow."

Evening, Friday, 8 September 1972

Many of my missed appointments and disappointments these past days have been due to my eagerness to talk with Otl Aicher, the man in charge of the Visual Department (Visuelle Abteilung) here at the Munich Games. I have been with agreeable assistants who try hard to tell me without actually doing so that Herr Aicher would prefer not to talk with fans. These same underlings communicate their excitement at being able to work on so grand a project.

Since positing myself as a sports critic and sports esthete, I have been seeking evidence or efforts for the mutual use of sport at its highest levels and art at its higher levels. This search is one of my tasks in life. At the Munich Olympics the grandest and frankest efforts to intellectualize or estheticize sport were some projects by a team of designers surround-

ing Otl Aicher. I fear that, particularly in the shadow of the ugly upheaval
at the Games, Aicher's most optimistic and original work may be passed
over. I cannot abandon Aicher and his work and so have come up with
this playful, though still earnest, effort to present or to suggest the significance of what he has been allowed to pull off here.

This is a heuristic proposal for an art exhibition:

Proposal for an Art Exhibition

Design at the Munich Olympics of 1972

I propose a spacious display of the designed materials, princi-
pally graphics, left behind by the organizers of the XXth Olympics
in Munich. The purpose of the exhibit is not only to offer for public consideration a variety of items of some esthetic interest but
also to present the evidence for a uniquely ambitious project in
contemporary engineering.

To an extent, the display will memorialize the ideas and energies of two men—Willi Daume, the president of the Organizing
Committee of the Munich Olympics of 1972, and Otl Aicher,
Daume's deputy who was given the assignment to integrate all visual aspects of that festival into a purposeful, internally logical
scheme.

Posters will dominate the show. About half were made in
huge runs for general, worldwide publicity. The more interesting
ones (at least from a social-engineering point of view) were intended to serve didactic, coordinating purposes among those who
labored to stage the most expensive and complex sports festival of
all time. Other displayed materials will be prescribed publicity bulletins, exhibition catalogs, some banners, uniforms, and souvenirs.
We can even display some meal tickets, identification cards, and favors. All of the above-mentioned items were part of a grand
scheme.

The visual aspects of the Munich Olympics were not a
unique example of the attempted integration of particular social
values, cybernetic concepts, and the visual rhetoric of ahistorical
symbols with the most advanced production techniques. The Oli-

vetti Company practices coordinated visual engineering in their
worldwide operations.

The aspirations of the German "visual engineers" (an apt term
actually employed in Munich) were strongly reminiscent of the
now-ridiculed (at least in chic art circles) optimism and messianic
encyclopedism of the later nineteenth century.

Though the objects proposed for exhibition are all distinctly
fresh and "modern" looking, what makes the material especially
worth brooding over is that the sum of things shown is a manifestation, possibly anachronistic, of notions much more characteristic
of a much older European social-critical milieu. I mean here ideas
such as those positing the social role or intrinsic meaning of textures and colors in general and the iconography of specific colors
in particular. Central in all of this, a century ago and now, is the belief that good design inspires good living.

A forebear and ideological relation to Daume and Aicher was
Frédéric Le Play (1806–82), the impresario of the Paris Universal
Exposition of 1867. This world's fair was the most ambitiously
philosophical and the most encyclopedic (in that it attempted to
display evidence of all of man's creative activities) festival of the
nineteenth century. Le Play offered an intellectual and artistic feast
for the world's teachers and students at the same time that he
proved the continued primacy of French creative power. Impelled
by a grand educational mission, he decreed the layout of the whole
exhibition, including the spatial aspects of the architecture, the ar-
rangement of the exhibits, and what should be included. His exhibits, the order of the programs, the catalogs, and the accompanying scholarly congresses all conformed to advanced scientific and
social knowledge. Le Play intended to demonstrate the accomplishments of his epoch, and his visitors in Paris in 1867 felt that he
had succeeded in especially vivid form. That the achievements of
this genius have since been passed over by the historians of politics, art, and ideas does not lessen Le Play's stature.

A more recent and definitely more acknowledged influence
on Otl Aicher was Walter Gropius (1883–1969), a titan of twentieth-century architecture who was the most celebrated director
(1919–28) of the closely observed art school, called the Bauhaus, of

Weimar Germany. Historians of the modern movements in art
have not adequately emphasized that Gropius was special in his
time in that he was a proselytizer of the view that designers should
work closely with scientists, social planners, and engineers to better the quality of life for all people.

In his ambitious-altruistic views of design and in his plans
for education, Gropius was opposing the conquering notion of l'art
pour l'art and was, therefore, himself a throwback. And he was, of
course, a good German, sentimentally rooted in the spiritual ideal-
ism and humanism of prepolitical, cosmopolitan Germany. One
can understand why Gropius and the Bauhaus were aversions for
Hitler and the Nazis. The Nazis suppressed the Bauhaus. Its teachers emigrated.

Otl Aicher (born 1922) is a Catholic of the socially committed
left. As director of the Hochschule für Gestaltung or College of Design in Ulm, his political activity has annoyed conservatives. Both
his enemies and his friends accuse Aicher of attempting to refound
the Bauhaus. A certain German willingness to surrender to large
philosophical schemes, an outdated belief in the social-melioristic
capabilities of good design, an ability to inspire others, strong sym-
pathies for democracy, an enthusiasm for modern synthetic materials, and a reputation for faultless taste were all combined in Aicher
when Willi Daume dug him out in 1967 just as Munich was definitely chosen as the site of the XXth Olympics of the modern era.

Daume, the securely rich steel manufacturer, amiable technocrat, and up-to-date all-arounder, had his own particular views
of the deeper purposes of the 1972 Olympics. Daume knew ahead
of time the moods his Games ought to induce in the world at
large.

But Daume also knew how to delegate. By the beginning of
1968 even minor aspects of design for the second German Olympics had to be cleared with Aicher, who was instructed and em-
powered by Daume. By visual means Daume and Aicher decreed
and enforced the notions that the Munich Games were to be efficient, lighthearted, modern, and most important, at the same time, international and German.

These ideas are quaint; they are outside the bordered fiefs established in the course of the past century of advanced art criticism. Indeed, it may only be possible for design to accomplish such objects in a social-intellectual milieu in which there are vague boundaries and art makers and consumers alike are tuned to the same system of activating symbols. If such a system of liaisons between art makers and art takers ever existed (and it probably did in classical Athens and in thirteenth-century France), we can be reasonably certain that the connections are especially weak now. Nevertheless, the attempt in Munich was courageously conceived and determinedly advanced. And this is the deeper basis of what makes the proposed exhibition worth mounting.

The exhibition, then, will pose two questions: the offhand, methodological one, "How was the attempt to impose art on a sports festival fashioned?" and the brutal one, "Were the aims of the organizers and the visual engineers accomplished?"

Aicher took with him a small staff from Ulm and augmented it with more young German artists. A starting point, posited by Daume and Aicher in the beginning and accepted by all, was the task of correcting the German impression of the previous German Games, those in 1936. The Nazi Olympics used the architecture of symmetry, grand vistas, overwhelming scale, bombastic ceremonies, and, most noticeably and unforgettably, neoclassical design motifs. They also employed those colors so beloved by all dictators—red and gold.

Aicher assumed that an enduring hangover of the Berlin Olympics was the universal view that the visual rhetoric characterized above represented what was the old menacing Germany. The new innocent (yet paradoxically sophisticated) Germany must counter lingering conceptions of what *was* German. The new Germans must reintroduce themselves visually to the world. Therefore, the Munich Olympics in the last third of the twentieth century should be human, playful, musical, and nonideological or, better said, unhistorical. Still, the Organizing Committee demanded a system of visual presentation that would be vivid and novel.

As a twentieth-century modernist, Aicher had to reject all historical styles. He knew that classicism has more often been a refuge for the sentimental longings of the good Germans than for the bad ones such as Hitler and Albert Speer. Aicher rejected classicism and its derivatives since they were equivocal and not affirmative. An early position paper barred the arch from any decorative elements or graphic designs.

Aicher's team also deflected some proposals to exploit the nervous, nostalgic chic throughout the West for another and not-so-old international style, Art Nouveau-Jugendstil. Aicher and Daume, both of them up-to-the-minute Germans of our time, also opposed traditional design elements that might be single-outable as Bavarian or even folk-German in any way. German cosmopolitans now sneer at folksy art. A position paper early in the planning stages of the design department stated that anything "Teutonic" must be shunned. The souvenir Waldis, the dirndls of the hostesses, and some of the grander sports facilities are all monuments to battles that Aicher lost. All the same, one did not find pretzels, beer steins, sausages, cuckoo clocks, or lederhosen at the Munich Olympics. All of this and comparable stuff were forbidden to those having access to the communications media.

Some interesting prose left behind by the visual engineers has to so with the six new official colors devised for the Munich Games. This is an early rationalization for the dominant color, a sort of sky blue: "The overarching color is a light blue. This is certainly an evocation of Bavaria. But blue is also the color of peace. It is the color of youth, just as it the color of the Bavarian lakes and the silhouettes of the Alps. This blue will be supported by a light green and a silver in order to stress and assure its freshness."

There are deft rationalizations for all the six colors devised for the 1972 Olympics. Despite the avoidance of the trite symbols of folklore, some color justifications evoke "Bavarian blue sky," "Bavarian green grass," "Bavarian silver clouds," or "Bavarian yellow meadow flowers."

Perhaps some of these are jokes by Daume and his press chief, Hans Klein. Maybe the designers smile secretly at this obfuscation for those who ponder their color codex, for it must have been apparent to them that the six official tones (two blues, two greens, and two yellow-oranges) plus silver are all rootless and artificial and have never existed in nature or in history. They could have been specified as well (in fact they have been scientifically specified and so are precisely reproducible) by Czechoslovakian or Canadian chemists as by German ones.

Color dictatorship was one means of enforcing some unity on the disparate festival. Other means were by the employment of a consistent typeface for the printed materials and a system of indicative and explanatory signs and symbols. Aicher settled on and imposed the strong and undatable Univers typeface, designed by an already successful Swiss designer, Adrian Frutiger (born 1928). Univers is unserifed and could be considered a corrective to (classical) Roman type and also an aggressive counter to the nationalistic German black letter revived and imposed by the Nazis.

Early on Aicher proposed a simple logo or official emblem of the Munich Olympics, a radiant ring suggesting (he said) the sun, flowers, and the stars. It was too much like the sun emblem used at the Tokyo Olympics in 1964 and also like the symbol (taken from an Aztec calendar stone) of the Games of 1968. Besides, it was too easily reproducible. The Organizing Committee rejected this project and held a design competition. Eventually they chose a complex spiral brought forth by a design team from Cologne. A lot of people do not like it, since it suggests vertigo and evokes the anguish of expressionism. Willi Daume was required to defend the eventual logo of the XXth modern Olympics, which he did. He declared it "the most beautiful design in the world."

Otl Aicher had his way in the positing of a system of nonverbal Esperanto for use in the polyglot sports jamboree. His *Piktogram* system (henceforth, "pictogram") offers unequivocal information or explanations for most of the momentary situations that a functionary or traveler can encounter in Munich. It has also been generously made available for free, cosmopolitan use after the Games. I might note here that Aicher blithely passed over an analogous, pre-existing (though far less complete) system of nonverbal information devised for the Tokyo Olympics of 1964 and altered and used in Mexico in 1968.

For the television viewer in the late summer of 1972, Aicher's pictograms for all the sports were well known. They accompanied or indicated each event. But these were just parts of a larger, com-

prehensive system that contained as well the design elements for
expansion. Late in the preparations for the Games, the Visuelle
Abteilung (Visual Department) had printed up a poster that was a
sort of dictionary of signs devised to that point and that included
symbols for saunas, baby-sitting, and car washes. These big sheets
intended for internal use at the 1972 Games will be parts of the
exhibit proposed and should be solid evidence that Aicher's ambitions were not confined to earning a reputation at the Munich
Olympics or in the art world of the galleries.

This observer in Munich was repeatedly awed by the assurance with which Aicher and his crowd assumed that the values
they declared to be lurking in certain colors, textures, or symbols
would be the values grasped without thought by the universe of
visitors in Munich. With what enviable insouciance they presumed
that they could correct a visual concept of Germany; that somehow
these synthetic colors, the neutral typeface, the geometric nonlan-
guage were all German! One is justified in asking, "If 'Teutonic' impressions were to be avoided, what is indeed German after all?"

Though the products of the Visual Department are arresting
for many reasons, the impression of the instant—that is, without
examining the rationalizing prose or the grandeur of the whole
scheme—is something like what one might now expect from the
most snotty and cynically run of the Italian design studios. The energized, leftist technocrats with good taste in Aicher's atelier were
largely building on (as everyone must) existing innovations—the
philosophical ones a century or more old as well as the visual ones
of much more recent vintage. Since the exhibition I propose
would be well supplied with translated captions taken from the
many position papers collected from Aicher's internal operation,
these pieces of prose should establish Aicher's views.

Perhaps for any large scheme there must be a plan, and we
can summarize by saying that the Olympic myth was one of several
serving heuristic purposes in young German hands. Let the spectator judge.

Following are a few examples of modern Olympic and, at the
same time, West German imposition and coordination:

I. For the motifs of the fifteen or so posters celebrating the major Olympic sports, the designers, in addition to rejecting the historical styles, turned against the exhausted, abstruse repertoire of abstract art and chose instead photographs. I quote a position paper: "The posters should give a fresh impression and be as understandable alike to a professor in Helsinki and to a construction worker in Accra." Action photos were simplified by a type of solarized developing (Aicher's team called it an "ischelic" technique) that reduced detail to crystallize the meaning of a particular sport. By submission to the color code of the 1972 Olympics, the sports posters were made to symbolize the Munich Games as a whole. All the sports posters emphasized movement from left to right.

II. The system of pictograms was built on a square whose geometric construction allowed only four directions of movement. Eventually, for signs displaying human figures, the team evolved a "body alphabet" of a "geometric man" consisting of head, torso, legs, and a few other elements. The stick figure indicating a females' toilet, for example, had symmetrical arcs suggesting a skirt.

III. The imposed, overall harmony extended to the working uniforms prescribed for sixty-eight different groups encompassing the 30,000 or more people who would be playing official roles in Munich. Distinctions would be made by color and by cut. Here, too, overall design consistency held. The darker yellowish orange that throughout was to indicate "technology" was established for the uniforms of the technical personnel. Green, intended for "communication," was to be worn for the uniforms of those serving the press. An underhanded, ideological imposition was Aicher's decree that the darker official colors were to be employed for the organizers and bureaucrats. The lighter, "fresher," brighter colors, signifying (or so it was posited) cleanliness, health, youth, and greater utility, were to be used by the actual working personnel at the Games.

There were three cuts of clothes: one used the blazer, and another used the waist-belted short jacket and was dubbed the "safari look." A third, the dirndl with calf-high socks, was worn by the hostesses. Bavarian politicians demanded the lumpy dirndl as a völkisch concession from Daume and Aicher. These two had unsuccessfully proposed for the highly visible hostesses a Courrèges-designed outfit of beaked hat, miniskirt, and characteristic white boots. The rustically cut dirndls, seen everywhere, were, however, made of synthetic fabrics of the official light, chemical blue. A poster intended for wide internal distribution, at the same time an art manifesto and an instruction for use, illustrates the various uniforms and explains the functions of the persons inside them. The uniforms were another characteristic attempt at coordination, analogous to the pictograms that took words away from concepts. The uniforms made people not people but preprogrammed and coded responses to anticipated organizational situations.

IV. There was in existence for a heady few months a large plan to impose a consistent, festive, decorative overlay on the whole civilian city of Munich. Aspects of the project were, in the end, radically truncated. This was done due to reasons of expense—one of the few known impositions of this stricture in the brief history of the spectacle at hand. In and around Munich the designers were held back to groupings of high, narrow, pole-held banners in white, light blue, and light green and a lot of distinctive, temporary directional signs for auto traffic.

At the Olympic complexes themselves, the design teams made murals, wall hangings, and huge, multilayered, plastic transparencies of the pictogram symbols. There were also freestanding poster displays and more official sports posters at pavilions and kiosks.

Despite the grandeur and the detail of Aicher's conceptions and the support that he had for them, there were areas that he could not cover. He had no voice in the first layouts of the site (which were almost fixed even before the International Olympic Committee accepted Munich's candidacy in 1966) and little in the architecture. Dutifully Aicher enthused over the sprawling roof and joined in the chorus of approval for the landscaping, although he had no part in creating them.

As the Games went on, it was easy to recall sardonically some of Daume's statements in the beginning that the Games would be "lighthearted and cheap." Neither Daume nor Aicher knew how to resist pressures—uncompromising in the case of various world sports federations—for "perfect" sports facilities. And they were passive before the generosity of various German public treasuries—for whom so few outlays were too great. There was, in the end, giganticism and bombast in many parts of the eventual presentation.

Aicher was ideologically opposed to the notion of VIPs and did not design their facilities, which therefore were sovereign outside his reach and repertoire. Willi Daume also staged a separate "art" poster contest with sport as a putative motif. Some other small fiefs slipped away. Nevertheless, the visual aspects of the Munich Olympics stand as the most ambitious attempt in modern times to impose ideologically buttressed design consistency on a grand, new environment.

The exhibitiongoers will see the artifacts of a conscious rejection of historical and national styles and another effort to assist in the decline of "spoken language." Significantly, the communications used internally in the Visual Department of the Munich Olympics employed a lot of English and Italian words where German would do. More cosmopolitanism at work here.

Dominating our entire exhibition will be the various internally used *Erscheinungsbilder* (literally, "appearance pictures"), the fascinating posters that might be roughly characterized as commands to all those who would have anything to do with what would be *seen* at the 1972 Olympics. They were done in small editions. Curiously, these pictures were not intended to be examined by the general public or even by the art-consuming and art-critical public. The first *Erscheinungsbild*, from late 1968, is merely a poster with some rectangles of the official silver, light blue, and light green. It contains the radical emblem of the Cologne design school and the five "traditional" Olympic rings.

A later "design manifesto" (I believe that this is about the most honest rendition of the meaning of these placards intended to declare and coordinate official taste) displays all the official colors and some suggested guidelines to those outside the central studios, for example, organizing committees in other countries, for devising Olympic publicity. The last design manifesto is a complex (though still quite pretty), large (ca. 3' × 4'), slickly printed sheet

containing miniatures of many posters to be seen full-size elsewhere in our exhibit, some pictograms, suggestions for devising
maps and other schematics, recommended sketches for landscaping, and even color schemes for beer cans and Waldis. Many of the
captions for other parts of our exhibit will be translated quotations
from the last Erscheinungbild's superconfident prose. This is evocative, anachronistic language declaring the healing or educational
capabilities of well-intentioned art.

As stated earlier, the bulk of this show will consist of posters.
Besides the first official poster showing the roof (perhaps the only
ugly piece of graphic art to come out of the 1972 Olympics—maybe the roof is to blame), there are twenty-one other official posters, one each for the major Olympic sports. Some dozen or so
more official posters advertise, with much more daring and looser
layouts, the many parts of the much-touted cultural program that
ornamented Bavaria during the summer of 1972. Only one poster
uses all the colors of the official spectrum. This is the one that cele-
brates the torch run from Olympia in Greece to the several sporting sites in Germany.

More interesting from an art-historical point of view and
possibly from an esthetic point of view as well are the posters for
internal use. Among these are the already mentioned pictogram
placards, the explanations and orderings for the official uniforms,
the maps of sites, and the schematic charts of various sorts, some
of which turn out to be quasi-abstract compositions of consider-
able power. One of the by-products of the Visual Department was
a new map of metropolitan Munich that is conventional in its layout but that deserves display in an art-sensitizing milieu because
of Aicher's delightful employment of his colors for supposed com-
municable as well as intrinsic use.

Another whole category of fine graphic designs are those of
the many posh catalogs, costly giveaways for the whole or for parts
of the Munich festival. A series of seven expensive brochures were
printed in large editions for periodic distribution, instruction, and
esthetic intimidation ahead of time to the thousands of members
of the accredited press. The layouts of these large folios follow the
examples set by Aicher. These various occasional publications con-

tain, incidentally, some risky sports photography of a new sort that is rarely seen outside Germany.

The Visual Department also laid out or supervised the making of catalogs for several sports-specific exhibitions in Munich. There was a historical display of the artifacts of sports rowing, a small display of Olympic medals, and a rather chilling exhibition of the technology that is used to record exactly, suddenly, and minutely the supreme levels of sports endeavor—the mechanism for doing photo finishes, for example. A small brochure on drugs, called "Doping," is done in the (we guess) sinister, darker colors.

In Munich there is a minor concession at the second German Olympics to the venerable German intellectuals' yearning for classical Greece. This is a proud, though publicistically downplayed, exhibition celebrating a century of exemplary German excavations at ancient Olympia in the Peloponnesus. It cannot be an accident that the catalog (with superb illustrations, text, and bibliographical apparatus) is a cold (and therefore revealing) example of the design department's attitude toward history. This 140-page book is unmistakably of Aicher's design but evokes minimally, perhaps with cruel intent, the neo-classicism that has been an integrated element not only of high German culture but also of the modern Olympic Games as well.

The remaining parts of this display of official taste will be more examples illustrating the degree to which visual engineering was extended. We could show some of the ephemeral, orange results sheets issued by the computers after each sports event was run, some of the fat books of final results printed the day after the Games ended, some fact sheets (printed, consistently enough, on green paper, meaning "information") for journalists, some rule books, and some stationery.

The identification cards, meal tickets, passes, and receipts were all devised with consistent design criteria in mind and may appear to some critics like a pushing of minutiae too far. However, the admissions tickets using colors to aid in the instant identifications of various sites, locations, and times are outstanding examples of nice design. Many of them are uncounterfeitable items that pragmatically managed large numbers of many-languaged people in difficult circumstances.

A couple of display cases revealing accommodation to the souvenir trade would be a gesture toward completeness. There were paperweights, ashtrays, bandannas, neckties, umbrellas, lap robes, ballpoint pens, and the ubiquitous Waldi, which was most successfully hawked as the ornament for a key chain. One could purchase "Olympic" phonograph records whose jackets held titles such as "Olympic Dancing Sound" and "Folklore of Munich." All, in design, in any case, were approved by Aicher and his staff, and those things that are repulsive are more so because of their zany functions rather than their colors and surfaces.

Ornaments for the show that might make it more fetching would be some of the large banners, murals, and ephemeral sculpture used at the site in Munich. I myself was particularly moved by the overlapping, huge transparencies of the pictogram for water sports that were used as a backdrop (and to give life to an intimidatingly huge interior space) at the diving competitions.

Some photo murals of the architecture raised for the Games might add an Olympic ambience for our crowds of pleasantly astonished visitors. The roof is simply too grand to be ignored. I would like to see at least some pictoral celebration for that cycling stadium.

The catalog will be small and consist mostly of amplifications of the historical parts of this prospectus. An effective adjunct for the catalog and a sort of favor for the visitor and the art world might be re-edition of the last *Erscheinungsbild* with the presumptuous text translated into English. We might give a boost to a little reform movement in design.

8

Finishes

If there have ever been underdogs at a big meet, the Malawians would fit the appellation. And, of course, I am a fan.

A "bright spot" (I employ Mike Nicholls's phrase) was the performance of Emesia Chizunga who, during her elimination heat in the 800-meter race, led the pack of seven runners for about two-thirds of the first lap of the two-lap race. I was on hand for this vignette at the full main stadium and cheered with abandon only to watch, pained and embarrassed, as the little woman in red fell back to finish last and sixteen seconds slower than the British woman who was sixth. Still Emesia's time of 2:19.2 was good enough to set a new Malawian record.

This morning I chat for a while, yet again, with Max Emery, Malawi's chief sports organizer. We are seated on a bright green, fiberglass park bench in the Village. We sip from plastic containers of Milo, the drink the

Nestlé people are providing free. How does Max feel about the performances of his team?

"Things could be worse. We're not breaking the [Malawian] records we had hoped, but we're making some good shows. Lots of 'personal bests.'"

When I wheedle for his observation about a certain sprinter who, like Emesia, finished poorly in his heat at the main stadium, Max replies smartly, "All right. Last, but not disgraceful."

The discipline of the team continues to slip. From morning until night the athletes wish most to stuff at the Mensa and at the no-pay Coke spigots. Their food at home is mostly maize porridge. Curiously enough, the sensational diet here is causing no intestinal difficulties—only the steady accumulation of bulk, experienced by all.

The favorite recreation of all hands has been to slouch in a darkened room before a television, keeping the sound on loudly, despite the fact that for them German might as well be Etruscan. Nor do they grasp the sequence of the action of the old movies of drawing room comedies, the talk shows, or even many of the Olympic sporting events—horse jumping, for example. At first they made no distinction between the color and the black-and-white sets in their rooms, but now they favor the fine color sets in the public lounges. This has made the members of the team even more difficult to locate for the enforcement of workouts.

The most serious personnel problem has been Wilfred Mwalwanda, "Malawi's best and most experienced athlete." As the Mark Spitz of Malawi, Wilfred has imperiously demanded exceptional considerations. He must be *warned* that he should come to practice. He is to be awakened gently. Wilfred thus establishes distinctions in rank that demoralize the rest of the team. Most nettlesome has been his insistence that he and he alone will decide when, in what fashion, and how much he will train for the decathlon. He trains but little.

Still, if raw publicity distributed to the world is a measure of the utility of a Malawian athlete, Wilfred has been a good investment, because the letters "MAW" were flashed many times on the great scoreboards of the full main stadium and, consequently, for the world's television viewers as Wilfred competed in his ten (count 'em) different events. His javelin throw of 71.28 meters (235'3") was almost ten meters better than that of Nicolai Avilov, the overall victor and therefore "the world's greatest athlete." Alas, Wilfred showed badly in almost all the other nine events, and of the twenty-two athletes who scored in all parts of the decathlon, his score, 6,227, was the lowest.

Max describes the muddle at the start of the individual road race for bicyclists. In Munich the distance was 182.4 kilometers (113 miles). Our two Malawian cyclists actually had to start at the back of the pack of 150 because the Malawian functionary with their entrance certification got snarled in traffic with the team Ford and never did arrive at the start. Langston Grimmon and Raphael Kazembe were pulled out by officials after they were lapped in the fifth of an eight-lap race.

"However," Max lowers his long eyelashes and stares hard in an attempt to induce shame in me, punishment, perhaps, for my occasional and instantly regretted employment of ironic intonations over the past few days, "not a single one of our athletes failed to appear for his event." He was cruelly alluding to the fact that Eddie Hart and Reynaud Robinson, my compatriots, had missed their heats for the 100-meter dash—admittedly a world-class screw-up. Everyone is still talking about it.

4:15 P.M., Sunday, 10 September 1972

The most intricate yet thrilling event of a big track meet is the final men's 4 × 100-meter relay. This event is a whirling climax of speed on the part of eight groups of four extraordinary individuals each. While at full power, the athletes must also manage the intricate, ever-perilous passing of the baton. Just now this event is imminent on this the last day of what may be the last Olympics. Those of us here have reveled in and perhaps suffered from drama these past two weeks. However, the playlet about to be enacted before us is overloaded with the potential for revived astonishment.

In the final today are, among others, the teams from East and West Germany, the Soviet Union, and the United States. Providentially, these are the teams that are leading in the medal counts. The anchor man on the all-black American team is Eddie Hart, perhaps the fastest man in the world, who had earlier been disqualified in the qualifying heats for the 100-meter dash. Valeri Borzov, the *declared* fastest man, is the leadoff runner on the Soviet team.

The full stadium heaves with excitement. For within this big piece of theater, there is the subdrama of a race between the East and the West Germans. I am with American newspaper reporters in the press section. We all know that our emotions are being shared by hundreds of millions of people—now.

The gun goes off. There is no false start. All of the runners and each of the three handoffs are so nearly simultaneous, all of the performances so apparently faultless, that one revels in a long rush of theatrical vertigo. The pleasurable disorientation is so keen that we are incapable of distinguishing high points of the winning performance, which lasts 38.19 seconds. One can, however, most easily follow the blacks because of their blackness and greater size.

As Eddie Hart, sure enough, breaks the tape, I bellow, "Gut!" in German which astonishes the thirty or so Americans, also in transports, around me. We all await confirmation on the big scoreboards. Soon the non-Americans around are noting, as indeed one might, that the spread in time between the first place and the eighth team in this event is less than a second.

This is a strategically placed athletic victory, but especially here and now. It is a partial vindication for the two men who missed their heats on 31 August. I and others also have to view the victory of the blacks as a flaunt to Avery Brundage who excluded two of their number from the other potent relay, the 4 × 400 meters. So, this win before the world is not just the garnering of a pack of gold Olympic medals, it is a complex triumph—the full potential of which has not yet been played out.

The joyousness of this triumph has not gone past the victors, Larry Black, Bob Taylor, Gerald Tinker, and the aforementioned Eddie Hart. Keenly, empathetically observed, their heads back the better to shout, they jump up, rubbing and slapping each other in voluptuous fits of mutual congratulation. Rapturous, reveling in their prominence, they hold hands in a chain and, a quartet, run around the track, the vast scene of their proven supremacy, screaming, punching the lovely air, bathing in triumph, smearing themselves with the pleasure of it. The crowd loves them, and they devour that love.

And then, at once, I know that in the energy of this crowd and of myself and of my fellow millions of watchers there is an apprehensive fear. We are greeting these glowing performers with such projected desire because we want this all to stay sporting and Olympic. We do not want to watch an anarchic third act in the drama of American blacks in Munich. We do not want them to mess up our festival now with a demonstration. But, all along, we understand. Would it not be tempting for them to employ for themselves the award ceremonies—already proven so crucial to the conservative and apparently incontestable value given to Olympic sacred rites?

The appropriate ritual approaches. Did these potential outlaws have discussions beforehand? What pressures are on them as Americans, as Olympic competitors, as private persons, as supercharged, auraed "niggers" to all of us? The tension within us all is steadily mounting.

And all along, some of us must yearn for disorder. I want to see it. The naughty child within sides with the devil in them. I project prayers to them to pull down their pants and hurl tendoned moons at Avery Brundage and the limousined barbarians who forced the Olympics to go on. And all along the conformist, peaceable adult passionately yearns optimistically with the crowd. What will they do?

Happily for our tense emotional state if not for the American fans, the womens' 4×100-meter event intervenes, producing only bronze medals for the U.S. team of three blacks and a white. Had they won, the symbolic burden they carried would have loaded yet more heavily the significance of the dubious sacraments we all fear now.

The victory ceremony for the four men will be the last act in a couple of playlets. One is the battle between the loose blacks and the tight organizers of this whole long show. Another one is the many-chaptered tale of rancor that ranking American organizers have been having with those they claim are corrupt international officials. I refer to such constantly, intricately rediscussed matters as the Rick Demont doping case, the wrangles with biased judges in diving and wrestling, and most especially the basketball game (which the Yanks lost in the last second) with the Soviet team.

The twelve athletes—four Yanks, four Soviets (including the poised-to-the-point-of-arrogance Borzov), and four West Germans—approach the little tribune for the hanging of four gold, four silver, and four bronze medals, all dangling from ribbons. All of us everywhere are in an agitated, chilled state of anticipation. There can be no doubt that the particular keenness of these moments is due to our super-fine esthetic sensitivities, tuned, alert to any slight beginning of a flick of a gesture that the splendid heroes might make. The four take the top-most platform. As dirndl-clad girls carry out the medals, one of the Americans in the middle affectionately and lightly nudges two of his companions, and my throat swells in hot terror and happy wicked anticipation. After all, I am at a historic event!

In a palpable willing of love, the entire world yearns for the quartet to behave. The men, meanwhile, are silent though possibly twitching a little (I think so anyway) as the crowd is in an uproar. Four dark-brown jocks have half the world in their control!

They face the flags poised to rise on the standards. Their faces are stern as the amplified music starts loudly:

"Oh say, can you see"

Faces impassive, in poses approximating military full attention, they are immutable, indecipherable. The stadium and the world are on the verge

"By the dawn's early"

of the inner grasp

"Light"

of assurance that these magic athletes, after threatening us, have it in their power to behave as good parts of the Olympic system and that

"What so proudly we"

probably they will

"Hail the twilight's last gleaming"

not demonstrate. And that all will end safely and well.

All of us are victors at this victory ceremony.

Black, Taylor, Tinker, and Hart leave the victory ritual in the midst of the crowd's projected gratitude. One feels a sort of peaceful wistfulness. A keen, familiar piece of theater had a proper ending.

There is another, intervening piece of tension a short time later when Frank Shorter, another American, enters the stadium from a dark tunnel and, looking as though he had not really tried very hard, wins the marathon. He circles the track of the stadium to a buzz of applause and more projected, generous affection.

7:00 A.M., Monday, 11 September 1972

We are taking in our by now standard huge breakfast in the Press Center's cafeteria. Paul Martin, the American expatriate, is my company.

My farewell to the Malawian team will be only representative. Max Emery has just left for London where he will try to talk some wealthy public schools into donating their extra sports equipment to the Malawian national effort. Mike Nicholls is organizing the imminent flight back to Africa for the rest. Between big forkfuls of scrambled eggs garnished with bits of deeply browned sausages and pale pink ham, Malawi's sole representative in the international press corps sums up:

"I often asked our athletes if they were frightened, and they as often insisted that they were not. It seems that some of them *had* to have been. We practiced gun starts in Malawi during our two-week training camp and here too. Still, they were usually left at the blocks for the sprints. They must have been overwhelmed by the feared performances of athletes who at these starts had been just beside them.

"As to the whole experience, I think that their general attitude might be best expressed as a stolid welcoming of the pleasurable-exceptional. That airplane takeoff out of Blantyre was a sort of socko sensation after which all that followed was remarkable but not really as stunning as that was.

"Munich and the Olympic Games, viewed in terms of the quantum leap from their everyday lives in villages, are not much more extraordinary than a trip to Harlem or to Hong Kong or to the moon. And Munich is certainly less realistic than a trip to London would be. As former British subjects, they have all heard of London, which they could in some small way anticipate."

"What do you mean when you say that they found it all 'pleasurable?' "

"It *has* been fun almost from beginning to end for them. Unfortunately and perhaps sadly, they will be incapable of describing the trip to their fellows in the villages. One reason is that the whole adventure has been so otherworldly that they will not be able verbally to distinguish many particular aspects of the three weeks—that to us would be distinctive—from the whole, very long march of dazzling events. Another matter is that Chichewa or any other language that they may regularly employ does not contain the words or the expressive possibilities to describe the Olympic Village, souvenir shopping at the Marienplatz, discotheques, European fatty luxury food, and the tumult of the crowds at the main stadium. Without language to fix these experiences, the adventures will rest in their imaginations, imprecise, garbled, incommunicable, and eventually uncertain."

"You mentioned discotheques. Was there any interracial hustling? Were they being hustled by members of other teams?"

"No. They're not brave enough for that. They looked in a bit at the big discotheque and watched with some amazement, I'm sure, the American blacks moving about with such flashy assurance. They kept to themselves, if you know what I mean."

"How did they feel about the Israeli deaths?"

"Sad, of course. Those whose events were not yet run were upset at being told that the Games might be stopped."

"Was there a sort of Malawian high point or a hero?"

"My hero was little Matthews [Kambale]. Relative to training, he did everything he was asked to do and volunteered to do more. All the rest were sometimes only going through the motions. And, you know, his performance in the marathon was beyond what we had a right to expect."

"How so?"

"Well, though he started with the big pack, he was quickly left behind by the giants. But he kept going at it gamely. He told us later, 'At first I felt I was too far behind, until I passed my first white man. Then I passed several other gentlemen and understood that perhaps I was doing quite well for a Malawian.'

"And Matthews' entry into the stadium occurred just after the award ceremonies for some event or other and three minutes after the runner who preceded him. Trotting at a smart pace the last 400 meters around the track, he and Malawi got solo applause the entire way. His time of 2:45.50 took more than a half hour off his previous best and, naturally, set a new Malawian record. He will be our Olympic hero."

"But really, Paul, as a whole the Malawians were the worst performers at these Olympic Games. Will Mike and his Olympics and Commonwealth Games Association try again for Montreal in 1976?"

"Oh, absolutely. I have been enthusiastic in my newspaper reports."

"The only newspaper reports," I interject.

"Max will be enthusiastic. The athletes are bound to be enthusiastic. We all gained needed seasoning. And just a short time ago we started from nothing. Until now there have been almost no sports in Malawi. And, as was explained to you, the whole trip didn't cost a hell of a lot of money."

"Lots of political benefits at bargain prices."

The only Malawian sports journalist of international rank taps his spoon around in his coffee cup for a while and then responds, "Yes, I suppose so."

We sip our good coffee for a while. Then Paul leans back in his chair to assume a soothsayer's look as he gazes into the heavens, at present blocked by fiberboard panels and fluorescent area lighting.

"Someday we're going to find a Keino lying around in the bush down there. All we need is one of these guys and then athletics will really go in Malawi."

Monday, 11 September 1972

Yesterday, as at all the sites, the journalists' perches were supplied with televisions. On overlay for the manifestations at the stadium broadcast on these sets (also periodically announced over the stadium loudspeakers) was the knowledge that far ahead of the other marathon runners was an American, Frank Shorter. And so, pleased, if not in a state of tumult, we awaited this harbinger of the end to enter the stadium on the last day of the contests.

At the expected moment the expected figure emerged from the marathon tunnel and detonated the mass of 80,000 and, we assume, the rest of the world. But it was not slender, elegant Frank Shorter. It was a floppy-haired, stocky fellow wearing the number 72, which was not on our official lists. Relishing the excitement, and looking bouncily fresh, the object of our attention approached the finish tape but did not break it. In the meantime Shorter, the real winner, entered for a welcome that was short of complete. He *did* break the tape, *did* get a gold medal in the obligatory ceremony with the obligatory national anthem.

The newspapers today tell us that the fake finisher had hidden himself in the crowd, run out 100 meters outside the tunnel, and performed as he wished. He was a twenty-two-year-old sports student from Mün-ster. It was a joke, he said, to remind us all that these were to be, as announced some eight years before, "lighthearted Games" ("heitere Spiele"). No coaches, schedulers, or International Olympic Committee members had any control over him. There were no ordinances in the Munich law books against such an offense. Amid historical Olympic pro-fundities, we lived an Olympic hoax but not disorder.

We were getting ready for the closing ceremonies.

Here again, I arrived long before the formal ceremonies were to begin, in this case, to wait while watching the last equestrian contest, a complex combined jumping event called the *prix des nations*. The stadium was nearly full. I was mystified, as almost everyone around was, and distracted as the various bar jumps and other equipment were hauled off by four-wheel drive Mercedes army trucks to light applause.

Then there were lots of formal and noncompetitive displays of lux-ury horses. There were girl acrobats on some circling, huge animals with steady, rapid gaits. There was a parade around the track of Bavarian so-ciety people in horse-drawn antique carriages. For a while in the gather-ing dusk some spotlights focused on a white Lipizanner. Some dressage horses repeated the routines they were trained to perform competitively at the palace of Nymphenburg. While inattentively observing this last performance, which I had also seen an afternoon of at Nymphenburg itself, I recalled that the scoring of this Olympic activity is so complicated that journalists expressing an interest in reporting on the event were invited to go to a "seminar" of several days in order to learn just what is going on.

It is worth noting that most of the equestrian jumping competitions for which medals were awarded took place far from this, the main site. The imposition of horses here and now seems like a strange throwback to ancient times, when a public display of sport horses, as in a chariot race, was an emphatic demonstration of the owners' wealth and position. And even today, though intrinsically useless, competition horses signify the great wealth necessary to display them. In Germany today, where grazing land is especially dear and a lot of great wealth is very new, a costly horse is a declarative symbol of high arrival. Here, too, I suspect that we were witnessing an attempt on the part of the organizers to enlist, demonstrate, and integrate into this grand confection sport horses, the

almost ageless symbols of oligarchic status, just as in the exceptional treat-
ment of VIPs.

Another odd thing about the closing ceremonies was that just then
the two-week period of dry warm days broke. The air thickened to
become murky, and the swooping roof looked vastly more distant, even
spooky. As it grew dark (the formal ceremonies were to begin at 7:30
P.M.), we all became cold and increasingly eager for the Games to end.

We already knew that our ceremonies, which were originally
planned for the day before, a Sunday, had been reformulated and much
shortened. Joachim Fuchsberger, the announcer, this time did not do
French and English translations. At the outset he declared, "The Games of
the XXth Olympiad began lightheartedly—they must end seriously."

There were some fanfares and brief pieces of modern music by
musicians of impeccable reputation broadcast over public address systems again functioning with astonishing clarity. A much-heralded "surprise" was not a surprise at all, since we could see it the entire day and
before we entered the stadium. It was elegant and memorable, though: a
plastic balloon, as long as the infield, filled with helium and adorned with
stripes of official Olympic colors, representing the five continents but
somehow looking indeed like a rainbow.

There was a scheduled march-in of athletes. But the number of
them was perhaps a third or a fourth as large as the troops who marched
in more than two weeks ago. And the athletes became disorderly almost
at once. Athletes from the various national teams did not carry flags but
rather were preceded by hostesses carrying miniature banners. However,
none of this proceeded very far. Phalanxes of dozens, perhaps hundreds,
fell apart and swarmed in masses about the field. There were swirling
circles and conga lines. At a couple of moments the sights of screaming
girls and boys lunging at police lines produced the near-throttling heart-
beats in the throat that were anticipating fear and the euphoric realization
that the orgies I had presaged with hallucinatory intensity were coming
about.

But no—the controlling anticipation of uncontrol was too good. A
couple of old-hand sports reporters, real ones, who had been at the
Games in Mexico City told me to expect this sort of disorder. They said
that the rioting at the closing in 1968 had been pervasive and nearly
complete. However, it was joyous, harmless, and had merely petered out

in genial noisiness. A sort of generational (an Olympic generation lasts but four years) passing of lore led the athletes, despite official warnings against doing so, to prepare for this episode of rule breaking when threats of punishment were idle.

It went on for about ten minutes, and then it looked like a new stage—one I had fantasized pleasurably—was taking over. A few spectators, drunks probably (mostly locals), made efforts to beat past guards, to pull down fences, and to get into the action on the center field. Reassurances were not working. Disorder spread. Now this *was* something!

A last effort calmed the assembly. The faultless loudspeakers broadcast Haydn's ancient hymn, again the national anthem. Many, many thousands of good Germans were required to stand at attention as they had learned in school. The foreigners joined in. There was quiet in the center field and a return to assigned locations—if not the serried ranks originally set for patient assembly.

I recalled dimly that a couple of my high school football games were de-rioted by this method—that is, by having our bands (always obedient) make us stop, stand up, and be quiet by means of the slow-tempoed "Star-Spangled Banner."

But, all along, this disorder, because I was forewarned that it would occur and would be harmless, *seemed* part of this ceremony that had to be at least partly sad because it was ending something splendid. Besides, it was getting dark and cold.

As we were warned in advance, it was now time to say farewell to Avery Brundage. How can one begin to suggest the significance of Avery Brundage at the final Olympic Games? I must go back and review a bit. As chairman of the United States Olympic Committee in the mid 1930s Brundage, largely by lying to himself and to others, had made the Nazis out to be respectable and had thus frustrated a boycott. Brundage had gone far to assure the success of the 1936 Olympics. Since that time he had battled the world in efforts to maintain the (always, even long before him) unmaintainable amateur-professional distinction. In the 1950s Brundage had been seduced by the Eastern European orthodox Marxists, specifically their sports functionaries, and had arranged for their admission to the International Olympic Committee and thus to the Games.

Of course this was in keeping with the meritocratic ideology of world-class sport, but it led to incessant lies over their amateurism and disputes over scandalously dishonest judges and rule breaking—most especially in the eyes of Americans.

Brundage declined and then disappeared in popularity in the United States and took his position as president of the International Olympic Committee ever more earnestly. He shifted almost all his attentions to Europe and bought a house in Bavaria. For Willi Daume, who relied for this information on the older German members of the IOC, Brundage was *the* VIP among the VIPs. His metallic blue Mercedes 600 was the longest one on the site. Its side and back windows had little fringed curtains that could be slid shut. Everyone knew that in the despair first following the atrocity to the Israeli athletes, Daume and the national politicians were too stunned to consider a festive future. They had no program for seeing the action through. Brundage had a program—the same old one: "The Games must go on!" And so that is why we were here shivering in the cold on a Monday night in autumn.

Though unsteady, Brundage was still big and was alone on a blue podium. The prepared speech was one of the Olympic clichés that were again for him loaded with meaning. The first paragraph was in his German with his ponderous American accent. The second paragraph was in English; the last in German. He walked off the field under narrow spotlights from a long way off. The huge main scoreboard with its thousands of computerized lights carried the message, "Thank you, Avery Brandage." All through this farewell there had been a final hoax. On the grand scoreboard, his name was misspelled.

Long before the old man's speech at the improvised memorial ceremony for the Israeli athletes, we had received an advance program for the closing ceremonies that would have had us all sing, "For He's a Jolly Good Fellow." This would have been a crueler joke. It has been dropped.

There was a lot more fine music, some dancing before us, and the lowering of flags. There was also a lot of shivering in the cold. The Olympic flame was slowly extinguished in silence and to great effect. But the real end of the Games—the end of several eras in sport, perhaps—was the moment Avery Brundage walked away from his last Olympic Games.

Tuesday, 12 September 1972

The two experts at their kiosk in the Press Center took back the Leicaflex SL, observed that it had been scarcely used at all, and said that they would cancel the rental fee of 1 percent of its value that we had agreed upon when I took the machine away with me some three weeks ago. Then they offered to sell me the thing for 875 marks, or less than one-half of its retail price. An American newspaperman nearby assured me I could get as much as that for it in a pawn shop—even in South Carolina. As I walked away without the Leicaflex, I felt that the salesmen were waiting for my query, "What is the least you'll take?"

The atmosphere of a potlatch, of a combative giveaway, continues, but it is all less agreeable, oafish even. We all want to leave. The party is over.

The Press Center has great piles of computer printout paper under coffee tables and in corners. The media people who are ready to leave are taking home with them only the small amounts of printed material that they will need. That is not much. Piles of new books are free for the taking, though there are no takers. Almost all of these are national teams' "Who's Who"s offered to the journalists. They are stuffed with statistical information and intended to lessen the need throughout the games for journalistic personal access to athletes. All the national organizing committees brought too many. There are especially large numbers of various editions—some with long entries and some with shorter ones—for the teams from all the Eastern European countries. The East Germans have brought tons of these directories, which are now useless.

What has made these lists particularly superfluous is that the medal ceremonies and records have radically altered the appearance of leveling honesty, the impartiality in these life dictionaries. In the world of top-level sport, a tiny number of the biographees are now elevated to super-hero status. The overwhelming rest have been rendered nullities by the scientific recording apparatus. The books portray a human situation the Games were intended to transform. The Games have transpired. The books are junk.

The biggest bar in the Press Center is busy as usual. At 6:00 this morning the scrimmage consisted almost entirely of Japanese and Africans who were very loud—about what, one could only guess. They are having a last blast at low prices at something nifty, the equivalent of which has no approximation at home. A sort of counter to the slick surfaces, either in the chemically prescribable official colors or in the bland plastic that is the usual surface for new things in postwar Germany, is the carpet around the Press Center bar. Once an institutional gray with a short-bristly nap, it is now a raised mass of crud: tramped-in shoe wipings, spilled yogurts and beers, mashed-in cigarettes, and vomit. It is dark and of no color at all—signifying the end of meaning here.

The orgy of participatory disorder never occurred or even seemed likely to begin. The dreamed-of chaos presaged by a falling pigeon, orac-ular dreams, hallucinations produced by vertigo, we now know were brought about by sensuous excess and unrivaled, unequalable festive eu-phoria.

The intersexual fooling around, of which there was a lot, seems to be taking place now only a little and randomly. The easy lays, who were energized day after day, now look passive, fed up with it all, the women un-made up with sagging mouths and smudges under their fogged eyes. There are good-bye hugs and kisses, the equivalents of "see you later" in lots of languages. I heard some versions of "see you in Montreal," but we all know there will be few subsequent rendezvous. An Olympic genera-tion, even for us, lasts four years. We are older now and will be yet older then.

A Munich daily commented that our celebrations were "the most beautiful Olympic Games that were ever destroyed" ("die je kaputt ge-macht wurden"). There was a calamity. But it was so sudden, so entirely unforeseen and unforeseeable by the party organizers, that it stands apart ever more from the long, sacred, participatory rituals now finished.

We are sure that the disaster to the Israeli team, the botched and deadly rescue attempt and the exposed incapability of all levels of Ger-man government to improvise will all enter the told and retold histories of the Munich Olympics of 1972. Almost all of us believe that the dreadful incident owes much of its horror to the assumption that our euphoria had just at that time reached its summit. The Germans themselves felt that they had been sacrificed in the upset. Hans Klein remarked, "We are not only some of the most sensitive but because of this also the most easily wounded people of the earth." Then he added, "It seems now that there is no place in which we could be wounded where we have not yet been hit."

No, there were no grand disorders. There were muddles that might have been interpreted as disasters had the general atmosphere not been so grossly and predictably altered by the calamity that occurred on the morning a week ago.

Epilogue

I

Tous qu'il est prévue, c'est magnifique, mais les autres choses . . .
c'est ridicule.
– Official in Munich preparing for 1976 Olympic Games in Montreal

On 26 August 1973, that is, a year after those stunning opening ceremonies, there was an anniversary party on the site of the Games. Had the organizers read the available history books carefully enough they would have known that after every Olympic festival there is a hangover. There are regrets and some bitterness. Yet, a year after, one could tell that the official, historical position on the 1972 Games was nearly in place.

There were still forty-eight employees cleaning up. Some were selling off material, particularly apparatus used in the Press Center, such as televisions, telexes, and the special desks provided for journalists at all the sites. Others, lawyers mostly, were negotiating to complete the transfer of Olympic facilities, land and buildings, to the organizations that would use them later. More lawyers were attempting to dispose of fifty still-pending lawsuits. Many of these lawsuits concerned the payment of overtime to contractors and workers on the site in the last hectic weeks of preparations.

There was an eagerness to come up with an accountant's final statement—a satisfactory one. Certain matters remained difficult to explain. Accountants declared that some of the newly provided facilities, such as the regatta site and the stadium for the jumping events for horses, were improvident. But indications of crookedness in the awarding of contracts were surely already suppressed. The swooping roof, which some claimed was already clouding over and darkening, was now referred to as "the baldachin of many millions" ("Millionen-Baldachin"). Half of the apartments in the former Olympic Village were still unsold. In an interview, Willi Daume, who now had an office in the Olympic Village, summarized: "Naturally one has to anticipate that for ignoramuses and the mean-spirited, there are ever possibilities to make unreasonable and small-minded criticisms—needless to say, as hindsight."

How would those responsible for settling affairs have behaved at the anniversary party if there had been no terrorist attack in the early morning of 5 September 1972? We can never know. For this unanticipatable event overcast all interpretations of what took place before and after that date.

The atrocity, it needs to be said, even then was scarcely mentioned in the host country. The botch of the rescue attempt, which *Spiegel* called "the darkest day of the Federal Republic," was nodded at afterward in the German press but then ignored. The official position within Germany has been to give the calamity some attention and then to move on to statistics and photographs demonstrating success. All the German publications, and most particularly the official reports of the summer Games of 1972, are expensively printed with hundreds of technically superb sports action shots—in color. All the German photographs I have ever seen of the interruption are badly focused and in black and white despite the fact that the German sports photographers are the best in the world. The only color pictures I ever saw of the shattered helicopters were in a late 1972 issue of *Life* magazine. Of the 1,178 pages of the richly produced official report, the accident itself, a pivotal event in the story of the modern Olympics, occupies but three pages. There is little text and several fuzzy black-and-white pictures of mourners.

The West German government disposed of some potential entanglements connected with the nasty matter. On 29 October 1972, Federal authorities were informed that some Arabs calling themselves "Black Septembrists" had hijacked a Lufthansa Boeing 727 on its way from Damascus, Syria, to Frankfurt. The three threatened to blow it up with its crew and passengers if their demands were not met for release of the three terrorists who had survived the Fürstenfeldbruck massacre.

The plane circled over Yugoslavia as the three prisoners, who were awaiting trial, were taken from their separate prisons, put in a Hawker Siddley 125 executive jet, and flown to Zagreb. There, the murderers were taken aboard the Boeing, which had refueled. All flew to Tripoli in Libya, where the passengers and crew were freed and the plane released. Immediately after the atrocity in September, the federal government, just as they released the bodies of the Israelis for burial in Israel, had released the bodies of the dead assassins for burial as martyrs in Tripoli. On 30 October, the Libyans again staged public celebrations for the "heroes of the Munich operation."

In the diary I did not offer an objective or detailed story of the interruption and the disposal of it. From the beginning I wanted to tell another story. Besides, the massacre is the subject matter of The Blood of Israel, a fine, readily accessible book by a French journalist, Serge Groussard.

Groussard and others believe that the disposal of the incident was simply too expeditious; that in order to get rid of the matter, there had to be preparatory collusion between Palestinian officials, high officers of Lufthansa, the west German secret police, and Bavarian politicians. In the weeks following the murders in Munich, Lufthansa was the most internationally exposed and therefore threatened of the many manifestations of the West German technocratic-financial-political oligarchy. The October 1972 solution is one of many mysteries that will not be clarified until long after all the German actors in this shameful abortion of justice, almost all of them still in place, are dead.

If the West Germans and the International Olympic Committee wanted to dispose of the memories of the dead Israelis, the living Israelis would have none of it. In a previous book (*Sport: A Cultural History* [New York: Columbia University Press, 1984], pp. 174–77), I have discussed the integration of sport in Zionism. In no modern nation have sport and physical education been so long and so closely integrated into ideology and inspirational institutions as in Israel.

Israel lost eleven citizens but gained martyrs whose great value was instantly acknowledged by the world. From the first news of kidnapping and murder, the nine still-living Israelis were written off. In a deep and unguessable sense, since they more deeply institutionalized the guilt on the part of outsiders that has been a basis for founding and maintaining the Jewish nation, they stabilized a little more the always-threatened country.

In a more particular sense, the victims have been the basis for monuments and solemn holidays and the foundation for foreign donations to one of the most magnificent sports education and sports training facilities in the world, the Wingate Institute, about twenty miles from Tel Aviv.

A legacy of the atrocity affecting the Olympic movement was an obsession with security—a sort of terror of terror. A large proportion of the enormous expenditures of all meetings of the Olympics since 1972 has been, directly or indirectly, devoted to protection and further isolation of Olympic athletes, the precious flesh of it all. Another observation related to this book is that in my lifetime there will be no more big sports festivals in the course of which harmless sneaks and lookers, such as this chronicler, will be able to move about with such delightful ease.

II

Until some sort of consensus was in place regarding the outcome of the Olympics in Montreal in 1976, it would be difficult—or better, tentative—for German bureaucrats to set forth an official view of the festival that had occurred in Munich in 1972. For, just as each Olympic festival is planned in the light (or shadows) of the Games that took place four years before, the appraisals of the working out are based on what takes place four years later.

The Montreal summer Games took place as planned in late July of

1976. However, in Canada and in international sports circles this festival is remembered for the evidence that the ambitions of the planners exceeded the capabilities of the French Canadians to carry them out. The main stadium and some buildings were never finished. The Games of 1976 were a financial setback for the various government entities that were obliged to pay the final bills. The legacy was debt and disillusionment—most particularly in the hosting city.

In retrospect, especially if one underplayed the massacre (as all German officials did), the Montreal Games buttressed a warm appraisal of the Munich Games. In the preparatory period from 1966 to 1972, a justification for the enormous outlays for improvement of Munich's infrastructure was that all this would have to be done someday. And, indeed, other large German cities have been, in the course of time, comparably fixed up. Munich was merely doing it about a decade in advance. Otherwise put, Munich got a ten-year jump on the rest of the big cities in the Federal Republic and, due to subsequent cost increases, got her improvements cheaply.

Everyone knew that after the Games Munich would be a different city. In the years that the preparations were under way, a pervasive fear—one that was discussed only in higher technocratic circles—was that enormous amounts of accelerated construction work would, after the party was over, lead to massive unemployment, particularly in the critical building and tourist sectors. Economists feared that the hangover in mood would be made concrete in a hangover in commercial and residential construction. Pessimists anticipated sudden declines in prices and wages and a consequent depression in Bavaria. None of this occurred.

Underlying this slowly revealed happiness was the continued strength of the West German economy. As the Games' expenditures more than tripled the early projections in 1967, a fortuitous working out of the debts was foreseen by just a couple optimists. The *Wirtschaftswunder* or "economic miracle" that began in 1948 and splendidly went on and on was only perceived as such by few shortly before preparations for the Munich Games began. The deficits in various governmental fiscs due to the Olympic subsidies could be gracefully accommodated because the tax basis of all of the Federal Republic grew steadily more robust.

A particularly felicitous consequence the 1972 Games was that Munich itself became a more obvious object of travelers from everywhere. I believe that Munich has been for some time the most agreeable and elegant city that ever existed. I did employ superlatives, but I feel that a lot of experienced travelers will agree with me. Added to the pre-Olympics Munich were several new areas for flaneurs, the most obvious of which was the geographically transforming Olympia Park (of which more later).

But much of the old, filthy city became an almost incessantly used pedestrian area (Fussgängerzone). Tiresome appeals before 1972 on the part of city authorities to the citizens to clean up the streets resulted in a permanent alteration in local attitudes. Munich is now tidy almost everywhere.

The straining to capacity of the city's concert halls and museums, assumed to be an expedient in 1972, has continued into the present. The new museum to treat respectfully the overflowing riches of the Alte Pinakothek, called, naturally, the Neue Pinakothek, is done to a high standard of finish. It is splendid, immensely costly, huge, and full of people all the time. In the meantime all the city's many other architectural treasures continue to get refurbished—sometimes re-refurbished.

To what extent the wooing in 1972 of VIPs is responsible for another change one can only guess. I resist believing that something so silly could have substantial consequences. But Munich, along with Paris, Rome, and London, has become a place for the rich from everywhere to spend lots of money. Cologne and Kassel may lead in radical art, Berlin in radical theater and nightlife, and Frankfurt in air traffic and banking. However, as a perch for the *Schickeria*, Munich has more art auction houses, more galleries, more antique stores, and more interior decorators per capita than any other city—perhaps in the world. The Bavarian city still lacks hotels and restaurants in grand numbers and grand sizes that rank with the oldest and noblest of Paris or Rome. But this situation may be in the course of correction. One always sees construction cranes everywhere. Since about 1985 a lot of this construction is for high-end luxury hotels and dwellings.

Munich is safe. There are large numbers of attractive local destinations—many of them perverse. One does not see police or think about them. And Munich is as loose as ever. On foot or with public transport one moves from one delight to another with breezy facility. The streets are full of strollers. The parks are full.

As an exemplary case for observation and to seal my point, I suggest that the experienced traveler, a long-distance runner on a workout perhaps, get to one of the grassy meadows in the English Garden, a huge park in the center of the city, on a summer afternoon. There he may watch the nude swimmers and sunbathers. Sometimes big-breasted girls, naked for their pleasure and ours, toss a Frisbee. One hears every language. You can stare as much as you want.

Besides the effects of the Games on the city of Munich, other critical issues in the wrapping up and in the subsequent official summing ups were a couple of solid, almost angrily maintained, decisions made long before the Games began. These decisions were rooted in the authorities' steady rage at two valid and inescapable criticisms. These carpings were not attributable to one ideological position but were everywhere. One of these was a prediction that the Games would lose vast amounts of money and the other was the accusation that at least some facilities were arrogant extravagances that would be useless after the Games. Consequently, it became necessary for Willi Daume, most notably, to demonstrate somehow that the Games made a profit and that there would be no "Olympic ruins."

It must be stressed again that the preparations for the 1972 Olympics were well integrated and scarcely opposed at all in German domestic politics. Most especially in the highest cadres, the leaders of postwar Germany were intelligent, unideological, and lucky. With the possible exception of Japan (which offers striking parallels), there has never been such a combined and sustained economic and political success. The directors of all this—orators, investment bankers, and high bureaucrats (who are tenured and well rewarded)—always have provided enough equivocal activities and dubious adventures to merit honest elections and to fill columns on the political pages of the newspapers.

But at the top is a geographically dispersed, mutually respecting, and mutually deferential oligarchy that has, over the decades, become ever less astonished at its success and ever more smug about it. In the late 1960s the oligarchy could not yet assume that its success was part of a solid, long-term trend.

It is a heritage of generations of German ideological wreckage that all political positions were able to find comfort in the Olympic ideology—whatever that is. In any case, there *was* an Olympic truce in German life as the Games were being prepared. Or, better stated, in the crab basket of competition for prestige in German public life, all struggled to identify themselves with the Munich Games, which were (to some extent, therefore) predestined to be a triumph. My session of "Journalists Ask; Politicians Answer" made this clear.

Willi Daume, Hans Klein and other officials who before 1972 made Olympic decisions with big financial consequences were secure in the investment banker–political adviser establishment. Daume, Klein, various construction entrepreneurs, design consultants, and comptrollers never really left the Bonn scene during their Olympic work in Munich, and many physically returned to centers of more purely political intrigue when the Games were over. All of the politicians who submitted to the Olympic truce of 1972 and who expected to gain thereby remained in strong positions after the Games, and almost all of those still living (Franz Josef Strauss died in 1988) are in unassailable positions today.

Domestically the second German Olympic Games *had* to be sanguinely viewed as the preparations were under way. The subsequent stability (or less kindly put, the ossification of the oligarchy) of the elite levels of German life assured that this reassuring official position would remain in effect.

There may come a day when a cold-blooded accountant is able to gather enough archival materials to determine if the Games of 1972 were a defendable business proposition. I believe they were, if one brings in the multiplier effect—by this I mean the Keynesians' assumptions about the magnified impact of changes in investment expenditures. Then, too, there are the unspecifiable long-term effects on Munich's appeal as the object of a journey, the local population's élan, and the whole area's greater appeal to big-spending outsiders. But all of these are impossible to quantify.

I will then reluctantly accept the claim that the whole show, as was declared just before it opened, cost just under 2 billion marks. Due to the writing off of huge parts of the government subsidies, "sales" of various facilities to government bodies and corporations, and the capitalization of the predicted income from various preserved facilities, several times in the early 1980s the Olympic Games of 1972 were declared "profitable." The problem of the "ruins" is discussed below.

Nightmarish recollections of the atrocity notwithstanding, the Munich Games grow in reputation. The disappointments of the Montreal Games of 1976 have been mentioned. The subsequent Moscow Games of 1980 were incomplete due to the disruption of really big politics—Soviet and American politics and the resultant boycotts of the Americans and their lackeys. The Germans' concern with the Rhodesian problem in 1972 seems paltry in retrospect. If the Soviet Games were distinguished by the sort of brilliant, cosmopolitan innovations that were attributed to Willi Daume and his milieu, the obfuscation that characterizes almost all innovation in the Soviet Union was in effect there too. Officially, the 1980 Games were a triumph.

Politics, most especially paranoia in the Kremlin, made the 1984 Los Angeles Games incomplete as well. A central issue was that the Soviet leaders were not able to get unconstitutional guarantees from American authorities that their defectors would be returned. The result was more boycotts—this time by the Soviets and their lackeys.

In any case, this undertaking, so American in every way, did provide opportunities for the exercise of administrative genius and for artistic innovation, most notably in the opening ceremonies. Since the 1984 Games ended happily and even made a capitalistic profit, they mark another turning point in the history of the Olympic movement. They also seal the esthetically messy intrusion of hugely moneyed television into the Olympic Games and so carry us way beyond our task, which was to examine the impact of the 1972 Games. It seemed like a lot of money in 1972—everyone talked about it—but the $7,500,000 ABC paid for the American television rights then is paltry, indeed almost laughably so, in retrospect.

The competently carried out Seoul Games of the summer of 1988 were far from the scene of European and American culture and their political entanglements. The Koreans did not mind, and a broad summary of the festival was that these Olympic Games were run by Koreans for their benefit. The Barcelona Games of 1992 already have lively, potentially dangerous political issues contained within them. The Catalan Games of 1992 will be a demonstration of regionalism in modern Spain and will be a stage to play out symbolically a lot of issues connected with the debates over European integration. But we are way ahead of our story.

III

Early one morning in late August of 1988 I paid the 4-mark fee and took the rapid elevator up to the restaurant near the top of the 290-meter-high Olympia Tower in Munich. There was light smog on a sunny day. I could nostalgize and survey the long-term results of the planners of the international festival of 1972. The main site was spread below. It was easy to trace my old running routes and the location of the former Press Center. The German Olympic Center, or at the time, DOZ, had, as promised, become a school for physical educationalists.

In the middle distance of about two kilometers, the former Olympic Village, now a fully occupied condominium complex, looked much better than it ever did. The many colored awnings and greenery cascading from the balconies were not there in 1972.

The acres of acrylic roof just below no longer gave a crystalline impression—there appeared to be a lot of patches, and in some places there were applications of opaque protective paint. But the *Dach* was stolidly there, having survived more than sixteen years of storms from the Alps. It was transmitting light and was as ever the overpowering architectural element of the whole area.

There had not been many visible changes. The park below was gardened and picked up. Although it was early in the morning, there were lots of strollers. Many had baby carriages. Already some sunbathers were gathering around one of the site's little lakes, which had a lot of ducks and swans in it. A high jet of water rose from the lake's center.

Under the rotating restaurant in the tower, in a darkened, carpeted room containing about fifty straight chairs, I put 2 marks in a slot and was the sole viewer of a thirty-minute film called "Olympiapark." It was a self-laudatory publicity piece by the society that now runs the main site as a commercial enterprise. I learned that the area is the largest sports facility available for public use in the world. It has been visited by some 80 million people. The film showed happy crowds in all sorts of situations. In addition to very large sports events such as football games and international swimming meets, the various enclosed areas are used for international congresses. The first large assembly after 1972 was for the world's Jehovah's Witnesses. There was footage of the German national contests for ballroom dancers and of indoor motorcycle races for kids under twelve.

Happily, there was good footage of the bicycle stadium, which was closed at the time of my visit since it was getting a new roof. The palace of esthetic vertigo is still regularly employed for large cycle-racing meets called track omniums. An addition to the Munich social calendar has been a yearly six-day bicycle race in which the center field (which I long before found so stimulatingly austere) is employed in an adjunct fashion as the grounds of a sort of mini-Oktoberfest with long wooden tables surrounded by eating and drinking and therefore joyous Bavarians. Supporting our preconceptions, there was footage of grinning, substantial waitresses carrying many beer mugs and platters of white sausages—just like at the Hofbräuhaus. The movie also had some winter footage of kids in snowsuits going down the highest rubble hill on little sleds.

The Olympia Park is, then, being used. The film, however, could not communicate a more substantial accomplishment. The vast facility with its attendant housing, parks, and schools and the foreseen addition to the city's public transportation network caused substantial geographical alterations in the whole area. Munich now had a powerful international draw in a huge area where there had been nothing whatever (except possibly the BMW assembly plant) worth a trip.

Planning or agreeable accidents determined that somehow, when one thinks of Munich, this new complex of several hundred acres is an extension of the old, outdoorsy, folksy, artsy city, which is, in fact, far away. The big medieval cathedral, the Frauenkirche, is five kilometers from the Olympic site. This area, which was lavishly built up and then employed in 1972, has turned into an extension of the city whose inhabitants, like those in Haifa or Marseilles, have traditionally been outside, looking at and enjoying each other. To repeat: Munich is better than it ever was.

Returning to an issue left open above, a unified object of the planners of the Games of 1972 was to block a basis for retrospective criticism by avoiding the evolution of "Olympic ruins." Corrosive commentaries were to be anticipated; critical historians headed off.

Of all the constructions, the one that provided for the rowing contests was one of the most profligate. It was crazily expensive. Even in the few days it was Olympically used, the stands holding 8,000 were rarely full. Nor, needless to say, was the standing room for 16,000.

In August of 1988 it was tough to get to. There were few indicative road signs, and (in a land where public transportation is nearly complete) no bus went there. Early on another morning, as I walked a narrow, linden-lined road toward a lot of barnlike sheds, I was shaken with nostalgia recalling the crowds and the splendor of the staged competitions sixteen years ago. For a while I heard only small birds.

Turning a corner, I saw again the stupendous panorama: the two-kilometer lake, the enormous, roofed stands put up for just eight days of action. As before, the site was vast, unlikely. But now there was no movement. It was like a mural of a ruin. Or was it? It merited more careful watching.

I walked further and approached a low dock where a man in proletarian coveralls of blue was mopping with a volatile paint some wood surfaces near the lapping water. Nearby were some nicely kept flower beds of geraniums and impatiens. In the far distance I saw boats. One was approaching. As I sat on a stanchion to await it, I saw trout in several sizes in the clean water.

It was a four-man boat—a canoe—it had a surface of gleaming mahogany—it held the national team of New Zealand. In back of me now there were five support people who had come from a storage shed.

Of course, one expects such people to talk, and probably New Zealanders abroad talk more than most voyagers do. A trainer explained that canoeing is a sport in which New Zealanders traditionally distinguish themselves internationally. This group of athletes, coaches, trainers, and technicians was one of many top-level rowing and canoeing teams scheduled to exploit this unequaled installation. The "Kiwis" (they called themselves that) had to stay in a hotel in Oberschleissheim, three miles away since the dormitory on the site (which also provided fine meals) was now full of Brits and Danes.

More national teams would be using the lake, which was widely known and treasured—there was rarely any wind. Provided correct arrangements were made long in advance, the Germans were generous in offering the attendant facilities and the lake for the use of athletes—but only those at the highest level of performance. The New Zealanders were preparing for some European championships in Denmark. After this, all their many boats would go in a container for shipment to Seoul. As we talked, I noticed, as I had not before, gardeners and more painters. There was the sound of a hammer and an electric drill at some repairs. So the place was not a ruin but was, as promised, being used—by a few people at least. This was surely a costly enterprise to keep going. I asked myself the interior, rhetorical question, "Who is paying the bills?"

The actual question was, "Doesn't it seem sort of odd to be training where it is so quiet and so isolated?"

"Yes, it is. The whole area is almost ghostly in daylight, but especially those great big stands over there, always empty, make us feel sometimes that we're in a mausoleum."

"Does anyone ever come here to fish out some of those nifty trout?"

"On weekends you might see a gaffer or two. The fish are too well fed. I don't think anybody catches much. One of the nice things around here is the girls who come 'round in the afternoons. They're all down there at the far end—to sun and take a dip. Since it's hot, there'll be a pack later in the day. They're naked you know. Sometimes the boys swing by for some hard looks. Gives 'em a buzz."

Bibliographical Note

An object of all of my writing about sport has been to ease the way for subsequent investigators of sports festivals. This short essay will focus mostly on the literature of the Munich Olympics of 1972 and will also include some general discussion of the earnest literature about the Olympic movement.

Little would be gained if I cited the many picture and statistical books on the Olympics of 1972 that appeared just after the Games. Almost all were published in Germany and are superficial. They are at the level of sports journalism. The same material is available in a fresher form in the microfilms of almost any good local newspaper of the time. The *Süddeutsche Zeitung*, Munich's most comprehensive newspaper, was published in fat editions before, during, and after the Games. It offered the most diligent and complete current coverage.

There is pathetically little secondary literature on the Olympic Games in Munich. This is a predictable misfortune after any Olympic festival but is particularly sad after the Munich Games, which are still recalled chiefly for the calamity that was their grisly summit and consequently are considered a low point in Olympic history. The detailed survey is Serge Groussard, *The Blood of Israel* (New York: Morrow, 1975, 464 pp.; original edition, Paris: Denoël, 1973).

Hans Klein and Willi Daume told me several times that they planned to write memoirs of this pinnacle of their rich lives, but so far these have not been published. Klein returned to public life in Bonn where he continues to be a spokesman for the government. Daume remains an administrator in the German and international Olympic movements. Because of his prominence, his speeches on sport get published. These are public performances and are mostly assemblages of sports clichés. They reveal almost nothing of Daume's remarkable wit or the basis of his manipulative, inspirational, and unfoolable administrative genius.

This is not the first diary inspired by the Olympic Games. Thilo Koch, a well-placed and compliant radio and television journalist, published his *Piktogram der Spiele* (Munich: Bruckmann, 1973, 153 pp.) (English subtitle is *Pictogram of the Games*. The English translation occupies pp. 77–153.). Koch's stature gave him ready access to the highest ranking politicians in Munich and the stars who were in the cultural program. He drops the names of most of them. Since I am not a "name," Koch referred to me as "an American Jew who has written a book on the 1936 Olympics and who seems to dislike Olympiads in general" (p. 131).

Per Olav Enquist is a Swedish novelist and social critic of international reputation. While in Munich he furnished a Stockholm daily with a lot of current and refreshingly skeptical commentary on the sporting competitions and the terrorist act. These writings were collected and published as *Kathedralen i Muenchen* (Stockholm: Norstet & Soners, 1972, 189 pp.). The French translation is *La cathédrale olympique: ou Munich 1972* (Aix-en-Provence: Pandora Éditions, 1980, 198 pp.). I can save diligent Americans some time by stating that I have located neither a Swedish nor a French copy of this book in the United States.

The official report is *Die Spiele: Der offizielle Bericht, herausgegeben vom Organisations komitee für die Spiele der XX. Olympiade München 1972*, 3 vols. (Munich: Prosport, 1974). Volume 1 is entitled *Die Organization*, 400 pp.; Volume 2, *Die Bauten*, 215 pp.; and Volume 3, *Die Wettkämpfe*, 564 pp. English and French translations were also published. The volumes are magnificently designed (Aicher was on hand here as well) and include an immense number of stunning sports photographs and a grand number of statistics but not much of what the probing might want to know. The report is intended to give an optimistic summary from an administrator's point of view.

For an appraisal of the truly vast amounts of other printed materials—almost all of it, aside from the official reports of the national Olympic committees, published before the Games—I must cite my article on sources for research on the Olympic movement, "The Modern Olympic Games: A Bibliographical Essay," *Sportwissenschaft* 6, no. 1 (Spring 1976): 89–98. As in that article, I will stress again that the best way to locate sources on any accomplished Olympic Games is to go to their site. One begins by poking about in public repositories and then asking where there might be other hoards. These searches are successful.

The standard professional approach—through a library catalog—produces insupportable frustrations due to confusion, mostly inconsistency, really, regarding the librarians' efforts to come up with authors or main entries. I can perhaps best illustrate this by quoting from a report made for me by the chief cataloger at the University of South Carolina:

> In checking *LC Books: Subjects*, 1970–1977, I found 88 items listed for the 1972 Olympic Games. Of these, 53 were entered under personal author, 16 under 11 different corporate names, and 19 under title.
>
> Of the 11 corporate names, only 4 were "formulated" headings. Two were established as conferences: *Olympic Games, Munich, 1972* and *Informelles Treffen Junger Europäischer Künstler, München, 1972*. One was qualified by country: *Nationales Olympisches Komitee (Federal Republic of Germany)*. The other was entered under the heading for a country: *Germany (Federal Republic, 1949–)*. The [cataloging] code [employed] is used in the U.S. . . . and most other English speaking countries.

The most important and most discouraging part of all of the above is that last sentence. For what this means is that almost any citation I might give of some official or semi-official document would be of little use in the German or other European libraries in which the researcher is likely to work. Again, if one wants to work on particular Olympic Games, it is essential to go to the spot and ask a lot of questions.

In Munich, the first place to go is to the Monasensia, a bucolically located former villa that is now the archive for materials dealing with the recent events in Munich's civic life. The librarians are amiable experts. The materials are reasonably well cataloged. Correctly, but perhaps perversely for the next investigators, the papers of the German National Olympic Committee and of the organizers and the liquidators in Munich are still in the process of being acquired and cataloged in the Bundesarchiv (federal government archives) in Koblenz.

Unfortunately for the diligent searcher of primary sources, the questions about the Munich Olympics that are the most enchanting may not be answerable for a long time. The public reputations of too many living and influential people are still at stake. In the course of my narrative I have suggested some of these issues. Examples: Who arranged the "Olympic truce" in German politics in the months before the opening, and how was it so quietly maintained? To what extent was Willi Daume in control of the preparations? Was the tone of it all as much due to him as others claim and I suspect? How were Otl Aicher's boundaries defined and maintained? What were some of the disputes concerning his jurisdiction, and what were the ideological justifications of the disputants?

A crucial problem would be to determine just how the incident of the terrorists was disposed of by helping the three surviving hostages get away in October of 1972. An exposé of this would reveal a lot about how the Federal Republic of Germany, at its highest levels, functions in emergencies. But we are dealing with the sort of intimate details about individual actions that one finds not in official archives but rather in memoirs and correspondence. We must wait many years for these revelations.

Acknowledgments

I am grateful to Willi Daume for providing the nest in the Press City and the passes that let me move about in the summer of 1972. Those who subsidized my adventure were, of course, the constituent bodies of German National Olympic Committee, and so I must thank them too.

The Universtity of South Carolina's Research and Productive Scholarship Committee gave me two grants after the Games of 1972 so that I could do some library work there. More work on the book was done as I worked on other projects as a guest professor in Germany. For the year 1973–74, I had an appointment as a research Fulbright Professor in the Sportwissenschaftliches Institut of the University of Bonn. The Richard Merton Stipendium, administered by the German Research Foundation, financed my professorship, 1976–77, at the German Sports College (Deutsche Sporthochschule) in Cologne. My appointment there was in the Institute for Sport History.

Bradley Bargar, a professor emeritus at the University of South Carolina, knows our language well. Over the years Bradley has constructively read everything I have written before it was published. He read and commented on this book twice. Careful readers of parts of this book were Patrick Scott and John Temple Ligon. A thorough reader was Charles Wendon. Another was Arnd Krüger. Dan Boice led me many times to push the Thomas Cooper Library to its limits. My younger two children, Max and Isa, also helped by reading early drafts of the book to locate those silly mistakes that their Daddy wished not to expose to others.

A grand figure hovering over this book and everything I have done in a constructive literary or scholarly way during the past decade is Allen Guttmann, who long ago was briefly my pupil and thereafter has been my teacher.

Index